D0046319

Economics and Politics

Economics and Politics

The Calculus of Support

Edited by
Helmut Norpoth, Michael S. Lewis-Beck,
and Jean-Dominique Lafay

Ann Arbor
THE UNIVERSITY OF MICHIGAN PRESS

1994   1993   1992   1991   4   3   2   1

Distributed in the United Kingdom by
Manchester University Press, Oxford Road,
Manchester M13 9PL, UK

Library of Congress Cataloging-in-Publication Data

Economics and politics : the calculus of support / edited by Helmut
   Norpoth, Michael S. Lewis-Beck, and Jean-Dominique Lafay.
         p.   cm.
   Revised versions of papers given at a meeting in 1987 at the Villa
Serbelloni in Bellagio, Italy.
   Includes bibliographical references.
   ISBN 0-472-10186-2 (alk. paper)
   1. Elections—Europe.   2. Voting—Europe.   3. Europe—Economic
conditions—1945–   4. Europe—Politics and government—1945–
I. Norpoth, Helmut.   II. Lewis-Beck, Michael S.   III. Lafay, Jean-
Dominique, 1944–
JN94.A956E27   1991
324'.094—dc 20   90–49340
                                                                CIP

British Library Cataloguing in Publication Data

Economics and politics : the calculus of support.
   1. Electorate. Voting behaviour. Economic aspects
   I. Norpoth, Helmut   II. Lewis-Beck, Michael S.   III. Lafay,
   Jean-Dominique
   324.6

   ISBN 0-472-10186-2

To the Pollsters of Economic and Political Opinion

Preface

This book took shape in a way that tells something about the interplay between economics and politics. It is the result of international cooperation, inspired more by free-market principles than those of state intervention. The various authors whose research is reported here operated very much on their own, with frameworks, data, and tools of their choice. No common plan was imposed, no roles were assigned. Yet anarchy, we believe, was not to be feared. If there was competition, rivalry, and controversy, so much the better for everyone.

All of the contributions focus on the influence of economic matters on political choices in the mass electorate; the authors have all cut their teeth in research on economic voting. Our goal was not to produce a country-by-country survey of the extent of such voting using a fixed format. Instead, we intended to present contemporary research on promising theoretical questions related to economic voting, regardless of where the research was conducted or on which country. That, inevitably, makes for a certain skewness in the coverage.

Where this volume tries to strike a balance, however, is between research that focuses on the individual voter as the key actor and research that focuses on the electorate as a whole. We are not wedded to the belief that one is inherently superior to the other; in fact, several among us have played on both sides of this field. We feel that each approach is able to provide certain answers that the other one cannot.

The authors included in this volume had the benefit of a week-long meeting in 1987 at the Villa Serbelloni in Bellagio, Italy, that received the generous support of the Rockefeller Foundation and the National Science Foundation. At that time, earlier versions of the articles assembled here were subjected to the test of public peer review, in a spirit of vigorous competition softened, perhaps, by the serene surroundings.

We are indebted to Colin Day for his encouragement and support in shaping the papers into a publishable volume. Two reviewers helped us with their comments to avoid the perils of too little or misguided regulation. We also gratefully acknowledge the permission of the *Review of Economics and Statistics* to reprint the article by Galeotti and Forcina.

This volume is dedicated to an unsung profession in the business of scholarly analysis: the pollsters of economic and political opinion. Their generosity in sharing data with the academic community has made it possible for us not just to trust our intuition on economic voting but to verify it.

Contents

Introduction   1
  Michael S. Lewis-Beck

Part 1: The Economy and Electoral Decisions

How Robust Is the Vote Function? A Study of Seventeen
Nations over Four Decades   9
  Martin Paldam

The Economy in U.S. House Elections   33
  Gary C. Jacobson

Unemployment and Elections in West Germany   49
  Hans Rattinger

Italian Economic Voting: A Deviant Case or Making a Case for
a Better Theory?   63
  Paolo Bellucci

Part 2: The Economy and Government Popularity

The Economy and Presidential Approval: An Information
Theoretic Perspective   85
  Nathaniel Beck

Economic Conditions and the Popularity of West German
Parties: Before and after the 1982 Government Change   103
  Gebhard Kirchgässner

Political Dyarchy and Popularity Functions: Lessons from the
1986 French Experience   123
  Jean-Dominique Lafay

The Popularity of the Thatcher Government: A Matter
of War and Economy   141
  Helmut Norpoth

Macroeconomics, the Falklands War, and the Popularity
of the Thatcher Government: A Contrary View   161
  David Sanders, Hugh Ward, and David Marsh

**Part 3:   Economic Perceptions
and Government Accountability**

Explaining Explanations of Changing Economic Conditions   185
  Stanley Feldman and Patricia Conley

Explaining Aggregate Evaluations of Economic Performance   207
  Henry W. Chappell, Jr., and William R. Keech

Public Perceptions of Parties' Economic Competence   221
  Manfred Kuechler

Ambiguous Intervention: The Role of Government Action in
Public Evaluation of the Economy   239
  James E. Alt

Part 4:   Models of Politico-Economic Behavior

Forms of Expressing Economic Discontent   267
  Bruno S. Frey

Political Loyalties and the Economy   281
  Gianluigi Galeotti and Antonio Forcina

Contributors   293

Introduction

Michael S. Lewis-Beck

In one way or another, when enough discontented individuals take systematic collective action, governments are likely to fall. As Machiavelli saw long ago, "for a prince it is necessary to have the people friendly; otherwise he has no remedy in adversity." Because of this, the politico-economic linkage is closely monitored. Politicians, journalists, and scholars routinely watch it. Moreover, the citizenry acts to redress economic grievances through all sorts of political means, from simple acts of voting to bloody street rioting. Which of these means a public chooses can be seen as a rational calculation, one that can be derived with mathematical rigor, following the demonstration in Frey's article.

One of the merits of the Western democracies is that they create strong incentives for choosing the peaceful avenue of political expression, voting. Scientific research on this critical nexus between economics and elections has acquired a lengthy, even distinguished, pedigree. Quantitative efforts tracking the influence of the business cycle on electoral outcomes date back as far as the early 1930s, if not earlier (Tibbits 1931). Survey studies of voter choices have long accorded economic issues a place in the electoral calculus (Berelson, Lazarsfeld, and McPhee 1954, 185), at least as "antecedents of political behavior" (Campbell, Converse, Miller, and Stokes 1960, chap. 14). But the scholarly spotlight of electoral studies was not fully turned on the economy until pioneering work that appeared almost simultaneously by Goodhart and Bhansali (1970) and Kramer (1971). These studies have spawned hundreds more. Does this mean all the important questions have been answered? No. They are still asked, but with more vigor and subtlety, traits fully exhibited in the current volume.

The perennial first question, a sine qua non, is "Do voters respond to the economy?" In the political economy literature generally, the overwhelming answer has been positive, with the classical exception of Stigler (1973). The papers at hand underline that verdict, reporting clearly significant economic effects on political behavior, save for Rattinger's challenging work on unemployment in West Germany. Overall, then, the basic hypothesis guiding the literature is reaffirmed:

when economic conditions are bad, citizens vote against the ruling party (coalition).

The corraborative findings on this central proposition are valuable, as far as they go, but much more remains to be said. In the first place, belief in the proposition rests essentially on the (positive) results of repeated statistical significance tests. Such testing has great utility in countries where few political economy studies have been carried out. While the tests encourage us to believe in the reality of such a relationship, they tell us little about the strength of that relationship. Hence, a second question arises, "How strong is the impact of economics on the voter?" Several of our authors find economic factors decisive. Lafay, for example, argues that the popularity of the French prime minister is driven by economic forces, even under conditions of a divided executive ("cohabitation"). In a popularity study from Britain, Sanders and his colleagues conclude that economic changes almost entirely accounted for the supposed Falklands War effects in securing the 1983 victory of Mrs. Thatcher's party. As counterpoint, Norpoth contends that the war, rather than economics, won it for Thatcher.

An implication of the Norpoth-Sanders debate is that the strength of economic issues ought to be judged relative to other issues. Kuechler, in his investigation of West German legislative election surveys, reports that economic issues are more predictive of voter intentions than noneconomic issues. By way of contrast, Jacobson finds that voters in U.S. legislative contests are only weakly responsive to economic issues, compared to matters such as constituency service and candidate quality.

Thus, on the second question, that of strength, the papers reveal less consensus. Perhaps that is because the relationship is conditional. That is to say, the effect of economics on elections depends on the values of other variables, such as these three: the time context of the election, the type of election, and the national setting. The first calls up the possibility that the importance of economic issues may vary, depending on the particular election (or election period) being considered; e.g., the 1968 versus the 1988 U.S. presidential elections. Kirchgässner examines such a possibility for West Germany, finding that unemployment influenced political support under the Social-Liberal coalition (1969–82), an influence that ceased when a Christian-Liberal government took office in 1982. The second refers to the institutional locus of the election; i.e., is it local or national, legislative or presidential? For instance, while Jacobson finds weak economic effects in U.S. House races, Beck uncovers a sharp economic impact on presidential support (with food price inflation the particular culprit). The third condition has to do with characteristics of the nation in which the elections take place. While several studies reveal a strong economic-electoral connection in, say, Britain, positive results in Italy are more fragile and uncertain, as the Bellucci article nicely illustrates.

Thus, one may view the display of different findings on the link between economics and elections—differences fully reflected here—as a useful demonstration of the critical role of conditional variables. Or, less optimistically, one may simply view it as evidence of an inherently unstable relationship. This possibility is hard to accept, at least when a brighter alternative exists, namely that the apparent instability may merely be a product of specification error. From that perspective, the observed differences would disappear, at least in principle, if the right model could be found. This notion inspires Paldam, when he asserts the following: "it is highly desirable if models are *general and institution free,* so that the same basic model works across countries and over time." In pursuit of this goal, he formulates a general model, and estimates it with a national time-series pool (197 elections, held from 1948–85 in seventeen nations). Unfortunately, the results are disappointing: the overall fit is poor and the key economic coefficients (on unemployment and inflation) generate unimpressive statistical significance values.

One potential reason for these weak findings is that Paldam's model specification, too, may not be error free. Another potential problem is data quality. Weak findings may be due to bad data. Worth exploring, then, are other data sources. At least four of the articles utilize data sets clearly different from the usual kind for examining economic voting in the countries covered. Lafay's study is the first French popularity function to employ the SOFRES opinion poll series, rather than that of IFOP. In their examination of U.S. presidential popularity functions, Chappell and Keech compare the traditional Gallup poll general performance rating to the more specific Harris poll economic performance rating. By way of contrast, Galeotti and Forcina, in their U.S. investigation, adopt voter turnout as the dependent variable, abandoning political support measures altogether. Finally, Rattinger's German study is unique, using the 327 counties (*Kreise*) as units of analysis.

The Rattinger investigation, played against the other German studies here, well illustrates another data problem: aggregation versus disaggregation. In dissaggregating data from ten separate federal elections (1953–87) down to the county level, Rattinger fails to uncover unemployment effects on the vote. However, Kirchgässner, in his national-level popularity functions, consistently finds unemployment to be a significant determinant. Perhaps the different findings can be ascribed to the different levels of aggregation, and the problem might be resolved by looking at individual voters themselves. This is done by Kuechler, who finds that economic issues, unemployment included, do have an impact.

Ambiguous or conflicting findings at the aggregate level, then, push the analyst to seek resolution through the study of individuals who, after all, are the actors making the voting decisions. When this happens, the question of model specification becomes more focused: "how do voters translate economic conditions into a vote choice?" Are their calculations in some way "rational"? Certain of these papers suggest so. In their U.S. survey analysis, Feldman and Conley show that respondents tend to attribute responsibility for overall economic conditions to the national government, but to assign responsibility for personal economic conditions to themselves. If voters do not blame the government for their own economic plight, then a vote against the government on personal economic grounds would not seem sensible; hence, the puzzle of missing evidence for pocketbook voting may be solved.

This does not mean that pocketbook calculations never enter into the voter's decision. Obviously, among those few who attribute their personal economic circumstance to government action, it does. But, it also exists in more subtle forms. In his imaginative survey research on the various types of economic voting in Italy, Bellucci provides the example of the Exchange Voter who, although unemployed, tends to favor the incumbent government (dominated by the Christian Democrats). While this goes against the standard hypothesis, it makes sense in the context of Italian political culture. Especially in Southern Italy, marginal political participants see politics in traditional patron-client terms, and mainly exchange their votes for a reward from the reigning DC bosses; in the case of the unemployed, the exchange might be for extended benefits or a patronage job. This pocketbook vote becomes "rational," once the cultural context is understood.

While the traces of pocketbook voting found by Bellucci are retrospective (backward looking), he also uncovered prospective (forward looking) economic voting, but of a collective nature. Among Opinion Voters, the most informed and issue-oriented sector of the Italian electorate, incumbent vote support was less likely when future economic prospects dimmed. More broadly, Alt suggests (from his British study) that the public forms subjective evaluations of economic performance from what government says *will* occur after an economic policy intervention, as well as from what has already occurred. Hence, subjective economic evaluations, which ultimately determine the vote, are both retrospective and prospective. Another way of putting it, as Chappell and Keech have done, is that voters are "sophisticated"; they assess the future as well as the past, and so might conceivably vote for a ruling party in bad times, if it promises a bright future.

Such "sophisticated" economic voting, to the degree it exists, has serious implications for the stability of the vote function. If voters are, indeed, "sophisticated," then they may respond to different economic variables, giving them different weights at different times. For instance, the slope coefficient for an inflation policy variable from a properly specified individual-level regression equation could be, say, .4 in one election and .7 in the next. Thus, the microlevel results would appear unstable. Further, such microlevel stability could produce instability in the inflation coefficients of macrolevel models. Similarly, if the individual-level distribution of attitudes toward inflation performance (e.g., the percent saying "better" or "worse") changed, more macrolevel instability of coefficients could be expected.

Given these circumstances, perhaps the high instability of economic voting across studies, evident here and elsewhere, is not to be decried. It simply resides in the changing nature of the phenomenon, a function of the way individuals make subjective assessments of economic factors, and how these assessments aggregate up to the national level. One research prescription, offered by Paldam, is to make models more bound to particular time periods. Another, which we offer, is to formulate models with economic indicators as global as possible. We assume that most research will continue to be divided along the two separate tiers of micro- and macrotheory, each with its own purposes. With regard to microtheory, researchers should develop well-specified models of vote choice that include general subjective assessments of economic performance, built from (or validated with) multiple items tapping different dimensions of the economy. With regard to macrotheory, a major danger is relying on too few national indicators, commonly unemployment and inflation, or real income. Others should be added (perhaps all combined into a principal component), such as exchange rates, public debt, interest rates, taxes, and income inequality. Only models with carefully built general economic indicators can hope to capture the shifting weighting scheme utilized in the political economic calculus of the democratic voter.

The contributions to this volume are organized in four broad sections. Part 1 examines the influence of the economy on electoral decisions. Part 2 utilizes, as the dependent variable, the more frequently monitored popularity ratings of governing parties or leaders. Part 3 presents different perspectives on the formation of individual perceptions of the economy and their role in evaluating government performance. The last section, Part 4, proposes formal models of political action, inspired by the economy, that go beyond partisan choice. Taken together, the contributions included here testify to the progress that has been made in understanding the role of the economy in the calculus of popular support.

REFERENCES

Berelson, Bernard R., Paul F. Lazarsfeld, and William N. McPhee. 1954. *Voting*. Chicago: Chicago University Press.
Campbell, Angus, Philip E. Converse, Warren E. Miller, and Donald E. Stokes. 1960. *The American Voter*. New York: Wiley.

Goodhart, C. A. E., and R. J. Bhansali. 1970. "Political Economy." *Political Studies* 18:43–106.

Kramer, Gerald H. 1971. "Short-Term Fluctuations in U.S. Voting Behavior, 1896–1964." *American Political Science Review* 65:131–43.

Stigler, George J. 1973. "General Economic Conditions and National Elections." *American Economic Review* 63:160–67.

Tibbits, Clark. 1931. "Majority Votes and the Business Cycle." *American Journal of Sociology* 36:596–606.

Part 1
The Economy and Electoral Decisions

How Robust Is the Vote Function?: A Study of Seventeen Nations over Four Decades

Martin Paldam

1. Introduction: The Stability Problem

A Vote function (hereafter V-function) is defined as a function explaining (the change in) the vote for the government by (changes in) economic conditions and other variables. A Popularity function (hereafter P-function) explains (the changes in) the popularity of the government—as measured by polls—by (changes in) the economic conditions and other variables. The two functions are so alike that I shall speak of VP-functions. The measure used for the vote or popularity is $C_{t,i}$, where t is time and i the country index. $C_{t,i}$ is calculated as a percent of all (valid) votes cast for the government, $G_{t,i}$, ruling *before* the election or, correspondingly, if it is a poll, *before* the poll was taken.

The literature on VP-functions has now increased to about 200 titles (see, e.g., Paldam 1981b, Schneider 1984, and Lewis-Beck 1988 for surveys). In spite of the considerable efforts very little is "cut and dried" in this field, and again and again discussions flare up when this or that result is found to be sadly lacking in stability.

The typical sequence is as follows:[1] First X presents an impressive study of the V- or P-function for country Z, with a nice theory and—most important—very fine econometric fits: a high R^2, very significant t-ratios, and, in addition, some new econometric trick like the $\zeta\zeta$-test from the latest issues of

Torben Poulsen served as my research assistant on this project. This article has a long history. It is hard to accept such negative conclusions as most of the ones reached in the chapter. However, I am now confident that the results are as presented (see also Korpi 1989 and Høst and Paldam 1990). I am grateful to many people, including a class of students whom I had working with subsets of the data for several months. Thanks also go to Fritz Schneider for comments and to "my" editor, Mike Lewis-Beck, for a thorough job.

1. This author knows of five such sequences that have been published in standard journals. There must have been more that remained unpublished. Some of the sequences are covered in Paldam (1981b).

Esoterica. Everybody is impressed, until a few years later Y demonstrates that, by one little change, X's result collapses. The change may be in the calculation period, the time-series used, or maybe Y applies another, even newer, econometric trick. Then X manages to get the results back by another little twist, etc. From time to time this causes writers to doubt that there is such a thing as a VP-function—or that the VP-function can survive a real thorough statistical test.[2]

One reason for this predicament is to be found in the sociology of our scientific societies (i.e., economics and political science). The literature is so huge that we can read only a fraction. We all prefer to read something smashing. The publication pressures on the few journals everybody sees are enormous, so articles have to be short to be accepted. All problems with results, qualifications, etc. are therefore normally cut away. People present only the best results obtained after many experiments. Consequently, the results are normally much too good relative to the true model. This is possible due to the flexibility of econometrics: we do have a large tool kit that allows us to work with models and improve fits until they become better than the "true model."

In a sense this is only normal: to establish a new field one needs advertisement. Smashing new results which are enthusiastically oversold.[3] Then (we) plodders, following with some lag, have to put the field, which is now established by the pioneers, on a basis that is more modest. This is the spirit in which the present article—which is replete with terribly poor results—is written. Those who want to keep the illusions that VP-functions are strong, robust tools should stop reading now! However, I should start by stressing that in my opinion there is really no doubt that there is a VP-function. This lack of doubt is not only due to the many (overly) significant results in the literature; but also to the very thorough tests done for a number of countries using large data sets and techniques that are model robust, such as spectral analysis and causality tests (see Kirchgässner 1976, 1985, and 1986; Whiteley 1986).[4]

---

2. The reader is referred to the literature on the econometrician as a "con man" (see Leamer 1983) and the ensuing discussion, with contributions such as Hendry and Mizon (1990) and others. The main thrust of the argument against the standard econometric technique is that regression techniques are too easy to use, in the sense that they are so flexible that they can always be made to deliver a nicely fitting model. In addition, there is the problem with the economic theories (not to speak of the maze of theories in political science) that one can always make a theoretical argument for any result.

3. One would be hard pressed to find a more elegant and convincing article than Kramer 1971, which sold the VP-function to the profession for a decade; today it is clear that Kramer's article promised more than the hard numbers can deliver. The two Frey and Schneider papers (1978a and 1978b), giving the second wave of VP-papers, are almost as elegant.

4. In addition to the theory-robust studies mentioned, a number of studies demonstrate the average fit of the model as well as its variability over time. See, e.g., Goodhart and Bhansali 1970

The stability problem has two operational aspects:

1. How general are the models, i.e., do we have to make different functions for different countries and periods or can we use the same functions?
2. How large is the e-fraction of the VP-function, i.e., how large a fraction of the changes in the voters' support for the different parties, at elections and polls, are due to economic factors? (The e-fraction is discussed in sec. 2).

The question of model generality is, as usual, the toughest one: obviously it is highly desirable if models are general and institution free, so that the same basic model works across countries and over time.[5] This does not necessarily mean that the model takes no account of country differences and institutions; but only that any relevant difference is explicitly modeled. The pure theory of the VP-function (as will be discussed in sec. 2) looks very much like the theory behind any other standard macroeconomic function, and as most macrofunctions it is presented as general and institution free. People are supposed to react to economic changes in a basic way, which is independent of institutions. Where institutions (may) matter is in giving the levels on which the reactions take place. Also, different institutions may allow us to see the reaction from different angles.

Thus, to estimate over long time periods and across countries we have to use first differences (Δ): To delete levels due to institutional differences we study how the change in the percentage vote (or poll) for the government, $\Delta C_{t,i}$, reacts to changing economic conditions, such as unemployment and inflation: Δu, Δp, etc. It has been widely discussed whether it is appropriate to formulate models in levels or in first differences. The two main general points in this discussion are as follows. (1) When we have to compare across countries and over long periods, it is very likely that levels matter in a complex way. We suspect that the average Italian cares much less about inflation than the average German, but it is not, a priori, unreasonable to expect that Italians and Germans react in the same way to *changes* in the inflation rate. (2) If we

---

and Pissarides 1980 for the United Kingdom; Paldam and Schneider 1980 for Denmark; and Lybeck 1986 for Sweden, etc.

5. Macroeconomics is built around the consumption function, the demand for money function, and the Phillips curve, because these functions are taken to be general ones. They are, of course, endlessly debated; nevertheless, we all know that at least the first digit of the coefficients in the most simple linear versions of these models is really robust. The big discussions concern the second digits, the dynamics, etc. Note that it is remarkably rare to find country specific traits in economic models. Models are normally presented as if they were totally institution free, following from pure theory.

have adjustments to the levels that exceed the time unit of the analysis, this creates biases, when the model is estimated in first differences. Our time unit is one year, we include lags, and the elections are removed by an average of three years from each other. As will be argued in the next section and demonstrated in the empirical sections, these lags are long relative to the adjustments known to exist in this type of model, so it should be safe to use first differences.

In my analysis, I cover all governmental elections over thirty-eight years in the seventeen main developed democracies: altogether 197 elections. Over such a large sample we expect to find the basic pattern of the VP-function—a basic structure that can once and for all lay any doubts about these functions to rest. That is, if these functions cannot, in fact, be doubted.

2. The Theory of the VP-function

The theoretical foundation for the VP-function is the responsibility hypothesis, i.e., the idea that people hold the government responsible for economic conditions. It follows that changes in economic conditions cause changes in the support for the government. Since we formulate the hypothesis in first differences, it is clear that it deals with swing voters.[6]

One may, as is often done, argue that the responsibility hypothesis follows from "basic" behavioral assumptions, as proposed by Downs (1957), and the ensuing Public Choice theory. A number of researchers have worked with various parts of the microfoundations (as we shall see); but nobody has, until now, made a strict micromodel of the VP-function and shown that it can be consistently aggregated to the macrolevel. It has actually been proved, by Arrow (1951) and the whole social choice school since then (see Sen 1986 for a recent survey), that individual preferences will not, in general, aggregate to a consistent social welfare function. This is not very surprising, as it appears that none of the standard macrofunctions can be derived by a perfectly consistent aggregation of microfunctions.

I shall return to this item in section 4. Till then I just note that the macrotheory of the VP-function rests on the same kind of "sloppy" microfoundations as (all) other macrofunctions. We have some general principles; but these principles are consistent with many operational models. This state of affairs is exactly why it is important to study the stability of the functions, using sufficiently large data sets. Let us, with this in mind, turn to the mac-

---

6. Whether or not voters who stay with their old party do so due to a rational or irrational party identification, class consciousness, religious beliefs, etc., is therefore not really relevant for the model. It is, however, relevant that there seem to be gross movements of 15 percent to 25 percent of the voters between the parties at the typical election in a democracy.

romodel of the VP-function. It has a set of economic and a set of political variables: an e-part and a p-part. In its most simple linear version the functions are:[7]

$$\Delta C_t = \{a_1 \, \Delta u_t + a_2 \, \Delta p_t + \ldots \} + [c_1 \, D_t^1 + c_2 \, D_t^2$$

$$+ \ldots] + \epsilon_t \tag{1}$$

Here Δ is used to indicate the first difference, C is either the vote or the popularity, for the government, in percent. The as and cs are coefficients to be estimated, and ϵ is the disturbance term. The braces contain the economic variables: the e-part of the model. Two of the economic variables are u and p, which the reader may think of as the rate of unemployment and the rate of price rises. The next set of variables, the ds, are the political variables forming the p-part of the model—it is found in the square brackets. The p-part is often modeled by dummies, i.e., artificial variables giving trends, individual government periods, etc. There are, from time to time, genuine political variables in these functions, but dummies are the most common form for political variables.

Sometimes the political factors may already be covered by the economic ones: if the main differences between right and left governments are the economic outcomes they generate we do not need a right/left variable, or rather there is multicollinearity between the e-part and the p-part. This is analyzed, with weak results in the theory of Partisan Cycles (introduced by Hibbs 1977; see Paldam 1990a and 1990b for empirical results). But we all know that people are interested in things that have no correlation to economic factors (however they are measured). Some highly relevant noneconomic factors are: the personalities of politicians, changes in party structures, foreign policy crises, scandals, hot issues (like abortion, nuclear power plants, etc.). Economists are likely to lump such noneconomic factors together as political factors.[8] And, as it is most often difficult to find good time-series for the political series we end up modeling all these complex factors with the usual set of political dummy variables.

Therefore, one problem with the VP-function is: there is a strong asymmetry in the quality of the modeling of the e-part and the p-part. It makes a

---

7. Hibbs's P-function model (1982) is more complex when it is expressed in absolute levels; when it is converted into first differences and linearized it is like the model presented here. However, if not linearized it generates elasticities instead of linear terms.

8. There are, of course, relations between the economic and political factors, but the trade-offs are often negative: i.e., politicians sometimes get popularity from foreign policy initiatives (such as empire building) that cost the taxpayers money, people are willing to pay more (and stand more pollution) to get electricity that is made from coal rather than nuclear energy, etc.

function unstable if important variables are modeled in a very weak and, essentially, arbitrary way.

The variables in equation 1 enter with some lags; but it is a standard result in the literature that the lags are short, so that everything takes place within one or, at most, two years. This is known as the *voter's myopia result*. It is notoriously difficult to determine lag structures in functions between series with a lot of autocorrelation so it is no wonder that some controversies have been going on here. Many authors have found ultrashort lags, like only a couple of months. D. A. Hibbs, Jr., has, however, in seven studies of five countries (recently reprinted, see Hibbs 1987) found that even when three-fourths of the popularity adjustment take place in the first year, something can be traced for almost two years. In any case the results speak of short lags. The voters myopia result is very well established indeed.

Incidentally, these short lags are crucial for the theory of electoral cycles where it is assumed that the relevant expectations in price/wage adjustments are less myopic, while the government has full foresight—an assumption that is highly dubious. Most economic policymaking would appear to take place with a similarly short time-horizon. The various theories of political business cycles are surveyed in Paldam 1981a, 1990a, and 1990b.

Furthermore, there seems to be a fairly general agreement that what people react to is their perception of the general economic situation, and not to their own economic grievances (see Kinder and Kiewiet 1979; Fiorina 1981; and Lewis-Beck 1988). The reason more people vote against the government when there is an increase in unemployment is not that they themselves have become unemployed, but that they perceive that unemployment is going up in general. A problem here, however, is that it has often been demonstrated—by polls testing people's knowledge—that they have a fairly limited understanding of macroeconomics. As will be discussed in a moment, it would be irrational if they invested much effort in understanding macroeconomics.

One of the first questions to pose about VP-functions is how large a fraction of the variation they explain. In principle, the e-part and the p-part in equation 1 should exhaust the universe. So we may ask how large is the e-fraction and how large the p-fraction—given that they add up to one. This obviously shifts a great deal over time; but the average orders of magnitudes are about one to three for the e-fraction relative to the p-fraction. The typical findings in the VP-function literature are that the two fractions can be made to reach an R^2-score of .8 to .9; but the dummies explain a lot, so that the e-fraction is in the range of 0.15 to 0.35. The results are in the high end for P-functions and in the low end for V-functions. I find such average orders of magnitudes quite reasonable, and would have been a bit worried if the e-fraction had been much higher. These findings cast new light on old discussions about the importance of economic and other factors in our political behavior, discussions where the intuitions of the founders of our sciences have differed.[9]

The findings, as just reported, also appear to tally with the theory of rational expectations: RE theory analyzes the way expectations are formed by the means of a theory of information, i.e., how much information is it rational to have given that there are information costs and benefits. The result is a whole spectrum of REs, of which the most interesting is the HIRE case (High Information Rational Expectations).[10] It is the case where it is rational for the relevant agent to form the best possible expectations. Think of the situation where you are investing \$1 million of your own. This will surely make you pick all the brains you can and collect all the knowledge you can find, in order to assess the most likely future development in all relevant fields. Hence, under the HIRE case, expectations are forward-looking, and likely to be volatile, reacting quickly to all new information. Obviously the situation is radically different when you are voting; but let us for a moment apply the HIRE case to the voting decision. In that case the voter has to use all available information, the best theories and advice from experts, in order to assess whether the opposition or the incumbent government is going to rule better. The relevant expectations will be forward looking. Economic conditions in the immediate past are not going to dominate such an assessment, as they do in the typical VP-function.

However, when we vote, we know that there are millions of other voters. Our influence on the election is infinitesimal. Furthermore, we know that the difference between alternative governments is, in most cases, quite small, seen from the point of view of the average voter. It is already a (well-known) paradox that people bother to vote. And, surely, the payoff one can get from improving one's expectations is extremely small. We clearly have to move to the other end of the RE spectrum, the LIRE case (Low Information Rational Expectations). The least difficult assessment one can make of any variable is to take it to be what you remember. As your memory becomes dimmer the more you go back, the LIRE case is simply the good old case of adaptive expectations where people form expectations on, e.g., Δp (the rate of inflation) by just what they remember about Δp. Hence we get a formula as:

$$E(\Delta p) = a_1 \, \Delta p_{-1} + a_2 \, \Delta p_{-2} + \ldots, \tag{2}$$

---

9. The intuitions of some of our classics are very different: Marx would probably have argued for a large and class-specific e-fraction, while Max Weber and Keynes would have argued for a low one.

10. This is the case mostly discussed in the literature under the name of RE, as it was the new and exciting case fifteen years ago, when these ideas became known (with R. E. Lucas as the main innovator). It is here one gets the paradoxical result that economic policies are inefficient.

where $\Sigma a_k = 1$, and $1 \geq a_k \geq a_{k+1} \geq 0$. Here myopia means that a_1 is already close to 1, so that the following as do not matter. The less people care to form expectations, the more myopic they become. The standard myopia result really means that people form the dumbest possible expectations; but this is perfectly rational given the payoff. This is well in line with the logic behind the paradox of voting, but there is some contrary evidence. Not only do most people vote; but it actually appears that they spend a lot of time on politics—especially around election time. They watch TV, read newspapers, and discuss politics with friends. Why are people investing that much effort? Is it simply that people like elections because they are a great show? Or, do we need a special "civic duty" concept,[11] so that we can say that people vote because they feel it is their civic duty? Or, do we all have some (irrational?) interest in understanding our environment?

In any case it is clear why the V-function must generally have a lower e-fraction than the P-function. When people answer an opinion poll they do so without much deliberation—we get their "gut feelings" right now. Here it is perhaps realistic to get simple adaptive expectations with a short time-horizon. An election takes place after a campaign where people have a lot of time to decide and collect information. Large amounts of effort and money are spent to influence people, and it appears that these efforts are successful in the following sense: polls have movements that are (at least) twice as large (per time-unit) in the six months surrounding an election as they have at other times.

There is one more reason for getting better results in P-functions than in V-functions. A P-function is generally estimated over much shorter time periods than V-functions. It is common to estimate P-functions on the forty quarters of a decade, where there are at most four elections. To obtain enough data to estimate a V-function one needs to consider a much longer period. Hence, if these functions are unstable, or have poorly understood medium-term dynamics, it is much easier to hit a "good period" by considering a P-function for a shorter time period. Furthermore, we may catch a lot of medium-term instability by trends and other dummies in the P-function, while we have to model these complicated matters explicitly in the V-function.[12]

---

11. It is possible to rationalize such concepts as socially desirable mechanisms allowing us to reach cooperative solutions in complex game situations, where it is expensive to monitor free riders. These rationalizations have a tradition, as it is a well-known anomaly in many practical situations (and experiments) that far too few people are free riders. But it appears that these rationalizations are hard to formalize convincingly.

12. There is a nasty argument that can be presented here, for it appears that many economic variables have medium-term trends like the popularities, so it should always be possible to find variables that "fit" together if one can fiddle around a bit with the lags and have some variables to choose among, provided the time period is sufficiently short.

One more problem is worth considering and it concerns the very foundation of the theory: the responsibility hypothesis itself. Is it reasonable to imagine that voters hold all governments responsible for the economic situation? If the government fails to have a majority, and rules for a short period only, how can it be responsible—it tried to rule, but did it actually influence things? It is a fact that nearly all of the fine looking VP-functions in the literature have been found for stable governments in countries with simple party systems, which either is, or is perceived as, a two-party system.

Only about half of the countries have such simple party systems—and the party system changes over time in several countries. About five of the countries have systems with as many as a dozen parties, a tradition of minority governments, and complicated parliamentary situations. In many such cases it is highly dubious which coalition government will be formed after the election even when the election outcome is normally very well predicted: in Holland, Belgium and Finland it often takes months of negotiations, following an election, to form the next government. In Denmark, most governments have been minority governments.

In our study of the Danish P-function, we found that no P-function generalized throughout the full period 1957–70, where we had data (Paldam and Schneider 1980). However, a very significant pattern appeared when we divided the data into two periods: (1) 1957–73, when the party system worked as a two-block system, and (2) 1973–79, when there were ten to fourteen parties. We only got the standard responsibility-pattern for the first period. For the second period we got the reverse pattern. Similar results have been found by Bellucci (this volume) for Italy. Our—necessarily tentative—interpretation was that in addition to the responsibility pattern working in the stable two-party environment, we also had a stability pattern in more complex party systems: here economic difficulties make the voters turn (back) toward stability and the old (respectable) parties. More evidence supporting this idea will be discussed subsequently.

3. The Structure of Election Results: Are the ΔCs from the Same Distribution?[13]

It follows from the previous section that the dependent variable should be the first difference, Δ, of the percentage vote, $C_{t,i}$, for the government, $G_{t,i}$ (the government ruling up to the election). The only Gs not counted are a few cases of Gs of civil servants formed with the sole purpose of ruling during the

---

13. This section summarizes the results in Paldam 1986, building on data up to 1980. We have more observations now, so the results are even stronger. However, the detailed statistical analysis will not be repeated here.

TABLE 1. Countries, Type of Elections, and Some Basic Averages, 1948–85

	Election Statistics			Average Result ΔC_t	
Country/Type of Election	N	StP	AP	A	S
Australia/House of Representatives	16	3	2.5	−1.92	(3.12)
Belgium/Chambre des Représentants	13	4	3.1	−3.24	(5.02)
Canada/House of Commons	13	5	3.1	−2.09	(8.96)
Denmark/Folketinget	15	4	2.7	−0.95	(5.56)
Ireland/Dáil Éirann	12	4	3.3	−3.27	(3.65)
Finland/Eduskunta	11	4	3.6	−1.73	(3.65)
France/Assemblée Nationale	9	5	4.5	−0.53	(13.90)
Germany/Bundestag	8(+2)[b]	4	3.8	0.80	(4.93)
Netherlands/Tweede Kamer	11	4	3.6	−2.00	(5.38)
Italy/Camera dei Deputati	8(+2)	5	4.5	−1.96	(3.59)
Japan/House of Representatives	14(+1)	4	2.7	−3.87	(7.54)
New Zealand/House of Representatives	13	3	2.9	−3.74	(3.75)
Norway/Stortinget	10	4[c]	4	0.59	(3.91)
Austria/Nationalrat	10(+1)	4	3.5	0.29	(2.55)
Sweden/Andra Kammaren[a]	13	4–3	3.1	−1.18	(3.68)
U.K./House of Commons	11	5	3.6	−1.36	(3.91)
U.S.A./Presidential	10	4[c]	4	−1.81	(11.32)
Sums and averages	197(+6)[b]			−1.61	(5.50)

Note: N is the number of elections, while P is the election period, statutory, and average. A is the average and S is the standard deviation. StP is the statutory period, while AP is the average period.

[a]The constitution has been changed in Sweden where election periods are now three years.

[b]The first two elections in Germany and Italy and the first election in Japan and Austria are excluded.

[c]No dissolution is possible. Dissolution is difficult in Germany and Italy too, but it has happened. Note that two of the positive averages occur in Norway and Germany.

election after a crisis—mainly in Finland. We shall, in the present, disregard how long time the G has ruled and, hence, the electoral cycle.[14]

One elementary condition that has to be fulfilled before we can even consider whether it makes sense to calculate cross-country results is that the election results can be shown to be generated by the same distribution. This is actually the case. Table 1 presents electoral results for seventeen main OECD countries. A few more of the least developed OECD countries have turned to democracies within the last decade (Spain, Portugal, and Greece) and we could have added a few small countries; but by and large this is the set of elections in developed countries since 1946 that are relevant for the formation of governments. All results are expressed as a gain in the percentage of the (valid) votes cast for the government ruling before the election, even if the

14. It appears that there normally is a "honeymoon" effect, so that a new government is more popular its first six to twelve months, then the popularity falls, reaching bottom about one year before the election when it turns upward once again.

government ruled only a few months. The gain is measured relative to the voting result for the same parties at the last election. The average gain (and its standard deviation) for all 197 elections is:

$$A(\Delta C) = -1.6\%$$

$$S(\Delta C) = 5.5\% \tag{3}$$

The negativity of the average result means that it does cost votes to rule. There are only three exceptions in table 1. The wrong signs occur in Norway, Austria, and Germany. These few exceptions do not need any explanation. Given the size of $S(\Delta C)$ relative to $A(\Delta C)$ there should be a couple of wrong signs. It is, nevertheless, interesting to note that two of these cases are in countries where it is impossible or difficult for the government to call an early election. Imagine a government ruling for three years, and then having to resign because of inner disagreement. If the parliament cannot be dissolved, a new government—presumably without a majority—will have to be formed. The election result will then be for the new government. For various reasons, such a new government is likely to win votes.

In an RE world it is a paradox that it costs votes to rule (I shall speak of the "paradox of ruling"), for the average government must rule exactly as could be expected by the rational voter, so why should they systematically punish the government? The fact that we get an extremely significant loss from ruling, therefore, speaks quite strongly against rational expectations. If we nevertheless want to be within the RE framework, we have to add something to the "pure" RE theory to explain the result, such as the voters like change or 1.6 percent of the voters are irrational.[15]

For each of the countries we have drawn the election results as probit-diagrams, figures 1 and 2 show four specimens of these diagrams.[16] We have chosen to compare extreme cases. Figure 1 compares the distribution of the ΔCs in Denmark, where the party system has changed most (from five parties to fourteen and now back to nine parties) during the period, and in

---

15. It is possible to explain anything by adding a special "taste" for the thing explained. To explain that $A(\Delta C) < 0$ by a "taste for change" is, therefore, a cheap explanation, it might nevertheless be true.

16. The reader will probably remember the technique; just in case, the probit curve for the N elections in a country is made in the following way. (1) The N election outcomes (the ΔCs) are first sorted with the smallest C value first, the second smallest as the second, . . . , the largest C value in number n. (2) Then the sorted observations are depicted against the cumulated normal distribution, so that the smallest corresponds to the $100/(n + 1)\%$-probability, the second to the $200/(n + 1)\%$-probability. In case the ΔCs are normally distributed, the resulting curve looks straight—the largest deviation from straightness (roughly spoken) should be below a certain value given by the Lilliefors test, as presented, e.g., in Conover 1971.

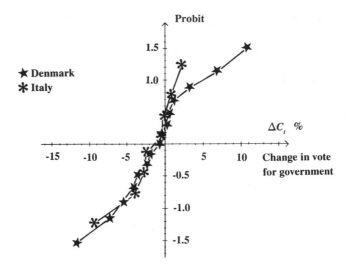

Fig. 1. The distribution of the ΔCs for Denmark and Italy

Italy, which is the closest we come to a one-party state. The reader will see that the ΔC distributions are indistinguishable.

When the probit diagrams for all seventeen countries are compared and the appropriate tests are made, it appears that for twelve of the seventeen countries the figures look as similar as one can possibly wish in the case of the

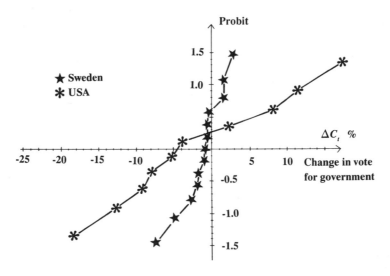

Fig. 2. The distribution of the ΔCs for Sweden and the United States

United Kingdom, Eire, New Zealand, Italy (fig. 1), Finland, Norway, Belgium, Australia, Germany, the Netherlands, Denmark (fig. 1), and Japan. Three countries are at the borderline: Sweden (fig. 2), Canada, and Austria. However, there should be a few outliers and the three countries do not have significantly different ΔC distributions. For all fifteen countries the variance is about fifteen, and when we apply the Lilliefors test for normality of the observations all countries pass, even when there are a few elections with a large shift in some countries (such as Japan and Canada). In these fifteen cases nothing has been found to indicate that we can reject the hypothesis that the results are generated from the same almost-normal distribution with the average, $A(\Delta C) = -1.6$, and the standard deviation, $S(\Delta C) = 5.5$.

Two countries, the United States (fig. 2) and France, do not appear to have a different average election result, but they are different by having a significantly higher variance in their elections. Note that it does not matter that the election laws and party systems are very different in the fifteen countries of the large group. The countries are different in size and in per capita GDP (by a factor 2.5). When we look at the distributions of the percentage change in the vote for the government (ΔC) there is no difference. In figure 2 I show one of the countries closest to the borderline, Sweden, which has a small variation but not significantly so, and one of the two "wild" countries, the United States.

The country in the main group that is closest to the borderline is Austria, with a very small variation. The Austrian case is due to the period of the "big coalition" where (almost by definition) there was no swing in the support for the government. Also, Sweden has a number of elections with a small variation (steep sections on the probit diagram). In Sweden the extreme stability occurred during the twenty-four year rule of Tage Erlander. Swedish election results have been normal since he retired.

However, two countries stand out as "high variability" countries, the United States and France. It is only too easy to explain these two cases. The United States has a presidential system and not a parliamentary one.[17] I therefore had to use presidential elections, which have twice the variability of congressional elections. In the same way, it is perfectly clear that France has had the most dramatic political history of the seventeen countries.[18] The most extreme French ΔCs do, in fact, correspond to the well-known dramatic

---

17. The United States is also different in having by far the lowest voting participation, in having the most heterogeneous political parties, etc. It is the largest and the most closed economy. It is an important point to remember that the United States tends to be an extreme case in all comparative studies.

18. France has had "near revolutions": one in 1958 and another (less serious) in 1968. Furthermore, the crisis in 1958 caused a change to its presidential system, with one of the most unusual presidents in our sample of politicians. It is not easy to find the right ΔC data for France

events in French history. However, as the game of explaining away strange cases is so easy, it is also intellectually unsatisfactory.

It appears from looking at all seventeen probit diagrams that the deviations from normality are just a few cases. Further we can present a good argument for the United States and France having an unusual number of "extreme" elections. Therefore, we have tried to work with the following general distribution:

$$\phi = \Delta C - A(\Delta C) \tag{4}$$

where $A(\Delta C)$ is the average ΔC, and

$$\Phi(\Delta C) = 2 \sqrt{(a\phi)} - a \tag{5}$$

for $\phi > a$,

$$\Phi(\Delta C) = \phi$$

for $-a \leq \phi \leq a$, and

$$\Phi(\Delta C) = -2 \sqrt{(-a\phi)} - a$$

for $\phi < -a$.

This distribution is quadratically normal at the tails ($\phi > a$ and $\phi < -a$) and normal in between. For $a = 2$ this transformation works very well. After the transformation, all seventeen countries have normal distributions, and we are unable to reject the hypothesis that all elections come from the same (normal) distribution.

This is perhaps an extremely "empiricist" result; but the reader will recall that theorists discussing how the social welfare function should look have often used quadratic formulations for many reasons. (Maybe, this is mainly because linear formulations lead to unrealistic corner solutions in optimizing problems.) So, if we take the extreme elections to be the ones dominated by one issue, then it is perhaps reasonable to get a quadratic normal result; if the election has more issues, then the result becomes normal as per the Central Limit theorem in statistics.

Hence, it does make sense to analyze vote results across countries; but

---

after 1958. For in addition to the president, there is also a prime minister. It appears that it is the latter who, in principle, has the responsibility for economic policies, so we have used the parliamentary election results.

maybe one has to use the transformation given above in equations 4 and 5, before one runs cross-country estimates.

3. The Basic Estimates

To check our result in the last section—that it makes sense to calculate cross-country estimates of the V-function—the first step is to try to obtain significant coefficients for institutional variables in cross-country regressions, such as the ones presented in table 2. The results given are typical for the results that are obtained. It is nice to see how little institutions explain—an R^2 score of .09 in a regression with six explanatory variables is remarkably low. The results confirm the ones given in section 2: the size of the country, the party structure, and the left/right variables fail to explain anything. We have also tried variables measuring the voting system (single constituency vs. more proportional systems, etc.) with the same lack of significance. Only one of the coefficients becomes significant, and that is the majority variable *Ps,* while the big coalition variable *Bc* is almost significant in (1b). These results will be discussed in a moment. One may see the results in table 2 as giving (strong) support to the preceding argument that while institutional variables may matter for the levels, they do not matter for the first differences.

The coefficient of the majority variable is −2.63 (or −3.51 for the raw ΔC data). Governments that have a majority, so that they can rule, lose more from ruling than other governments. This, of course, makes the paradox of ruling, discussed above, deeper: the majority governments must be the most

TABLE 2.   Model 1: Explaining ΔC by Institutional Variables

(1a) Raw ΔC data, $N = 190$				$[R^2 = 0.07$, SE $= 5.70$, $F(6,183) = 2.44]$		

$\Delta C = \quad -0.67 \quad +0.23 \; St \quad +0.09 \; Pa \quad -0.12 \; LR \quad +0.07 \; Ye \quad -3.51 \; Ps \quad +1.50 \; Bc$
$\qquad\quad (0.45) \quad (0.70) \qquad (0.59) \qquad (0.29) \qquad (0.87) \qquad (3.64) \qquad (0.96)$

(1b) Transformed data, $N = 190$				$[R^2 = 0.09$, SE $= 3.97$, $F(6,183) = 2.87]$		

$\Delta C = \quad +0.75 \quad +0.17 \; St \quad +0.06 \; Pa \quad -0.12 \; LR \quad +0.05 \; YE \quad -2.63 \; Ps \quad +1.53 \; Bc$
$\qquad\quad (0.70) \quad (0.72) \qquad (0.55) \qquad (0.41) \qquad (0.94) \qquad (3.91) \qquad (1.40)$

Note: Figures in parentheses below coefficient estimates are *T*-ratios. The transformation mentioned is given by eqs. 4 and 5. Seven elections are missing, all first elections where economic data are missing.

$\quad St \;$ = country size as measured by the log of the population,
$\quad Pa \;$ = party structure, the number of parties in the parliament before the election,
$\quad LR \;$ = Left/Right variable, −1 if the party ruling before the election is left, +1 if it is right, and 0 in a few cases where the orientation is unclear (the variable is discussed in Høst and Paldam 1990),
$\quad Ye \;$ = number of years the government has been in power,
$\quad Ps \;$ = 1 for a government ruling before the election having a majority, and zero otherwise, and
$\quad Bc \;$ = "big coalition" variable, 1 if the government has a majority of 80 percent or more of the parliament before the election, otherwise zero.

predictable ones, i.e., the ones about which it is most easy to form rational expectations. It is also interesting that the constant becomes insignificant and unstable. It turns out that the entire cost of ruling $(A[\Delta C] = -1.6)$ has to be paid by the governments who can actually rule. One interpretation of this result is that only the governments that are responsible are so held by the voters; but since more responsibility leads to a greater loss, we have to accept that people just don't like to be ruled, or, at least, that they do like changes.

We define a big coalition as a government supported by more than 80 percent of the parliament—not surprisingly all such governments include both the largest left and the largest right party of the country, and it is well known that such governments fight a lot internally. Nevertheless, it appears that big coalitions are often quite stable. In this light it is interesting that the coefficient for the big coalition variable is positive: $+1.5$ percent. Maybe the vote gains can help explain the stability. However, most big coalitions come about as an emergency measure, when it has proved difficult to form a normal government. One consequently may interpret the positive coefficient as a sign that a stability factor enters into the vote.

In table 3 I have added the three main variables in the VP-function literature, one at a time, to the model in table 2. The results are either insignificant or explain very little indeed. A number of experiments gave similar results. It did not improve the results to delete the institutional variables and to include two or three economic variables at the same time. Also, it did not help to include more lags.

However, as the responsibility hypothesis is the basis for the theory of

TABLE 3.   Adding One Economic Variable at a Time to Model 1, from Table 2

Raw ΔC Variable	ΔR^2	Transformed Variable	ΔR^2
Unemployment (u)			
-0.18 (0.37) Δu	0.001	-0.24 (0.71) Δu	0.002
-1.12 (2.03) Δu_{-1}	0.024	-0.78 (2.02) Δu_{-1}	0.023
Consumer Price Rises (p)			
$+0.08$ (0.72) Δp	0.003	$+0.05$ (0.09) Δp	0.002
$+0.13$ (1.81) Δp_{-1}	0.021	$+0.07$ (0.09) Δp_{-1}	0.016
Growth of Real GDP (y)			
-0.08 (0.74) Δy	0.004	-0.07 (0.99) Δy	0.005
$+0.02$ (0.15) Δy_{-1}	0.005	$+0.03$ (0.40) Δy_{-1}	0.006

Note: ΔR^2 is the change in the R^2 score brought about by adding the given variable.

the VP-function it is arguable—as in the last section—that certain other patterns should turn up in the results once we divide up the results into more or less "stable" systems. This is done in tables 4 and 5, where the party system is divided into more or less simple or stable systems. Let us first consider table 4. There is a tendency that the closer we are to a simple two-party system, the better the traditional VP-function pattern appears, and the more complex the system becomes the more the signs change to the reverse. However, it should also be noted that none of the results are very good—we get at most one significant coefficient and the R^2 is always very low.

Table 4 suggests that one reason for getting the poor fit in table 1 may be that the results from stable and unstable countries offset each other. This is further examined in table 5, where we get results in (3) that look a bit like the standard ones in the literature, even though they are (still) unsatisfactory. Note also that the two results for the unstable governments do look different. If the results in (3) and (4) are compared, the coefficients to Δp are significantly different, and the same applies when (2) and (5) are compared. If (3) and (5) are compared, the coefficients to Δp are significantly different, and the coeffi-

TABLE 4.   Dividing the Election Results according to Party Structure

Making the Structure More Simple	Making the Structure More Complex
$Pa < 7, N = 142$	$Pa > 2, N = 171$
-0.19 Δu $+0.03$ Δp $R^2 = .001$	-0.06 Δu $+0.06$ Δp $R^2 = .002$
(0.44) (0.29)	(0.19) (0.80)
$Pa < 6, N = 115$	$Pa > 3, N = 123$
-0.20 Δu $+0.06$ Δp $R^2 = .004$	$+0.07$ Δu $+0.00$ Δp $R^2 = .000$
(0.43) (0.50)	(0.17) (0.00)
$Pa < 5, N = 87$	$Pa > 4, N = 103$
-0.25 Δu $+0.18$ Δp $R^2 = .016$	-0.11 Δu $+0.01$ Δp $R^2 = .000$
(0.50) (1.22)	(0.24) (0.15)
$Pa < 4, N = 67$	$Pa > 5, N = 75$
-0.73 Δu $+0.34$ Δp $R^2 = .09$	-0.23 Δu $+0.07$ Δp $R^2 = .005$
(1.46) (2.04)	(0.44) (0.63)
$Pa < 3, N = 19$	$Pa > 6, N = 48$
-2.56 Δu -0.35 Δp $R^2 = .07$	-0.25 Δu $+0.25$ Δp $R^2 = .025$
(1.41) (0.66)	(0.47) (1.38)

Note: The institutional variables are left out. Pa is the number of parties in the Parliament before the election. The results presented are for the transformed ΔC variable; but they are very similar for the raw variable.

TABLE 5. Dividing into More and Less Stable Governments

More Stable Governments	Less Stable Governments

(1) Majority governments, $N = 136$
  -0.32 Δu -0.07 Δp $R^2 = .00$
  (0.71) (0.67)
	(4) Minority governments, $N = 54$
	  -0.08 Δu $+0.05$ Δp $R^2 = .00$
	  (0.14) (0.43)

(2) Governments ruling > 2 years, $N = 138$
  -0.59 Δu -0.12 Δp $R^2 = .02$
  (1.23) (1.05)
	(5) Governments ruling < 2 years, $N = 33$
	  -0.23 Δu $+0.16$ Δp $R^2 = .04$
	  (0.36) (1.61)

(3) Stable Governments, $N = 115$
  -0.94 Δu -0.14 Δp $R^2 = .03$
  (1.73) (1.06)	

Note: The institutional variables are left out. The results presented are for the transformed ΔC variable; but they are very similar for the raw variable. Stable governments are defined as a majority government ruling a full election period, i.e., at least 80 percent of the election period.

cients to Δu are different in the desired direction. This is an interesting result indicating that there is a highly significant difference in the way voters react to stable and unstable governments.

So we can conclude that the VP-function does contain a stability dimension. If an economic deterioration occurs under a weak, unstable government it makes people "gather" around the government, so the result is the reverse of (or much weaker than) the usual pattern. In fact, this finding would appear to give some additional support to the responsibility hypothesis. People hold the government responsible for economic conditions if the government is seen as ruling. However, when the opposition has the majority but is unable to rule, people take the opposition to be responsible.

4. Consequences for the Theory of VP-Functions: How Deep Is the Instability?

From the preceding argument it appears that the VP-function belongs to the family of awkward macrofunctions that have the following four characteristics: (1) they are statistically highly significant for some countries and time periods, (2) they nevertheless suffer from great instability as they disappear in some other countries and time periods, (3) they are needed to play an important role in a lot of theory and in practical forecasting and analysis, and (4) there is no better alternative. Other distinguished members of that family are the accelerator model of investment and the Phillips curve.[19] These func-

---

19. Especially in regard to the Phillips curve, it appears, however, that if we take a similarly large data set, as the one used above, we get a very significant negative coefficient a_1 for unemployment u, when explaining wage rises, w, by $w = a_0 + a_1 u$, even when the average R^2 for the simple Phillips curve is as low as .25.

tions are frequently declared null and void, but they nevertheless always return to life because there is "something out there," and we need a function explaining what the said function does.

My analysis has suggested one way to make the VP-function more stable: systematically build in the stability of the government. However, even if that is done there is probably still a great deal left before the function is really satisfactory.

The next question to pose is this: How deep is the instability? Is all that is required just one little trick, and then the function stabilizes? Perhaps some mathematical reformulation, one crucial new variable, etc., and then the function works. Or, is the instability so deep that there is no hope of finding a satisfactory VP-function? Three schools of thought suggest that the instability is deep indeed.

First, a VP-function is, of course, an empirical social welfare function. Seeing such results as those presented above, the social choice theorist is likely to rub his or her hands, grab Arrow's 1951 book and say something like: "This is what we, following our master, have been saying all along (a survey of all the nonexistence proofs in Social Choice theory is found in Sen 1986). Individual welfare functions cannot be aggregated into a meaningful social welfare function. Therefore, if you go ahead estimating one, you are likely to find nothing really solid has actually happened to you."

We, who have estimated such functions, have several answers to this general argument. The best answer probably is to turn to the following well-known parallel case: index theorists have developed a large number of proofs that the perfect price index does not exist.[20] As a consequence, the perfect real product does not exist. However, we do have a number of trusted methods to estimate imperfect price indices. They give results within a fairly narrow range, and there is a well-known pattern in the deviations between the results, so we can calculate price indices that are much better than nothing. In the same sense it would not have been overly worrying that the perfect social welfare function fails to exist, as long as we can estimate an approximation that is reasonably robust.

The same argument can be taken one step further. Nearly all economists (and, presumably, political scientists as well) believe that our goal is to obtain an integrated theory where the macrorelations are reached by aggregation of microrelations obtained from individuals maximizing explicitly formulated utility functions.

Second, some economists—let us term them the anti-macrotheorists—argue that macrotheory is a dubious field. What we have to do to obtain

---

20. The technique of the proofs is very much like Arrow's. You start by making a list of seemingly innocent axioms to which, as a minimum, the "true" index should obey. You then demonstrate that the set of indices that would fulfill the axioms is empty. Eichhorn and Voeller (1976) list eighteen such nonexistence proofs, and more have been made in the last decade.

satisfactory VP-functions (or any other macrofunction) is to start all over again and follow an "ideal" program. First we have to build a solid micro-theory on axioms that are thoroughly tested and logically consistent, and only aggregate to the macrolevel after a thorough examination of the properties of the aggregations has been made. If this is not done we will have to live with the instability.

The main problem with this ideal program is that there are so few—if any—examples where it is applicable.[21] Maybe in a century or two this would be the right way to go; in the meantime we need all the information we can possibly get from both the micro- and the macrolevel to build up a better theory.

Third, RE theorists will, as already mentioned, say that in their favorite case of high information expectations (the HIRE case) these functions should be unstable. Maybe one has to see our results as indicating that the relevant expectations are, after all, forward looking and based on a much broader information set than just the extremely simple myopic adaptive process. However, if this is the case, then the paradox of voting and the paradox of ruling would appear to become even more pressing. Suppose voters spend a lot of time trying to develop the best expectations possible. Then why do they vote at all, systematically punishing governments and, especially, stable governments?

Hence, there are three schools who would all appear to argue that the instability of the VP-function is of such a basic character that we cannot expect to do anything about it. The instability goes to the very core of the function. Our findings, as reported, are perhaps slightly less negative than the theoretical arguments of these three schools, but they are certainly not very encouraging.

On the other hand, it is obvious theoretical economists, political scientists, and policymakers need VP-functions. We very often see arguments in theoretical papers and in policy statements, from all kinds of governments, that explicitly or implicitly use a social welfare function. In fact, once we use a multiperiod framework in our analysis, it is very hard to get anywhere analytically without making welfare assumptions, which imply something about the macrowelfare function. The only really feasible way to get an empirical handle on that function seems to be the VP-function approach.

5. What Next

The whole argument above is that the VP-function is a function that is on the one hand unstable and, on the other hand, often highly significant. This

---

21. There is a horrifying tendency for the strictest formal theories never to lead any-where—the number of intellectual games one can play with, say, twenty axioms is so big as to be,

combination has led to great research efforts, for the combination of significance and instability appears to suggest that we are just missing one little trick that would make the function stable. It may be a mathematical reformulation, the inclusion of a crucial missing variable, or something else; once the trick has succeeded, everything is pushed forward with a full decimal point. There is, of course, a great incentive to write the paper presenting the trick. It would surely become one of the most quoted papers—so I am trying.

However, the arguments in section 4 suggest that perhaps the problem is deeper. The problem is not just one little trick. In that case, there appear to be three main lines that may lead to a breakthrough.

1. Improved microfoundations. If the problem is in the aggregation, we have to make better microtheories. From the attempts made, it does not appear to be clear that this is the way, but it is worth discussing.

2. Analyze periodicity more systematically, trying to identify the periods where the functions work the best and periods where they break down. Some researchers are already pursuing this line of attack, producing papers that sometimes appear to lead to short-run modeling of the political process, looking almost like political history (see Lafay, this volume).

3. Construct better political series. This possibility is perhaps the most promising, in the sense that it can be done. When done, it is sure to answer some questions; even if the answers turn out to be negative, they will still be interesting. What I am thinking of is the construction of quantitative indices of various types of "political events" from media coverage. For example, how much space is devoted to certain types of events in the main newspapers and TV channels per month? Only if we, in this or a related way, manage to construct adequate political series to use together with the economic series will we get truly politico-economic models; obviously this is the job for the political scientist.

Altogether it would therefore appear that there is enough that can be done to improve our knowledge in the important field of VP-functions. There is no chance or risk that research in the area will dry out in the foreseeable future.

REFERENCES

Arrow, J. K. 1951. *Social Choice and Individual Values.* 2d ed. 1963. New Haven: Yale University Press.
Conover, W. J. 1971. *Practical Nonparametric Statistics.* New York: Wiley.
Downs, A. 1957. *An Economic Theory of Democracy.* New York: Harper and Row.
Eichhorn, W., and J. Voeller. 1976. *Theory of the Price Index.* Lecture Notes in Economics and Mathematical Systems 140. Berlin: Springer.

---

in practice, unlimited. So even the first step in the ideal program tends to stall by its own inner dynamics.

Fiorina, M. P. 1981. *Retrospective Voting in American National Elections.* New Haven: Yale University Press.

Frey, B. S., and F. Schneider. 1978a. "An Empirical Study of Politico-Economic Interaction in the US." *Review of Economics and Statistics* 60:174–83.

Frey, B. S., and F. Schneider. 1978b. "A Politico-Economic Model of the United Kingdom." *Economic Journal* 88:243–53.

Goodhart, C. A. E., and R. J. Bhansali. 1970. "Political Economy." *Political Studies* 18:43–106.

Hendry, D. F., and G. F. Mizon. 1990. "Procrustean Econometrics, or Stretching and Squeezing Data." In *Modelling Economic Series,* ed. Clive Granger. Oxford: Oxford University Press.

Hibbs, D. A., Jr. 1977. "Political Parties and Macroeconomic Policy." *American Political Science Review* 71:1467–87.

Hibbs, D. A., Jr. 1982. "On the Demand for Economic Outcomes: Macroeconomic Outcomes and Mass Political Support in the United States, Great Britain, and Germany." *Journal of Politics* 44:426–62.

Hibbs, D. A., Jr. 1987. *The Political Economy of Industrial Democracies.* Cambridge, MA: Harvard University Press.

Høst, V., and M. Paldam. 1990. "An International Element in the Vote? A Comparative Study of Seventeen OECD Countries, 1948–85. *European Journal of Political Research* 18:221–39.

Kinder, D. R., and D. R. Kiewiet. 1979. "Economic Discontent and Political Behavior: The Role of Personal Grievances and Collective Economic Judgments in Congressional Voting." *American Journal of Political Science* 23:495–527.

Kirchgässner, G. 1976. "Rationales Wählerverhalten und optimales Regierungsverhalten." Ph.D. diss. Universität Konstanz.

Kirchgässner, G. 1985. "Causality Testing of the Popularity Function: An Empirical Investigation for the Federal Republic of Germany, 1971–1982." *Public Choice* 45:155–73.

Kirchgässner, G. 1986. "Economic Conditions and the Popularity of West German Parties: A Survey." *European Journal of Political Research* 14:421–39.

Korpi, W. 1989. "Unemployment and Distributive Conflict in a Long-Term Perspective: A Comparative Study of Eighteen OECD Countries." Institutet för Social Forskning, Stockholms Universitet. Manuscript.

Kramer, G. H. 1971. "Short-Term Fluctuations in U.S. Voting Behavior, 1896–1964. *American Political Science Review* 65:131–43.

Leamer, E. E. 1983. "Let's Take the Con out of Econometrics." *American Economic Review* 73:31–43.

Lewis-Beck, M. S. 1988. *Economics and Elections: The Major Western Democracies.* Ann Arbor, MI: University of Michigan Press.

Lybeck, J. 1986. *The Growth of Government in Developed Economies.* Aldeshot: Gower.

Paldam, M. 1981a. "An Essay on the Rationality of Economic Policy: The Test-Case of the Electional Cycle." *Public Choice* 37:287–305.

Paldam, M. 1981b. "A Preliminary Survey of the Theories and Findings on Vote and Popularity Functions." *European Journal of Political Research* 9:181–99.

Paldam, M. 1986. "The Distribution of Election Results and the Two Explanations of the Cost of Ruling." *European Journal of Political Economy* 2:5–24.

Paldam, M. 1990a. "Politics Matters after All (1): A Comparative Test of Alesina's Theory of Partisan Cycles." Forthcoming in *Recent Developments in Business Cycle Theory—Methods and Empirical Applications,* ed. N. Thygesen and K. Velupillai. London: Macmillan.

Paldam, M. 1990b. "Politics Matters after All (2): A Comparative Test of Hibbs's Theory of Partisan Cycles." Forthcoming in *Markets and Politicians,* ed. J. M. Guttman and A. L. Hillman. Doordrecht: Kluwer.

Paldam, M., and F. Schneider. 1980. "The Macroeconomic Aspects of Government and Opposition Popularity in Denmark 1957–78." *Nationaløkonomisk Tidsskrift* 118:149–70.

Pissarides, C. A. 1980. "British Government Popularity and Economic Performance." *Economic Journal* 90:569–81.

Schneider, F. 1984. "Public Attitudes Toward Economic Conditions and Their Impact on Government Behavior." *Political Behavior* 6:223–52.

Sen, A. 1986. "Social Choice Theory." In *Handbook of Mathematical Economics,* vol. 3, ed. K. J. Arrow and M. D. Intriligator. Amsterdam: North-Holland.

Whiteley, P. F. 1986. "Macroeconomic Performance and Government Popularity in Britain: The Short-Run Dynamics." *European Journal of Political Research* 14:45–61.

The Economy in U.S. House Elections

Gary C. Jacobson

If democracy works at all, economic conditions ought to shape election results. Modern governments have assumed broad responsibility for the economic welfare of citizens. Governing parties and leaders should thus be
rewarded or punished at the polls according to how well they manage the
economy. Apparently they are: other things being equal, the more robust the
economy, the better for parties in power. But we are far from understanding
precisely how economic conditions are translated into election results.

Such a translation is especially complex in elections to the U.S. House of
Representatives. In the aggregate, House elections reflect national economic
conditions: the stronger the economy, the more seats the administration's
party wins. Yet an unusually decentralized, candidate-centered system of
electoral politics renders the strength of the connection contingent and variable. It is contingent on the political strategies pursued by candidates and
other political activists, and it varies according to how effectively economic
issues are exploited by particular campaigns in individual states and districts.
The electoral effects of economic conditions are by no means a simple expression of economic rationality among voters; a good part of the economy's
influence is indirect, mediated by elite activities. The electorate's ability to
sanction economic performance thus depends to an important degree on strategic politicians.

Economic Voting in Congressional Elections

Congressional election results respond, broadly, to the national economy.
Analyses of aggregate time-series data by Kramer (1971), Tufte (1975 and
1978) and various of their critics and defenders[1] have produced abundant, if
not entirely unchallenged, evidence that variations in votes and seats won by
House candidates reflect variations in economic conditions. Economic expan-

---

1. For a brief summary of this literature, see Jacobson and Kernell 1983; for more detailed
accounts, see Monroe 1984 and Weatherford 1986.

sion, lower unemployment, and rising real income lead to more victories for House candidates of the president's party; contrary economic trends produce more defeats. Collectively, the electorate behaves like V. O. Key's "rational god of vengeance and reward" (1964, 567).

Although the aggregate evidence is silent about its own genesis, the assumption underlying most of this work is that collective economic rationality reflects individual economic rationality. "Rational voters are concerned with their real income and wealth" (Arcelus and Meltzer 1975, 1,234) and so vote in response to their own economic experiences under different administrations. But when this proposition was initially tested with survey data, the results were at best inconclusive, and most often negative. Individual analogs of national economic conditions (change in family income, experience with unemployment) appeared to have little or no impact on voting for House candidates (Kiewiet 1983).

Attempts to resolve this conflict between findings based on aggregate and survey data have followed two paths.[2] One line of research has continued to probe survey data more deeply for signs of rational economic voting. For example, Hibbing and Alford (1981), Alford and Hibbing (1982), Fiorina (1983), and Weatherford (1986) have shown that personal financial experiences have a stronger impact on voters' decisions in congressional districts held by incumbent members of the president's party, particularly when the economy is performing poorly. The effects are not especially strong or stable across election years, but they offer some support for the idea that voters reward or punish congressional candidates selectively in response to personal economic experiences. Other work has shown that more general economic assessments—of business conditions, of the administration's economic policies and performance, of party competence on economic matters—sometimes influence individual voting decisions, though once again few relationships remain stable across election years (Fiorina 1981; Jacobson 1983; Kiewiet 1983; Abramowitz, Cover, and Norpoth 1986).

Although it is possible to interpret these findings as evidence of rational economic voting in the conventional sense (Fiorina 1981; Kiewiet 1983), it is not at all clear that such an interpretation can be sustained. For any attempt to account for electoral choice as a pure manifestation of instrumental economic rationality runs up against the reality that anyone who thinks his own con-

---

2. Kramer (1983) proposed a third alternative by demonstrating that, in theory, there need be no conflict because intertemporal effects may not show up in cross-sectional analyses; Rivers (n.d.) finds evidence to support Kramer's theory in his reanalysis of presidential election surveys but has not yet applied his solution to surveys of congressional voters. But because the anomaly also shows up in panel studies, it is unlikely that Kramer's (and Rivers's) approach will resolve the problem. See Jacobson and Kernell 1983.

gressional vote will actually affect his economic welfare one way or the other is plainly *irrational*.[3]

As Downs (1957) recognized, pure utility maximizers will not vote at all if the only reason for voting is to affect the outcome. The benefit of having the preferred candidate win, discounted by the probability that an individual's vote will be decisive, is vanishingly small, because the probability of casting a decisive vote is vanishingly small. If voting costs anything—and there are always opportunity costs—rational people will not vote. But the same problem confounds theories of economic voting by people who *do* vote. Because the likelihood that a person's vote for a congressional candidate will affect his economic welfare in any way is, for all practical purposes, zero, there would be no reason to expect instrumentally rational economic voting even if the electorate were composed entirely of microeconomists.

Rational choice theorists have finessed the turnout problem by attributing utility to the act of voting itself (Riker and Ordeshook 1968). People vote because the act is intrinsically satisfying; it fulfills their duty as citizens and provides an avenue for political self-expression. But there is no equivalent solution for economic voting. Americans are not brought up to believe that they have a duty to vote according to how satisfied they are with changes in their real disposable incomes. No particular focus of political self-expression is normative. The question of what the vote is about, what it should express, is open.

Even when voters are persuaded that the vote should be about the economy, the question of what an economic vote should be about remains open: Retrospective personal or family finances? ("Are you better off than you were four years ago?") The national economy? (Are business conditions better or worse?) Future economic expectations, either personal or national? (Should we "stay the course" despite recession? Which party will be better at handling unemployment or inflation?) There is no conventional answer to these questions and, thus, it is not so strange that the measured effects of individual economic experiences and evaluations vary so much across districts and election years. An open question invites persuasive argument; the effects of economic issues depend, in part, on how they are portrayed and exploited by candidates and other activists during the course of election campaigns. And insofar as candidates and campaigns compete to cast economic issues in the form that helps them most (or hurts them least), the economy becomes an endogenous factor in the election. The evidence for this view is still fragmen-

---

3. The exception would be when the vote is purchased directly by a candidate—difficult since universal adoption of the secret ballot and, by all accounts, an extremely rare occurrence in recent congressional elections.

tary and largely indirect, because systematic district-level information on the content of campaigns has never been available for study (Abramowitz 1984; Jacobson 1983 and 1986); but it is consistent with survey findings, as well as with a second approach to dealing with the anomaly that accords a pivotal role to strategic political elites.

Strategic Politicians

An alternative approach to understanding how the economy shapes congressional election results takes as its point of departure some familiar idiosyncratic features of electoral politics in the United States. The entire electoral process is loosely coupled. The president and members of Congress are elected separately. Parties do not control congressional nominations and, in most places, do little or nothing to recruit candidates. Congressional candidates are necessarily self-starters and, for the most part, must rely on their own efforts to mount election campaigns. Party loyalty among voters is weak; most Americans think that they should vote for the "better" person regardless of party and regularly divide their votes between Republicans and Democrats. Congressional candidates adapt by emphasizing their personal virtues and accomplishments rather than commitment to national parties or programs. As a result, the focus of electoral politics is predominantly local and personal.

The same surveys that offer but little evidence of economic voting offer abundant evidence of candidate-centered voting. What voters know and like or dislike about the particular pair of candidates running in the district has a major influence on the vote decision; evaluative comments about candidates refer far more often to personal characteristics and constituency services than to parties, policies, or issues (Jacobson 1987b). At the same time, aggregate data reveal electoral trends to be remarkably idiosyncratic across districts. In elections from 1972 through 1984, for example, the mean absolute interelections vote swing in House districts contested by incumbents was 3.3 percentage points, but its standard deviation averaged 8.7 percentage points, and its range averaged 57 percentage points (Jacobson 1986).

Cross-district variation of this sort is by no means random. As would be expected in a candidate-centered electoral process, it is directly related to variations in the quality of congressional candidates and the vigor of their campaigns. Most of this variation is supplied by challengers to incumbent members; in particular, the more challengers spend on campaigns, the more votes they receive and the more likely they are to win (Jacobson 1985, 1986, 1987a, and n.d.).

Variations in the quality of challengers and the vigor of their campaigns is not random, either. As a group, ambitious, experienced career politicians make the most formidable candidates for Congress; they have the greatest

TABLE 1.   The Likelihood of Election and Quality of Nonincumbent
Candidates in U.S. House Elections, 1946–86

Type of Race	N	Percentage Who Won	Percentage of Total N Who Had Held Elective Office
Open seats			
No general election opposition	34	100.0	82.4
Held by candidate's party	821	75.0	62.6
Held by neither party	188	50.0	54.8
Held by opposite party	821	25.0	33.7
Challengers to incumbents	6,174	7.8	25.5

Source: Data compiled by author.

incentive and opportunity to develop the political skills and connections that produce effective candidacies. They also risk the most in trying to move to higher office, for defeat may retard or even end a political career. Thus the best candidates will also be the most sensitive to the odds on winning and to the conditions that affect the odds.

Initial evidence for this point is found in table 1. Here and throughout this chapter, candidate quality is measured by a simple dichotomous variable—whether the candidate has ever held elective public office of any kind. Candidates who have been elected to public office are considered high-quality candidates; the rest are not.[4] The table ranks electoral circumstances facing nonincumbent House candidates in the order of their proportion of victories in general elections from 1946 through 1986. Candidates for open seats who are unopposed naturally win every time; challengers to incumbents have the lowest success rate. The odds facing candidates for open seats who are opposed depend on which party, if any, previously held the seat. Clearly, the greater the chance of victory, the greater the proportion of high-quality candidates. In addition, an experienced candidate is more likely to challenge an incumbent the slimmer the incumbent's margin of victory in the previous election and the more favorable the local partisan balance (Bianco 1984; Bond, Covington, and Fleisher 1985; Canon 1985; Krasno and Green 1988;

---

4. More elaborate and nuanced measures of candidate quality have been developed (Bond, Covington, and Fleisher 1985; Canon 1985; Krasno and Green 1988), but I stick with this simple dichotomy (which biases the findings in favor of the null hypothesis) because prior office is the single piece of background information relevant to quality most frequently mentioned in the sources I rely on for data covering the first half of the postwar period. For this period, background information was taken primarily from newspapers archived in the Library of Congress; since the early 1960s, much of this information is available in *Congressional Quarterly Weekly Report*'s special preelection reviews of all House races.

Jacobson 1989). The best candidates are highly sensitive to local conditions that affect electoral odds.

Local electoral circumstances are not the only strategic considerations that affect the quality of candidates. Because congressional candidates must mount and conduct their own campaigns with comparatively little help from local or national parties, money and other campaign resources are crucially important. Astute career politicians will not enter contests without some promise of sufficient funds. People who control essential campaign resources also deploy them strategically. Regardless of their motives for contributing, they do not invest much in hopeless causes; better odds inspire more generous donations to nonincumbent House candidates with the appropriate views (Jacobson 1980). Among the things potential donors consider is the quality of the candidate. Better candidates attract more money, just as the availability of money attracts better candidates.

Potential candidates and contributors take an additional strategic factor into account: whether it promises to be a particularly good year for one party (and so a particularly bad year for the other). Because they believe that economic conditions affect election results, the economy shapes perceptions of election odds and thus strategic decisions about running and contributing. When economic conditions appear to favor a party, more of its ambitious careerists decide that this is the year to go after a House seat. Promising candidates of the other party are more inclined to wait for a more propitious time. People who control campaign resources provide more to challengers when the economy is expected to help their preferred party, more to incumbents when economic conditions put it on the defensive. Because the effects of campaign spending are sharply asymmetrical—marginal returns on campaign spending are far higher for challengers than for incumbents in House elections (Jacobson 1985 and 1990)—converging offensive and defensive strategies produce a net gain for challengers of the party favored by economic conditions.

The aggregate result of individual strategic decisions is that the party expected to have a good year fields a superior crop of well-financed challengers, while the other party fields more than the usual number of under-financed amateurs. Strategic decisions skew the choice between pairs of candidates across House districts, so voters need only respond to the local alternatives to reflect, in their aggregate behavior, the economic conditions that shaped elite strategies. Personal economic experiences may still influence individual vote decisions, but a pervasive habit of economic voting is not, in theory, necessary to produce a connection between the national economy and congressional election results.

Taken to its logical extreme, the argument implies that prophecies about a party's electoral prospects could be purely self-fulfilling. But decisions based on illusion are hardly strategic; the economy must have *some* independent effect for the argument to make sense. There is good reason for thinking that the economy does affect voting, even in a system of electoral politics dominated by local candidates and campaigns. For the economy can be turned into a local campaign issue—if a smart candidate has the resources to do it. Poor economic performance, for example, offers a challenger of the party out of power a tool for undermining the personal support an incumbent commonly enjoys. Whether or not the incumbent suffers real damage from the issue depends, however, on whether the challenger has the means and skills to exploit it. Thus, at the aggregate level, a party will benefit more from advantageous economic conditions the better its challengers; superior challengers will prosper to the degree that the economy can be turned against incumbents. It is this interactive combination of exploitable national issues and vigorous challenges that should change the makeup of Congress.

The Economy, Strategic Politicians, and Election Results

Since Kernell and I developed the argument that strategic politicians pursuing their own careers play a crucial, if unintentional, role in translating economic and other national conditions into aggregate congressional election results (Jacobson and Kernell 1983), doubts have been raised about one or another of its features (Uslaner and Conway 1985; Born 1986; Krasno and Green 1988). Thus in this section I review some of the evidence in its defense.

For the argument to be valid, several conditions must hold. Objectively superior challengers (by my definition, those who have previously held elective office) have to win more often. More of them must appear when economic (and other) conditions favor their party, fewer when the contrary holds. And their numbers must affect wins and losses apart from, or interacting with, economic conditions.

The first condition is easily met. Table 2 shows that challengers and candidates for open House seats who have held elective office are much more likely to win. Experienced challengers are almost four times as likely to defeat incumbents. Candidates for open seats with prior office are also more likely to win, their chances depending also on whether their opponents are similarly experienced (as well, of course, as on which party already held the seat). For (new) open seats held by neither party, experienced candidates win four of five contests with candidates who have never held elective office ($N = 59$; data not shown).

The success enjoyed by experienced challengers is not merely a consequence of more careful selection of targets, though such strategic behavior certainly contributes to it. They have a higher probability of winning, even

TABLE 2. Political Experience and the Frequency of Victory in U.S. House Elections, 1946–86

	N	Percentage Who Won
Open seats		
Only candidate of party currently		
holding seat has held elective office	347	86.8
Neither candidate has held elective		
office	192	76.6
Both candidates have held elective		
office	199	65.3
Only candidate of party not currently		
holding seat has held elective office	95	49.5
Challengers to incumbents		
Candidate has held elective office	1,714	17.7
Candidate has not held elective office	5,020	4.5

Note: For open seats, percentage of victories for party currently holding the seat.

taking the opportunities presented by local and national politics into account. And although high-quality candidates do better in part because they spend more money on the campaign, they are more likely to win even when their level of campaign spending is taken into account. This is demonstrated by the probit estimates reported in table 3.

The first probit equation in table 3 shows that local political circumstances (measured by the incumbent's vote margin in the last election) and national partisan tides (the change in the partisan distribution of the national House vote from one election to the next) both strongly influence a challenger's chances of victory. An idea of how much difference national partisan swings can make is given in the lower half of the table. Under probit analysis, relationships are nonlinear; the effect of any variable depends on the level of probability established by all of the other variables. So to interpret the results, the first column in the lower section of table 3 lists an initial probability, and the other columns indicate how this probability would differ under the condition specified at the head of the column.

The second column thus lists the probability that a challenger will win, given a shift of 3.4 percentage points in the national House vote (the mean absolute shift for the years covered in the table) in his or her party's favor, compared to the probability of winning with no partisan shift (shown in the first column). For example, a challenger who otherwise had a .10 probability of defeating the incumbent would have a .22 probability of winning if the national vote swing to his or her party was 3.4 percentage points; an initial .15 probability would increase to .30 under the same conditions. If there were an

TABLE 3.   Probit Estimates of a House Challenger's Probability of Winning, 1972–86 (N = 2,377)

Variables	3.1	3.2	3.3
Intercept	−4.214***	−4.122***	−3.117***
	(0.277)	(0.279)	(0.326)
Challenger's party's district vote in last election	.063***	.057***	.029***
	(.006)	(.007)	(.008)
National partisan swing, $t − 1$ to t	.147***	.141***	.134***
	(.015)	(.015)	(.018)
Challenger has held elective office		.454***	.318**
		(.095)	(.109)
Log challenger's campaign expenditures ($100,000s)			.911***
			(.088)
Log incumbent's campaign expenditures ($100,000s)			−.387***
			(.088)
Log likelihood	−444.0	−432.8	−345.8

Interpretation of Results[a]			
	Partisan Swing (Eq. 3.1)		Challenger Has Held Elective Office
Initial Probability	+3.4%	−3.4%	(Eq. 3.2)	(Eq. 3.3)
.01	.03	.00	.03	.02
.05	.13	.02	.12	.09
.10	.22	.04	.20	.17
.15	.30	.06	.28	.24
.20	.37	.09	.35	.30
.25	.43	.12	.41	.36

Note: Standard errors are in parentheses.
[a]Computed from maximum likelihood coefficients in probits.
*$p < .05$.   **$p < .01$.   ***$p < .001$.

equally large shift against a challenger's party, the .10 likelihood of winning would drop to .04, and the .15 likelihood would fall to .06.

The second equation in table 3, interpreted by the fourth column, demonstrates that high-quality challengers have a substantially greater chance of winning than would be expected from national and local political circumstances alone. For example, if conditions gave an inexperienced challenger a 5 percent chance of success, an experienced challenger would enjoy a 12 percent chance of success. Indeed, experience makes as much difference as a favorable 3.2 percentage point shift in the national party vote. Equation 3.3, interpreted in the fifth column, shows that, although some of the advantage superior candidates enjoy is attributable to better financing, experience itself makes an important independent contribution to the chance of winning. It is worth almost as much as a 3 percentage point swing in the national vote in favor of the challenger's party.

The second condition—that parties field more high-quality challengers under favorable economic circumstances, fewer under the contrary—is also largely met, as the regression equations in table 4 attest. The dependent variables in this set of equations are the percentages of Democratic (equation 4.1) and Republican (equation 4.2) challengers who have held elective office, and the difference between the two parties on this score (equations 4.3). Two control variables are included: the party of the administration (1 if Democratic, -1 if Republican) and the percentage of House seats the Democrats already hold. The former affects other variables because of the way the model is specified; the latter acknowledges that the more seats a party holds, the greater the number of inviting targets it presents to challengers of the opposing party regardless of other circumstances.

The state of the economy is measured by the percentage change in real disposable income per capita over the year ending in the second quarter of the election year.[5] In using real income growth to proxy the economy, I follow a majority of scholars working in this area, who appear to have two main reasons for adopting this measure. One is theoretical: it corresponds to the (dubious) assumption that economic voting is about personal finances. The other is that real income growth is usually more highly correlated with election results than any of the plausible alternatives: GNP growth, and levels of, or changes in, unemployment and inflation. In fact, it seems to be a good summary measure of economic performance on all of these dimensions. Because the administration's party (not just the Democratic party) is supposed to be rewarded or punished for its management of the economy, this variable is multiplied by -1 when a Republican sits in the White House. The figure for the second quarter (April–June) of the election year is used because this is the time period during which most *final* decisions about candidacy must be made.

Both economic conditions and the level of public approval of the president have a significant and substantial effect on the quality of Democratic challengers. Neither one matters for Republicans, who are sensitive only to the opportunities offered by the current level of Democratic strength in the

---

5. Data to compute quarter-to-quarter changes in real per capita income through 1976 are from *The National Income and Product Accounts of the United States, 1927–1976, Statistical Tables* (1981). Data for later years are taken from various issues of *The Survey of Current Business*. Year-to-year changes are computed from data in *The Economic Report of the President, 1987*. Quarterly data are not available for 1945–46, so the yearly figure is substituted for that observation in the regressions in table 4.

TABLE 4. The Economy, Presidential Approval, and the Quality of House Challengers, 1946–86 ($N = 21$)

Variables	Democrats 4.1	Republicans 4.2	Democrats Minus Republicans 4.3
Intercept	37.54**	−2.95	40.49**
	(11.40)	(9.61)	(14.64)
Party of administration	−9.24**	1.70	−10.94**
	(2.85)	(2.40)	(3.66)
Percentage of seats won by	−.12	.33*	−.45
Democrats, $t - 1$	(.20)	(.17)	(.25)
Change in real income per	1.67***	−.07	1.75**
capita (second quarter)	(0.45)	(.38)	(0.58)
$\bar{R}^2$	.41	.09	.40
SER	5.25	4.43	6.74

Note: The dependent variable is the percentage of challengers who have held elective office; SER is the standard error of the regression; standard errors of the regression coefficients are in parentheses.
$*p < .05.$ $**p < .01.$ $***p < .001.$

House. A composite index measuring the relative quality of challengers is affected significantly by all of these variables. Democratic challengers are clearly more "strategic" than Republican challengers by these measures. Yet it turns out that the quality of Republican challengers has just as strong an impact on election results as does the quality of Democratic challengers. Indeed, the fact that candidate quality is not strictly collinear with economic and other conditions makes it easier to show that it does have an independent influence on House election results.

The third condition also holds: the aggregate quality of each party's challengers has a major effect on election results apart from the impact of the economy (or the president's standing with the public). This is evident from the series of regression results reported in table 5. The dependent variable is the change in the percentage share of House seats held by Democrats from one election to the next. I chose to examine changes in seats rather than votes— the other dependent variable common in the literature—because seats represent the electoral bottom line; in any case, the results are not at all sensitive to this choice, because seat and vote swings are very highly correlated (Jacobson 1989).

The two control variables are again included, the first for the same reason as before, the second in recognition of the reality that the more seats a party already holds, the more difficult it is to win additional seats (Oppenheimer, Stimson, and Waterman 1986). The other variables are measured as before,

TABLE 5.   The Economy, Strategic Politicians, and Interelection Vote Swings in Elections to the U.S. House of Representatives, 1946–86 ($N = 21$)

Variables	5.1	5.2	5.3	5.4	5.5
Intercept	44.20***	23.80*	19.46*	18.97*	22.38**
	(14.64)	(10.02)	(8.72)	(8.25)	(7.74)
Party of administration	−9.52**	−2.90			−5.18*
	(2.82)	(2.81)			(2.37)
Percentage of seats won by	−.69**	−.44**	−.43**	−.44**	−.42**
Democrats, $t − 1$	(.18)	(.15)	(.14)	(.13)	(.12)
Change in real income per capita	1.41**	.39			
	(.45)	(.46)			
Quality of Democratic		.49**	.60***		
challengers		(.17)	(.11)		
Quality of Republican		−.61**	−.65**		
challengers		(.19)	(.18)		
Difference in quality of				.62***	.35*
challengers				(.09)	(.14)
Interaction between quality and					.09*
income					(.04)
$\bar{R}^2$		.59	.78	.79	.80	.83
SER		4.80	3.52	3.42	3.33	3.06

Note: The dependent variable is the percentage change in House seats held by Democrats, $t − 1$ to t; SER is the standard error of the regression; standard errors of regression coefficients are in parentheses.

$*p < .05$. $**p < .01$. $***p < .001$.

except that real income change is the average for the election year (this is the time period most commonly used in the literature).

Equation 5.1 in table 5 estimates the impact of the economy alone (except for the two control variables) on changes in partisan strength in the House. According to this equation, the impact is substantial. A one percentage point difference in real income growth is worth about six House seats ($1.41 \times 4.35 = 6.2$); a difference of one standard deviation (3.16) is worth almost 20 seats; the gap between its highest and lowest values (11.1) translates into 69 seats. So far, nothing unusual. These are typical results for equations of this kind.

The second equation (5.2) adds the challenger quality variables for each party to the analysis. Both have a strong, statistically significant effect on seat swings in the expected direction, and the overall explanatory power of the equation increases sharply (compare the R^2s). Moreover, the effects of real income growth drop by three-quarters and cease to be statistically significant. In fact, results are predicted more accurately if the economy and the administration's party are ignored, as in Equation 5.3.

Because the magnitudes of the coefficients on the challenger quality variables are indistinguishable, it makes sense to combine them into a single measure (quality of Democratic challengers minus quality of Republican challengers), as in equation 5.4. With only two independent variables, both referring to candidacies—current Democratic strength in the House and relative quality of challengers—this parsimonious specification accounts for 80 percent of the variance in postwar House election results. The regression coefficient indicates that a one percentage point difference in relative challenger quality is worth 2.6 House seats; a change of one standard deviation in this variable (8.95) translates into 24 seats; the difference between its highest and lowest values (34.2) covers 92 seats.

An estimate of the contribution strategic politicians make to interelection seat shifts in specific elections can be calculated by multiplying the regression coefficient in equation 5.4 by the difference between relative candidate quality for each election and its average, then dividing by the net share of seats that changed hands. For all postwar elections, an average of 44 percent of the seat shifts can be attributed to variations in relative candidate quality. The larger the seat shift, the greater the contribution of strategic politicians; in election years with net shifts of more than twenty seats, an average of 75 percent of them could be attributed to strategic politicians.

Although the economy has little direct effect on House elections, equation 5.5 indicates that it works interactively with candidate quality to influence the results. The interaction term (real income growth multiplied by relative challenger quality) is statistically significant and improves the equation's overall fit. The economic variable is not entered directly into equation 5.5 because preliminary analysis showed it to have no significant effect; all of the action for real income growth is in the interaction term. Candidacies and economic conditions do indeed appear to reinforce one another's effects. These results suggest that a party benefits from favorable economic conditions only to the degree that superior challengers are available to take advantage of them.

Such a conclusion is consistent with some other findings. For example, interelection vote swings are, by themselves, very poor predictors of successful challenges. In House elections from 1972 through 1986, if we tried to predict challengers' victories simply by adding the mean partisan swing to the share of votes won by the challenger's party's candidate last time, we would be wrong about 69 percent of the predicted winners and would miss 64 percent of the actual winners. On average for these years, the vote swing to winning challengers is about ten points greater than the vote swing to losing challengers of the same party. Again, cross-district variations in the vote swing are strongly related to the quality of candidates and to the financial resources they can mobilize. Most important, even in the most favorable years, weak (inexperienced, underfunded) challengers have little chance of winning (Jacobson 1986).

Conclusion

Taken together, these findings leave no doubt that economic conditions, the quality of candidates, and election results are connected in ways fully consistent with the theory. They indicate that challengers pursuing rational career strategies play an essential mediating role in translating economic conditions into changes in party control of House seats. A party expected to have a good year because of the economy fulfills expectations partly because it recruits better challengers, which in itself produces more victories, and partly because its high-quality challengers are given an effective issue with which to attack incumbents. This helps produce a striking bivariate relationship between relative quality of challengers and election outcomes. For example, the Democrats' advantage in number of high-quality challengers is correlated at .88 with the number of House seats they gain or lose (Jacobson 1989).

The relationship between relative quality of challengers and congressional election results is a good deal stronger than the relationship between the economy and election results. Considering the candidate-centered nature of electoral politics in the United States, this is not so surprising. Variation in the quality of challengers is not fully explained by either local or national political conditions. This, too, is to be expected in a fragmented, decentralized political marketplace in which office seekers operate largely as individual political entrepreneurs. But it means that the electorate's ability to exercise democratic control by acting as a "rational god of vengeance and reward" is contingent and variable, depending on elite decisions that are not fully determined by the economy or other systematic national political forces. The economy creates problems or opportunities for congressional candidates, but how they are handled or exploited makes a great deal of difference, and this varies among candidates, between parties, and across election years. So, therefore, does the influence of the economy on congressional elections.

REFERENCES

Abramowitz, Alan I. 1984. "National Issues, Strategic Politicians, and Voting Behavior in the 1980 and 1982 Elections." *American Journal of Political Science* 28:710–21.

Abramowitz, Alan I., Albert D. Cover, and Helmut Norpoth. 1986. "The President's Party in Midterm Elections: Going from Bad to Worse." *American Journal of Political Science* 30:562–76.

Alford, John R., and John R. Hibbing. 1982. "Pocketbook Voting: Economic Conditions and Individual Level Voting." Presented at the annual meeting of the American Political Science Association, Denver.

Arcelus, Francisco, and Allan H. Meltzer. 1975. "The Effects of Aggregate Economic Variables on Congressional Elections." *American Political Science Review* 69:232–39.

Bianco, William T. 1984. "Strategic Decisions on Candidacy in U.S. Congressional Districts." *Legislative Studies Quarterly* 9:351–64.

Bond, Jon R., Cary Covington, and Richard Fleisher. 1985. "Explaining Challenger Quality in Congressional Elections." *Journal of Politics* 47:510–29.

Born, Richard. 1986. "Strategic Politicians and Unresponsive Voters." *American Political Science Review* 80:599–612.

Canon, David T. 1985. "Political Conditions and Experienced Challengers in Congressional Elections, 1972–84." Presented at the annual meeting of the American Political Science Association, New Orleans, LA.

Downs, Anthony. 1957. *An Economic Theory of Democracy.* New York: Harper and Row.

Fiorina, Morris P. 1981. *Retrospective Voting in American National Elections.* New Haven: Yale University Press.

Fiorina, Morris P. 1983. "Who is Held Responsible? Further Evidence on the Hibbing-Alford Thesis." *American Journal of Political Science* 27:158–64.

Hibbing, John R., and John R. Alford. 1981. "The Electoral Impact of Economic Conditions: Who Is Held Responsible?" *American Journal of Political Science* 25:423–39.

Jacobson, Gary C. 1980. *Money in Congressional Elections.* New Haven: Yale University Press.

Jacobson, Gary C. 1983. "Reagan, Reaganomics, and Strategic Politics in 1982: A Test of Alternative Theories of Midterm Congressional Elections." Presented at the annual meeting of the American Political Science Association, Chicago, IL.

Jacobson, Gary C. 1985. "Money and Votes Reconsidered: Congressional Elections, 1972–82." *Public Choice* 47:7–62.

Jacobson, Gary C. 1986. "National Forces in Congressional Elections." Presented at the annual meeting of the American Political Science Association, Washington, DC.

Jacobson, Gary C. 1987a. "Enough Is Too Much: Money and Competition in House Elections, 1972–84." In *Elections in America,* ed. Kay L. Schlozman. New York: Allen and Unwin.

Jacobson, Gary C. 1987b. *The Politics of Congressional Elections.* Boston: Little Brown.

Jacobson, Gary C. 1989. "Strategic Politicians and the Dynamics of U.S. House Elections, 1946–86." *American Political Science Review* 83:773–93.

Jacobson, Gary C. 1990. "The Effects of Campaign Spending in House Elections: New Evidence for Old Arguments." *American Journal of Political Science* 34:334–62.

Jacobson, Gary C., and Samuel Kernell. 1983. *Strategy and Choice in Congressional Elections.* 2d ed. New Haven: Yale University Press.

Key, V. O., Jr. 1964. *Politics, Parties, and Pressure Groups.* 5th ed. New York: Thomas Y. Crowell.

Kiewiet, D. Roderick. 1983. *Macroeconomics and Micropolitics.* Chicago: University of Chicago Press.

Kramer, Gerald H. 1971. "Short-Term Fluctuations in U.S. Voting Behavior, 1896–1964." *American Political Science Review* 65:131–43.

Kramer, Gerald H. 1983. "The Ecological Fallacy Revisited: Aggregate- versus Individual-Level Findings on Economics and Elections and Sociotropic Voting." *American Political Science Review* 77:92–111.

Krasno, Jonathan S., and Donald Philip Green. 1988. "Preempting Quality Challengers in House Elections." *Journal of Politics* 50:131–43.

Monroe, Kristen R. 1984. *Presidential Popularity and the Economy.* New York: Praeger.

Oppenheimer, Bruce I., James A. Stimson, and Richard W. Waterman. 1986. "Interpreting U.S. Congressional Elections: The Exposure Thesis." *Legislative Studies Quarterly* 11:227–47.

Riker, William, and Peter Ordeshook. 1968. "A Theory of the Calculus of Voting." *American Political Science Review* 62:25–42.

Rivers, Douglas. N.d. "Microeconomics and Macropolitics: A Solution to the Kramer Problem." *American Political Science Review.* Forthcoming.

Tufte, Edward R. 1975. "Determinants of the Outcome of Midterm Congressional Elections." *American Political Science Review* 69:816–26.

Tufte, Edward R. 1978. *Political Control of the Economy.* Princeton: Princeton University Press.

U.S. Council of Economic Advisors. 1987. *Economic Report of the President.* Washington, DC: U.S. Government Printing Office.

U.S. Department of Commerce. Bureau of Economic Analysis. 1981. *The National Income and Product Accounts of the United States, 1929–76, Statistical Tables.* Washington, DC: U.S. Government Printing Office.

U.S. Department of Commerce. Bureau of Economic Analysis. Various issues. *Survey of Current Business.*

Uslaner, Eric M., and M. Margaret Conway. 1985. "The Responsive Congressional Electorate: Watergate, the Economy, and Vote Choice in 1974." *American Political Science Review* 78:788–803.

Weatherford, M. Stephen. 1986. "Economic Determinants of Voting." In *Research in Micropolitics.* Vol. 1, ed. Samuel Long. Greenwich, CT: JAI Press.

Unemployment and Elections in West Germany

Hans Rattinger

1. Introduction

In politico-economic research there are two major approaches to the study of the relationship between unemployment and politics. They differ in what they take to be the dependent and the independent variable. The first approach investigates the impact of political control of the economy and, specifically, of labor market policies on unemployment; the second approach attempts to clarify the effects of unemployment on political outcomes, i.e., mainly on voting or other indicators of political support or alienation. This chapter falls into the second category by presenting some findings on how voting outcomes in the ten German federal elections from 1953 to 1987 have been related to unemployment.

Studies of the impact of unemployment on political outcomes have a tradition dating back over fifty years. In terms of research design they have diversified considerably. Using a combination of the two dichotomies of aggregate- versus individual-level analysis and of cross-sectional versus longitudinal designs, most of the early investigations, in the context of the economic crises of the 1920s and 1930s, can be characterized as cross-sectional aggregate data studies (see, e.g., the pertinent chapters in Rice 1928, or the review of the literature in Rattinger 1980). The renaissance of studies of empirical political economy, stimulated by the seminal articles by Goodhart and Bhansali (1970) and Kramer (1971), on the other hand, tended to focus on the longitudinal impact of unemployment on voting or "popularity functions," usually at the highest level of aggregation, i.e., the national level (see Paldam 1981).

In addition, the spread of survey technology has also inspired attempts to ascertain the political effects of unemployment at the individual level. In this type of analysis, these effects have mainly been treated as being due either to the role of unemployment as a political issue (how bad is it, how salient, who is to blame, which political force is competent to solve the problem, etc.) or to personal experience with unemployment (see Schlozman and Verba 1979;

Krieger 1985). This diversification of approaches has not led to truly cumulative research with a solid theoretical integration of empirical findings from these various designs. Instead, empirical contradictions have been reported (see, e.g., Rattinger 1981), and (not quite convincing) claims to propose the "one and only" research strategy have been advanced (e.g., Kramer 1983).

This chapter does not claim to overcome the theoretical and empirical puzzles surrounding the quest for the political effects of unemployment. Instead, it goes back to the old-fashioned type of data mentioned first (i.e., cross-sectional aggregate data) in an attempt to see what they reveal about this relationship for the Federal Republic of Germany (FRG) if—instead of a single cross-section—a series of such sets of data is analyzed. In this way, one of the major shortcomings of cross-sectional aggregate data analysis can be avoided, i.e., the lack of any temporal or dynamic dimension. This type of analysis has only now become possible for the FRG at a reasonably low level of aggregation, because appropriate data (see sec. 3) have only recently been compiled.

2. Theory

Before describing data, methods, and findings, a few words on what to expect are in order. To what extent one regards such considerations as "theory" is a matter of taste. For this author, the temptation to put quotation marks around the title of this section is almost irresistible. Even at the individual level I have some difficulty discerning any truly theoretical formulations linking unemployment (as an issue, a threat, or a personal experience) to political attitudes or behavior (probably the classical Downsian calculus of voting or some sociopsychological theorizing about the effects of "deprivation" come closest). But here we are dealing with territorial units that are described by their unemployment and their distributions of political preferences. Where is the pertinent theory?

Even if we ignore all dangers of cross-level theorizing, and proceed as if we could argue in the context of aggregate data analysis as we would for individuals, we can only start with a few general notions that are sometimes contradictory and in need of further conceptual distinctions. This latter necessity is obvious both for dependent and for independent variables. For the political outcome variables, we first have to distinguish between a political mobilization versus demobilization component and a partisan support component. The latter has to be subdivided, again, into a conventional versus an unconventional component. Theoretically, unemployment thus can be related to the *level of political involvement* (for the aggregate level this mainly means turnout, of course), to the *distribution of power* among the forces established within the political system, and to the incidence of more fundamental *discontent and alienation* from the political system.

For our independent variable (i.e., unemployment) the necessary distinctions depend upon the level of analysis. With cross-sectional aggregate data, unemployment is indicative of at least two different things. First, it tells us something about the regional distribution of economic well-being and opportunities, and it reflects local economic structure. Second, the distributions of changes in unemployment mirror the local impact of the global business cycle. Both dimensions are not independent, but their interrelationship does not have to be uniform over time (and it is not, empirically).

The lack of predictive theory can be expressed very simply: We have little solid theoretical ground from which to infer which component of unemployment should be related to which dimension of the political outcome in which functional way. If we stick to the simple calculus of the rational voter's decision as developed by Downs (1957), and if we are willing to ignore problems of aggregation, we could derive some straightforward predictions based upon incumbency: high and/or rising unemployment should distract from the electoral support of incumbent parties. However, this basic logic of "bad times hurt the ins" tells us little about who would benefit, whether it should be the major opposition parties, radical fringe groups, or the "party of the nonvoters." Moreover, the simple incumbency-oriented logic has not remained unchallenged, because it ignores long-standing partisan identifications and the relation between the economic interests and the political affiliations of social groups or classes (see Hibbs 1977; Kiewiet 1983). Policy-oriented reasoning that takes such considerations into account would not predict, for example, that a left-wing government should be hurt by unemployment to the same extent as a right-wing government would be.

These arguments suffice to illustrate the difficulties that arise when familiar theorizing on the political impact of economic conditions is applied to the cross-sectional, aggregate-level linkage between unemployment and elections. Therefore, the rest of this chapter does not contain rigorous hypothesis testing. Instead, it aims at a reasonable description of the development, over time, of the cross-sectional relationship between some aspects of unemployment and electoral outcomes in the FRG, briefly interpreting these findings within the rudimentary conceptual and theoretical framework that has just been referred to.

3. Data and Research Design

Any attempt to relate West German election results to unemployment in a longitudinally comparable way at an aggregate level below the states (*Laender*) faces two problems. First, the territorial units for both types of data are not the same; federal constituencies do not correspond to the regional structure of the labor administration. Second, neither of these two territorial units has remained constant over time; constituencies have been redistricted, and the labor administration has (with some time lag) attempted to keep up with the wave of territorial reforms that swept the FRG from the 1960s to the mid-1970s.

For these reasons a comprehensive aggregate data set for the 327 counties (*Kreise*) of the FRG in their current boundaries was constructed that, besides numerous other data, contains results of federal elections and unemployment rates. These two subsets from the comprehensive data set are the basis for most of the analyses in this chapter. Unfortunately, however, results of the 1987 federal election had not yet become available at the county level at the time of writing, so that for this most recent election, data for constituencies (*Wahlkreise*) had to be used. Thus, we have one data set containing election statistics for 1949–83 and annual September unemployment rates for 1951–86 for the 327 counties (due to missing data for Lower Saxony and Saarland, *N* is only 274 for 1949, and 321 for 1953), and a second data set containing the same data for 1983–87 for 248 constituencies. Table 1 reports average partisan vote shares, unemployment rates, and changes of unemployment rates over the preceding year for the ten federal elections during 1953–87. Note that unemployment and partisan percentages in this table are not identical with the official aggregate statistics, because they are computed as

TABLE 1.   Mean Values of Party Vote Shares and of Unemployment, 1983–87

Year of Election	N	Turnout	CDU/ CSU	SPD	FDP	Green Party	All Other Parties	Unem- ployment Rate	Change in Un- employ- ment
1953	321	83.7	46.7	26.0	9.4	—	17.9	6.4	−0.7
1957	327	84.3	52.0	28.9	7.4	—	11.7	2.3	−0.1
1961	327	82.1	48.2	33.5	12.1	—	6.3	.5	−0.1
1965	327	81.9	50.7	36.3	9.4	—	3.6	1.2	0.3
1969	327	82.2	49.8	39.0	5.3	—	5.9	.5	−0.4
1972	327	87.3	48.5	43.1	7.5	—	1.0	1.0	0.2
1976	327	88.7	52.1	39.8	7.3	—	0.9	4.2	−0.6
1980	327	87.7	47.8	40.4	9.7	1.5	0.4	3.7	0.4
1983	327	88.2	51.8	35.7	6.8	5.2	0.5	8.2	2.5
1987	248	84.3	44.1	37.2	9.0	8.3	1.4	9.2	−0.4

Note: Unemployment rates are for September preceding the election. Change in unemployment is defined as the September unemployment rate preceding the election minus the rate one year earlier. Unless otherwise noted, all subsequent analyses are based on the numbers of cases indicated in the second column of this table.

averages across counties; also note that vote percentages are those cast for party lists (*Zweitstimmen*).

I suspect that bivariate correlations between turnout and party vote shares, on the one hand, and unemployment rates and their changes preceding elections, on the other hand, are spurious due to a common dependence of both unemployment and electoral outcomes on the social structure of countries, notably the shares of blue-collar or unskilled workers. As the data set does not yet contain data on the social structure of counties, its effect cannot be controlled directly. Failing to do so somehow, however, would not only produce spurious findings, but would also exaggerate the stability of associations between unemployment and election outcomes over time. Both party strength and the structural aspect of unemployment correlate considerably over time, indicating that parties tend to remain strong and unemployment tends to remain comparatively high where this has previously been the case, at least in the short- to medium-term perspective. In other words, cross-sectional unemployment rates and party votes shares for subsequent elections measure similar things, and thus should be related similarly.

Since data to control for the social structure of counties were not available, a simple alternative was pursued. First, turnout and party vote shares were regressed on the corresponding variables from the preceding election, and then residuals from these regressions were used as dependent variables in subsequent steps of the analysis. Provided that the impact of structural background variables on the regional distribution of voting patterns remains roughly the same in two subsequent elections, which can be reasonably assumed, these residuals should correlate only very little with such background variables. The strong temporal stability that described most percentages of party votes, in fact, is largely absent from these vote residuals.

Before investigating the impact of unemployment and of its change on the cross-sectional distribution of these vote residuals, two more problems of this research design have to be addressed. The first is whether controlling for structural correlates of party strength by analyzing residuals from autoregressive models really leads to similar results, as explicit controls of such variables would. Fortunately, the 1987 data set at the constituency level contains some variables of this sort in addition to unemployment and voting. Therefore, 1987 constituency election results were not only regressed on 1983 vote shares, but also (in separate zero-order models) on the number of people employed in mining and production per thousand inhabitants, on the percentage of wage-earners employed in the service sector, on the number of farms, of newly completed housing units, and of people moving to the constituency per thousand inhabitants, and, finally, on the overall percentage change in the number employed. These zero-order models explain between about 30 percent (for turnout) and about 60 percent (for CDU/CSU and SPD) of the constituency variance in 1987 election outcomes. Their residuals were again saved and regressed on the unemployment rate and its change preceding the election. If one compares 1987 results for the two types of voting residuals, i.e., from autoregressive and from structural zero-order models, it is obvious that the correspondence between the two sets of findings in terms of direction and strength of associations is quite close, so that the approach adopted here can be assumed not to distort substantive findings.

The second problem concerns the difference in units of analysis for 1953–83 versus 1987. This difference is not only in the number of cases (327 versus 248), but, more important, in the size distributions of the units. Constituencies in 1987 ranged from 165,000 to 315,000 inhabitants, but counties (in their current boundaries) are as small as only 35,000 people, and as large as cities like Munich or Hamburg with upwards of a million. Therefore, for 1983 the county-level analysis was duplicated with constituency data in order to ascertain whether the use of constituency data for 1987 should be expected to lead to discontinuities against the 1953–83 findings. Comparing these two sets of 1983 results shows that there is no strong systematic deviation.

4. Results

The results obtained by regression party vote residuals from the autoregressive models on the county unemployment rate and the change of this rate preceding each election are presented in tables 2–4. Inspecting them for continuities and meaningful patterns of associations between unemployment and election outcomes, one feels confronted with the proverbial glass of water: Is it half full or half empty? Some relationships appear to be stable over time and to make sense in terms of the theoretical speculations presented earlier; others appear to be more random. In addressing these findings one by one, we will start with the effects of unemployment as they emerge from these data, later turning to changes in unemployment over time.

The series of coefficients linking unemployment rates to turnout (table 2) indicates a predominantly negative effect (seven out of ten coefficients). This might, to some extent, still reflect structural influences, e.g., the dimension of urbanization. However, what is puzzling is the occurrence of three quite strong positive coefficients (in 1957, 1976, and 1987), two of which are significantly different from zero, which forces us to conclude that a universally negative impact of unemployment on the regional distribution of turnout cannot be established with these data, even though a tendency to this effect is clearly visible.

Ambiguity is even stronger concerning the impact of unemployment on the combined vote shares of the parties of the governing coalition (table 3).

**TABLE 2.   Standardized Coefficients for
Regressions of Turnout Residuals on
Unemployment, 1953–87**

Year	Unemployment Rate	Change in Unemployment Rate	Constant
1953	−.19**	−.05	0.83
1957	.11	.10	−0.34
1961	−.09	.20***	0.45*
1965	−.29	.35*	0.03
1969	−.11	.08	0.27*
1972	−.04	−.08	0.20
1976	.29***	−.01	−3.09***
1980	−.13*	.04	0.53
1983	−.48***	.38***	0.66**
1987	.33***	.13*	−0.65***

*p < .05.   **p < .01.   ***p < .001.

Seven of these ten coefficients are positive, but only twice (1961 and 1972) can they really be said to be different from zero. On the other hand, for 1965, 1983, and 1987, we find moderate to strong negative coefficients. Considering the party composition of the government, one can say that no federal government with Social Democratic participation (1969–80) has been hurt electorally by unemployment. In view of the number of cases one would not want to invest too much confidence in this assertion, however.

Turning now to the three established parties of the FRG, we see that

**TABLE 3.   Standardized Coefficients for
Regressions of Government Vote Residuals on
Unemployment, 1953–87**

Year	Unemployment Rate	Change in Unemployment Rate	Constant
1953	.09	.00	−0.92
1957	.06	.06	−0.34
1961	.37***	.10	−2.38***
1965	−.37*	.40*	0.53
1969	.07	.20**	0.14
1972	.43***	.03	−1.38***
1976	.05	.15*	−0.06
1980	.02	.03	−0.46
1983	−.15	.05	1.84
1987	−.32***	.18**	1.66***

*p < .05.   **p < .01.   ***p < .001.

TABLE 4. Standardized Coefficients for Regressions of Party Vote Residuals on Unemployment, 1953–87

Year	Unemployment Rate	Change in Unemployment Rate	Constant
CDU/CSU			
1953	.25***	−.11	−2.86***
1957	.18**	.14	−1.02*
1961	.43***	.14**	−2.44
1965	−.34*	.37*	0.50
1969	−.12***	.09	0.56**
1972	−.26***	−.16*	1.20***
1976	−.06	−.18**	0.04
1980	−.01	−.05	0.38
1983	−.13	.07	1.11
1987	−.17**	.01	0.73*
SPD			
1953	.06	.09	−0.21
1957	.28***	−.05	−0.83***
1961	−.10	.03	0.41
1965	.49**	−.47**	−0.92
1969	.08	.29***	0.36
1972	.50***	−.03	−1.90***
1976	−.03	.09	0.24
1980	.06	.04	−1.06
1983	.24**	−.06	−3.14***
1987	.49***	−.32***	−3.70***
FDP			
1953	−.16*	.12	0.79**
1957	−.35***	.02	1.41***
1961	.09	.02	−0.37
1965	−.17	.14	0.17
1969	−.10	−.02	0.11
1972	−.30***	.28***	0.37**
1976	−.15*	.18**	0.47**
1980	.12*	−.08	−0.38
1983	−.67***	.20*	2.26***
1987	−.01	.22***	0.12
Green Party			
1983	−.20*	.02	0.72**
1987	−.40***	.15**	1.00***

(*continued*)

TABLE 4—*Continued*

Year	Unemployment Rate	Change in Unemployment Rate	Constant
		All Other Parties	
1953	.23***	−.15*	−1.83***
1957	−.01	−.18**	−0.07
1961	−.14*	.01	0.40*
1965	.04	−.28**	0.44**
1969	.00	−.15*	−0.20
1972	−.23**	.00	0.08***
1976	.03	.01	−0.01
1980	.06	−.15**	0.00
1983	.02	−.32***	0.13***
1987	−.57***	−.17***	0.75***

$*p < .05.$ $**p < .01.$ $***p < .001.$

unemployment has affected the distribution of their electoral successes or disadvantages in a somewhat more consistent and stable fashion (table 4). The most coherent picture is obtained for the SPD; the cross-sectional deviations of this party's actual vote from expected vote shares have almost always been positively related to local unemployment. The two coefficients not conforming to this pattern (1961 and 1976) are very small; all five significant coefficients are positive.

For the Christian Democrats there is a reversal of this association between the 1950s and the period since the mid-1960s. In the first period we have a strong positive relation between unemployment and CDU/CSU vote shares above expectations; since the 1965 election this relationship is negative. Possible explanations may be found in two respects. First, in the 1950s, the CDU/CSU was the party identified most closely with the rapid economic recovery of the country (*Wirtschaftswunder*); its absorption of other right-wing parties, which were still quite strong in the first three federal elections, had plenty to do with this identification. So, excess support for the CDU/CSU in areas with still higher unemployment might have reflected the hope of catching up with the national downward trend of unemployment under this party's leadership. Second, unemployment in the 1950s was concentrated not only in urban-industrial areas, but also in rural areas where the CDU/CSU has had its strongholds from the beginning. With the concentration of the party system and the disappearance of unemployment as a pressing national problem, the relationship between unemployment and the electoral fortunes of the two major parties could develop into a lasting zero-sum constellation.

For the Free Democrats (FDP), high unemployment has almost consistently meant vote shares below expectations. Only 1961 and 1980 have deviated from this pattern, the latter deviation being statistically significant. Since this party could never be considered to have a particular appeal for those social strata most affected by unemployment, this finding does not come as a surprise. For the residual vote shares of the new Green party and of all other parties combined, the relationship with local unemployment is also predominantly negative. This is very clearly so for the Greens, but for the remaining parties five coefficients are positive and five are negative. However, out of the five positive coefficients only the very first one (1953) has a more than negligible magnitude. We can thus summarize these findings by saying that only the Social Democrats' residual vote shares have covaried positively with local unemployment over the 1953–87 federal elections, whereas (apart from a few exceptions for the CDU/CSU up to the early 1960s) the opposite has been the case for all other parties.

Conceptually and empirically, levels of unemployment and their changes over time are not the same. Therefore, we should not necessarily expect findings on the electoral correlates of the changes in unemployment preceding elections to be identical with those just described for unemployment levels themselves. For turnout and the combined share of government parties, our data clearly show that these variables tend to be above expectations in areas where unemployment grows more strongly or falls less quickly than average. For turnout, three coefficients, and for the government parties only one coefficient, have a deviant sign; all of these are very small. For both variables, four positive coefficients are significantly different from zero. Thus, while turnout residuals usually covary negatively with unemployment levels, they are associated positively with changes of unemployment. While deviations of government vote shares from expectations did not have a uniform relationship with unemployment levels over time, they have almost consistently (but only mildly) covaried positively with changes in local unemployment. This finding, of course, can be set directly against the incumbency-oriented hypothesis: in repeated cross-sections for West German federal elections it is flatly contradicted.

At first sight, coefficients for the two major parties, the CDU/CSU and SPD, appear to vary randomly; positive signs balance negative ones, and coefficients in both directions are significantly different from zero. One could provide speculative case histories of individual elections, of course, drawing upon contemporary macroeconomic conditions and relevant issues to account for these variations. For lack of space this will not be attempted. Instead, I would suggest that these changes might have something to do with a party's participation in the government. Remembering what has just been said about government vote shares, it is striking that for the CDU/CSU, except in 1953, all coefficients are positive when this party was in power, and vice versa.

Similarly, for the SPD the same holds with the exception of 1953, 1961, and 1972, these deviant coefficients being very low in magnitude. That the major party of government coalitions cross-sectionally receives vote shares above expectations with unemployment rising more or falling less than average conforms to the results about government vote shares, but again contradicts hypotheses about anti-incumbent effects.

The same thing can be said about the FDP, which almost always has been a part of the government coalition. Eight out of ten coefficients are positive, four of them significantly different from zero, and the two negative ones (one in 1969, when the FDP was in the opposition) are very small. Together with the results for the two major parties, this clearly is consistent with the equations for residual government vote shares.

In terms of the relation between its vote shares and changes in unemployment, the Green party is unlike the other minor parties. Whereas positive coefficients are obtained for 1983 and 1987 for the Greens, this association for all the other parties is strictly negative. Seven out of ten coefficients are negative and significant; the other three are practically zero (1961, 1972, and 1976). Neither high levels nor increases in unemployment have ever been conducive to the electoral success of minor parties in the FRG in a cross-sectional perspective. In sum, given the research design used here, we cannot observe many of the political consequences that are often ascribed to changes in unemployment. There is little indication of a response pattern resembling apathy (which probably is too grand a term when dealing with fluctuations of turnout), there is no anti-incumbent effect (rather the opposite), and the more exotic parties at both extremes of the political spectrum do not benefit (rather the opposite again). They succeed above expectations where both unemployment levels and their changes are less of a problem than elsewhere. Whether the regional distribution of the successes of the Green party will establish a lasting exception to this pattern remains to be seen.

I now carry the cross-sectional analysis one step further. In politico-economic research, the idea has often been expressed that economic variables should not necessarily be expected to have uniform effects at all levels. Some important notions in this context are those of "negative voting," of "asymmetric response" to boom or recession, or of threshold levels that determine whether or not there will be any political effect (see, e.g., Bloom and Price 1975; Kernell 1977). A simple version of such considerations is that political responses could be different (i.e., as a rule stronger) in regions that are more affected by the problem if compared to regions that are less affected. Thus, each unemployment level in the data set was split into two variables, according to whether a county was below or above average, with one new variable being identical to the original variable in all above-average counties and zero elsewhere, and the second new variable being identical to the original variable in all below-average counties and zero elsewhere. The same split at the mean was performed for changes in unemployment, and the whole analysis for tables 2–4 was rerun with these four new variables, instead of the two original unemployment variables.

Due to limitations of space, only the major results can be highlighted. Generally, this split of variables does not change the overall fit of models a great deal. However, there is a clear difference between the level of unemployment and changes in unemployment in the extent to which this split is useful and leads to the expected patterns. For unemployment levels, the expectation that political responses will be stronger at higher levels than at lower ones is borne out by the data almost without exception. For changes in unemployment, this is less clear; for more than half of these coefficients this split either leads to results that are inconclusive or contradict the expectation. This suggests that the assumption of uniformity of relationships is much more clearly contradicted for the first type of data than for the latter one. This attempt to carry the analysis a little further thus also demonstrates that some of the puzzles still present in the series of coefficients in tables 2–4 could possibly be resolved if the assumption of cross-sectional uniformity of the political impact of unemployment were given up in favor of a systematic search for structural sources of regional variations of this effect.

5. Conclusion: Problems for Further Research

This chapter has presented only a few findings on the political correlates of unemployment in the FRG that can be derived from this data base, and it has followed a simple research design. What can and should be the next steps? Obviously they can be separated into those that adhere to the cross-sectional design pursued here, and those that try to fully exploit the longitudinal component of these data. Following the logic of the first approach, it would appear useful to have a closer look at individual elections, especially if some of the parameters reported here appear odd. This could involve a more thorough breakdown of territorial units according to their unemployment experience along the lines briefly demonstrated at the end of the previous section. Repeated analyses of cross-sections could also be further differentiated according to relevant social characteristics of the territorial units; e.g., the political impact of unemployment in an urban-industrial context could be set against that in a rural environment. In this way, the shifting composition of unemployment in the FRG from the 1950s to the 1970s and 1980s could be taken into account.

The step from repeated cross-sections to a truly longitudinal approach could be taken in (at least) two ways. First, the coefficients linking unemployment to election outcomes computed here (or from more complex cross-sectional designs) can be regarded as time-series to be related to, e.g., incumbency, objective or perceived macroeconomic conditions, or changes in overall social structure. Some of the previously proposed interpretations correspond to such a logic of assuming that the changes of these coefficients over time can be systematically explained by third variables. In this way, the notion of an overall threshold level of unemployment at which political responses become visible could be empirically tested.

Second, and this is a possibility offered only by this data set, the data could be rearranged to allow pooled analyses across all elections and counties (for an introduction to the methodology see, e.g., Mundlak 1978; Sayrs 1989), an approach that is rarely found in empirical politico-economic research (for an exception, see Pollard 1981). Moreover, the data could also be used for time-series studies for individual counties or for any meaningful aggregation of territorial units. In contrast to pooled analysis, where cross-sectional and dynamic components could be estimated simultaneously, such regionalized time-series studies would have to face a serious degrees-of-freedom problem (for this type of analysis see, e.g., Bellucci 1984), but the addition of state elections could help in this respect. Longitudinal investigations at the county level could, again, produce classifications of territorial units that might prove useful for further cross-sectional study. These few remarks do not exhaust what can and should be done in the future, but they put the first step taken here into perspective and outline the agenda.

REFERENCES

Bellucci, Paolo. 1984. "The Effect of Aggregate Economic Conditions on the Political Preferences of the Italian Electorate, 1953–1979." *European Journal of Political Research* 12:387–402.
Bloom, Howard S., and H. Douglas Price. 1975. "Voter Response to Short-Run Economic Conditions: The Asymmetric Effects of Prosperity and Recession." *American Political Science Review* 69:1240–54.
Downs, Anthony. 1957. *An Economic Theory of Democracy*. New York: Harper.
Goodhart, C. A. E., and R. J. Bhansali. 1970. "Political Economy." *Political Studies* 18:43–106.
Hibbs, Douglas A. 1977. "Political Parties and Macroeconomic Policy." *American Political Science Review* 71:1467–87.
Kernell, Samuel. 1977. "Presidential Popularity and Negative Voting: An Alternative Explanation of the Midterm Congressional Decline of the President's Party." *American Political Science Review* 71:44–66.
Kiewiet, D. Roderick. 1983. *Macroeconomics and Micropolitics*. Chicago: University of Chicago Press.
Kramer, Gerald H. 1971. Short-Term Fluctuations in U.S. Voting Behavior, 1896–1964. *American Political Science Review* 65:131–43.
Kramer, Gerald H. 1983. "The Ecological Fallacy Revisited: Aggregate- versus

Individual-Level Findings on Economics and Elections and Sociotropic Voting." *American Political Science Review* 77:92–111.

Krieger, Hubert. 1985. "'Anti-Regierungs-' oder 'Klientelenthese'? Wirkungen persönlicher Betroffenheit von Arbeitslosigkeit (1980–1985)." *Politische Vierteljahresschrift* 27:357–80.

Mundlak, Yair. 1978. "On the Pooling of Time Series and Cross-Section Data." *Econometrica* 46:69–85.

Paldam, Martin. 1981. "A Preliminary Survey of the Theories and Findings on Vote and Popularity Functions." *European Journal of Political Research* 9:181–99.

Pollard, Walker A. 1981. "Macroeconomic Effects on U.S. Presidential Elections: A Study of Pooled State-Level and Time-Series Data, 1932–76." Washington University. Typescript.

Rattinger, Hans. 1980. *Wirtschaftliche Konjunktur und politische Wahlen in der Bundesrepublik Deutschland.* Berlin: Duncker and Humblot.

Rattinger, Hans. 1981. "Unemployment and the 1976 Election in Germany: Some Findings at the Aggregate and the Individual Level of Analysis." In *Contemporary Political Economy,* ed. Douglas Hibbs and Heino Fassbender, 121–36. Amsterdam: North-Holland.

Rice, Stuart A. 1928. *Quantitative Methods in Politics.* New York: Knopf.

Sayrs, Lois W. 1989. *Pooled Time-Series Analysis.* Newbury Park: Sage.

Schlozman, Kay L., and Sidney Verba. 1979. *Injury to Insult.* Cambridge, MA: Harvard University Press.

Italian Economic Voting: A Deviant Case or Making a Case for a Better Theory?

Paolo Bellucci

Certo che il governo Craxi ha operato bene. Non per niente era imbottito di democristiani. ([Certainly, the Craxi government has done a good job. It was, after all, packed with Christian Democrats.] Interview with Christian Democratic Treasury Minister Giovanni Goria on the forthcoming 1987 national elections, *La Repubblica,* March 6, 1987)

On June 14, 1987, Italians elected the Tenth Parliament of the Republic. Earlier in April a crisis ended, after thirty-three months, the rule of the five-party coalition government led by Mr. Craxi, the first Socialist Prime Minister and only the second non–Christian Democrat to head a government in post-war Italy. A minority Christian Democratic government failed to gain a confidence vote in Parliament and general elections were called, once again before the statutory end of the legislature.

During the electoral campaign, newspaper articles and political commentators strongly emphasized two results of the Craxi government: the government's stability and its economic record. Both were to figure prominently among the main issues of concern in the campaign. Indeed, the 1,316-day tenure of the Craxi government was extraordinary compared to the average ten-month length of previous governments. According to business leaders, this cabinet stability was of primary importance in explaining Italy's economic performance.

Past government crises were little more than exercises in musical chairs, with a substantial stability insured by the continuity of the political ruling elite (Calise and Mannheimer 1982). Nevertheless, it is fair to consider that government stability under Craxi contributed to the expansion of the Italian economy in the first half of the 1980s. When the Craxi government took office, the inflation rate was 15 percent and the GNP growth rate was −0.2

I wish to thank Mike Lewis-Beck for valuable comments on an earlier version of this chapter.

63

percent; four years later inflation had dropped to 4 percent and the GNP growth rate had averaged 2.5 percent. (Unemployment, however, rose from 10 percent to 14 percent.)

On the one hand, it can obviously be argued that both positive and negative economic results are not to be uniquely attributed to the government's economic policy, especially since Italy is an open economy depending on international economic trends. The inflation rate dropped to 8.5 percent in February, 1985, due partly to the Government action in curbing the wage indexation. But the decisive decrement in the inflation rate came later, thanks to the falling trend of both the dollar and oil prices.

On the other hand, ruling politicians are eager to take full responsibility for the country's positive economic performance, exploiting the economic record to elicit a proincumbent vote. Both Christian Democratic and Socialist leaders explicitly followed such a strategy. Of course, their eventual success was dependent upon the attitude of the electorate whose assignment of responsibility for economic performance to government action, it was hoped, would lead to a progovernment vote.

Is this what actually happened? In other words, did the basic economic issue enter into the 1987 voting decision? Or did the vote follow the traditional ideological and subcultural allegiances? And, even if the electorate might have been willing to consider economic performance, which party would have been considered responsible for it? There are several possible sources of responsibility: the party of the prime minister, the Socialists (PSI); that holding the Treasury, the Christian Democrats (DC); the Finance ministry (the Republicans, PRI); the Budget ministry (the Social Democrats, PSDI); or the Industry ministry (the Liberals, PLI).

To answer such questions means to assess the extent and the conditions under which economic concerns may influence Italian electoral behavior. Before addressing this general issue, it is worth investigating the impact of aggregate economic conditions on the 1987 electoral results.

The government parties as a whole fared well: they gained an extra 1.0 percent of the national vote compared to the preceding 1983 elections. However, this overall result hides two quite different trends: the two major coalition partners increased their electoral share (i.e., the PSI = +2.9 percent and the DC = +1.4 percent) while the three minor parties lost considerably (i.e., the PLI = −0.8 percent, the PRI = −1.4 percent, and the PSDI = −1.1 percent). The apparently zero-sum electoral game that took place within the government coalition points to a differentiated reaction of the electorate to the coalition parties' actions, showing the electoral impact of having the primary responsibility of governing, as is the case for the Socialist party. In an analysis of interparty electoral shifts, Corbetta, Parisi, and Schadee (1988) partially confirmed the zero-sum explanation, showing that the main DC gains came from the PLI, PRI, and PSDI electorates while the new votes for the PSI originated both from within the government coalition (the PRI electorate) and from outside (the Italian Communist Party, PCI, which lost 3.9 percentage points since 1983). Unfortunately, they do not offer an analysis of the electorate's vote motivations. It is open to speculation, then, whether the economic issue affected the favorable outcome of the elections.

The eventual relevance of economic conditions in the 1987 elections can be tested by relating the electoral outcomes to a set of economic variables in a cross-regional analysis of the vote. The demand function of an electoral economic cycle is the following:

$$V_t - V_{t-4} = a + b_1 I_{t-1} + b_2 P_{t-1} + b_3 U_{t-1} + e_t \qquad (1)$$

where

$V_t - V_{t-4}$ = changes in the party(ies) share of the vote 1987/1983;
I_{t-1} = yearly percentage growth of per capita regional income, with a lag;
P_{t-1} = yearly change of the regional inflation rate, with a lag;
U_{t-1} = yearly change of the regional unemployment rate, with a lag; and
e_t = the error.

According to the standard paradigm, one would expect, if economic conditions exerted an influence in the 1987 elections, to find the incumbent government parties overall favored by improving regional economic conditions, with the opposite being true for the opposition. The OLS estimates presented in table 1 only partially support such expectations.

Taking the government coalition as a whole, one hardly finds a confirmation of the rational actor approach that has guided research on political-economic interactions. Both the unemployment and inflation coefficients show a positive sign (but only the latter is statistically significant at the .05 level, $t > 2.1$, two-tailed), so as to suggest that in regions with a deteriorating economy (or with a slower relative growth) the government is electorally favored. Moreover, an increasing income reduces government support.

An alternative to rejecting the standard economic approach is to assess the impact of economic conditions on the different coalition parties, testing a somewhat differentiated electoral response of the parties' respective electorates that may be blurred if one looks at the aggregate government result.

The DC estimates confirm the preceding discussion: the Christian Democratic electorate does not seem sensitive to short-term economic fluctuations, at least as expected according to the incumbency hypothesis. In fact, the DC is

TABLE 1. Cross-Regional Analysis of Economic Effects in the 1987 Italian National Election (OLS)

Dependent Variables	Constant	Percentage Growth per Capita Income	Change in Inflation Rate	Change in Unemployment Rate	R^2	N
Government						
Full coalition	2.3	−.10 (−0.31)	.65 (1.0)	.69 (2.2)*	.29	19
DC	2.8	.01 (0.06)	.83 (1.7)**	.24 (2.1)*	.20	19
PSI	−0.82	.48 (2.4)*	−.93 (−2.3)*	−.08 (−0.40)	.43	19
PLI, PSDI, PRI	0.34	−.59 (−2.9)*	.74 (1.8)**	.53 (2.6)*	.58	19
Opposition						
PCI	−0.53	−.41 (−2.7)*	.48 (1.6)	.05 (0.75)	.40	19

*$p < .05$.   **$p < .10$. Both significance tests are two-tailed.

t-ratios in parentheses.

Definition of variables: The dependent variables are the changes (first differences) in the parties' share of the Camera dei Deputati regional vote (the region Valle d'Aosta is excluded) from 1983 elections (Ministero dell'Interno 1987). Income is defined as the yearly real (adjusted by GNP deflator) percentage change in regional per capita gross product with one year lag (Unioncamere-Instituto G. Tagliacarne 1988). inflation is the yearly change (first differences) of the regional inflation rate with one year lag; unemployment is the yearly change (first differences) of the regional unemployment rate with one year lag (Istat, various issues).

favored electorally in regions with poor economic performance, as indicated by higher inflation and unemployment. Thus, either the party is not held responsible for the regional economic downturns, or support is given in exchange for future rewards (government jobs, individualized policies, etc.) whose need is highlighted by the very poor economic indicators and which the government makes available.

On the other hand, the incumbency hypothesis is sustained in the PSI case: increasing income and reduced inflation are significantly associated with its electoral support both in statistical and substantive terms. The electorate (at least part of it) appears to hold the governing Socialist party responsible for economic performance, rewarding it with votes. More precisely, a one percentage point increase in real per capita income produces, on average, half a percentage point increase in the socialist support; a 1 percent drop of the inflation rate is rewarded with an almost equal extra vote share (0.93 percent).

The economic impact on the three minor coalition parties mirrors that of the Christian Democrats, in the sense that their losses are heavier in the regions with higher income growth and reduced in those with a worse economic performance. These results, compared with those of the Socialist party, are in line with the analysis of Corbetta, Parisi, and Schadee (1988). They found vote transfers between these parties and the PSI: economically content voters (i.e., some voters in growing income regions) tended to identify the Socialists as the party to reward for the government performance (compare the income coefficients for the PSI, .48, with that for the three parties, $-.59$, both statistically significant at the .05 level).

Turning finally to the opposition, it can be seen that economic discontent translated into a vote for the Communist party: increasing inflation is positively associated with its electoral support, whereas growing income decreased it.

What can be concluded from the analysis of the impact of aggregate economic conditions on the 1987 election results? Such an impact took place, but it was not evenly distributed among the parties of the government coalition. The net beneficiary was the Socialist party, consistent with the rational incumbency theory of economic electoral interactions. The other government parties' results seem to be less sensitive to short-term economic fluctuations, at least according to the rational approach. The Communist opposition, however, was electorally penalized by a rising income and favored by higher inflation, results that are again in line with an economic analysis.

In more general terms, the 1987 election confirms the difficulties a researcher encounters when studying the economic impact on electoral results in a country with a multiparty government and a polarized electorate. This concerns both the asymmetric effect of economic accountability of the government parties (which translates, for the electorate, into the difficulty of identifying positive or negative party responsibility), and the subsequent pattern of voting behavior of the electorate, issues that will be addressed next.

Economic Issues and the Italian Electorate

The general framework that has guided research on the impact of economic conditions on electoral outcomes is well known. Following Downs (1957):

—the voter is seen as a rational actor who casts a vote according to the individual utility derived from government activity;
—therefore the electorate rewards, with the vote, a positive government performance, while it casts a vote for the opposition in case of a negative performance.

Since the rational-actor model of voting behavior is a general one, its range of applicability covers both economic and noneconomic utilities. While there is much discussion with respect to the assumption of individual rationality applied to noneconomic interests (see Pizzorno 1983 for a critique of the rational approach) there are fewer questions about individual rationality with respect to economic utilities.

Results from research on the relationship between economic conditions and electoral outcomes in a series of Western European countries and in the United States are not all consistent with the incumbency–rational actor framework (Whiteley 1980 and 1986; Hibbs, Fassbender, and Rivers 1981; Lewis-Beck 1988). Differences of results tend to follow a line that discriminates between two-party and multiparty political systems. As Paldam wrote: "The very existence of the Vote-Popularity functions should no longer be doubted . . . the evidence is strongest that voters punish governments that preside over bad times; but considerable evidence also shows that voters reward governments associated with good times. *The main exceptions to the responsibility pattern occur for weak and unstable governments in multiparty systems . . .*" (Paldam 1981, 194; emphasis added).

An inverse relationship between economics and voting in multiparty systems is also assumed by Alt and Chrystal (1983). Their analysis of the retrospective type of rational voting model clearly states that in multiparty systems, retrospective voting is "inhibited" by the salience of the social cleavages that contributed to the formation of the multiparty format.

In assessing the potential impact of economic voting in a multiparty system, then, two aspects appear important: the presence of coalition governments and the degree of polarization of the electorate (see Sartori 1976 and Sani and Sartori 1983 for theoretical and empirical analyses of this interdependence).

Coalition governments make it difficult for the electorate to identify which of the parties in the coalition is eventually to be held responsible for economic performance (as outlined for the Italian case above). Even if this happens, a rational voter can switch his or her vote within the coalition. In this case, a voter's negative evaluation of the government's economic performance simply yields a redistribution of votes among the cabinet partners.

As for the second aspect, the degree of polarization of the electorate reflects the strength of the social cleavages that shaped the party system and the parties' electoral allegiances. The stronger the polarization, the stronger the party loyalties and the weaker the impact of short-term economic evaluations on the vote.

The Italian party system presents both of these aspects, plus an intervening variable that further complicates a study of economic voting, namely the lack of alternation of coalitions in power, given the dominant presence of the DC in every government. This makes it obviously difficult to distinguish between policy and incumbency economic voting, that is, between a vote for given economic policies and a vote that rewards (punishes) governments that preside over good (bad) economic times.

Given these formidable barriers, one might wonder whether there is any purpose in studying economic voting in Italy. The answer is twofold: first, earlier studies (see Bellucci 1985 for a review) have shown that economic conditions do exert some impact on Italian electoral choice; second, and most important, Italian electoral behavior seems to be undergoing an important change, attenuating the relevance of traditional ideological attachment with parties, thus allowing other factors to intervene in the electoral choice, as the 1987 elections analysis has partially confirmed.

Results from earlier aggregate studies (Lewis-Beck and Bellucci 1982; Bellucci 1984; Santagata 1981 and 1985) have shown that the economy matters at election time: rising inflation favors the PCI vote; rising income depresses the DC vote, while higher unemployment augments it. These findings are fully in line with earlier research on the geographical distribution of the parties' electoral strength (i.e., the PCI electorate tends to be more urban while the DC is stronger in less urbanized areas and in the south, where per capita income is lower). Still, the results contrast with the rational voter approach. Inflation is, in fact, the only variable whose sign is in the direction predicted by the model, while the other two variables have the wrong sign.

The explanations advanced to account for such trends, namely the parties' regional strength and the DC patron-client network in poor areas with high structural unemployment (Chubb 1982; Graziano 1984), rely on indirect inference and therefore do not shed light on how individual voters react to economic change.

For this reason, Lewis-Beck's recent (1986 and 1988) comparative research with survey data on five western European countries represents an important contribution to the understanding of economic voting in multiparty systems. Lewis-Beck's findings show two basic points:

— collective evaluations of government management of the economy are likely to elicit a vote for the incumbent, as opposed to personal economic grievances that show no impact on the vote;
— the strength of economic voting varies by country, with the strongest effect in Great Britain and the weakest one in Italy.

As for the second basic finding, Lewis-Beck advances three hypotheses to explain the cross-country variation. The first refers to a government's effectiveness, responsiveness, and stability, with Great Britain scoring high on all dimensions and Italy low. Therefore, a rational voter would not express his or her economic discontent with the ballot, given the perception of government inefficacy in meeting the demand. This hypothesis is stimulating and should be empirically tested, correlating the voters' perception of government efficacy with their demand for economic outcomes. The other two explanations offered by Lewis-Beck deal with the number of partners in the coalition, and the strength of traditional determinants of the vote choice. A hypothesis can be advanced that both could be related to the same phenomenon, namely the polarization of the electorate. If we accept, as Sani and Sartori (1983, 309) seem to do, that issue politics covary negatively with ideological politics, then the salience of economic evaluations will be negatively related to the ideological polarization of the electorate. Indeed, if we compare the Lewis-Beck country ordering of the extent of economic voting to Sani and Sartori's index of polarization we observe that Italy's high polarization contrasts sharply with Britain and Germany's low values.

Turning to Lewis-Beck's main finding concerning the irrelevance of personal economic concerns, in the next part of the chapter it will be shown that both personal and collective economic concerns moderately influence the vote choice in Italy. However, their impact is not cumulative; i.e., both concerns do not coexist for the same voter. On the contrary, they are expressed by quite different strata of the electorate. These differences must be taken into account for a better understanding of the economic impact on the vote, since it imrlies a variety of behavioral voting models within the electorate.

Opinion Voters, Exchange Voters, and Attachment Voters

In order to explain the unusually high volatility of the Italian electorate in the 1970s, Parisi and Pasquino (1977) proposed a typology of voting that includes three votes types (see table 2).

According to the two authors, in explaining electoral behavior it is

TABLE 2.   A Typology of Voting

Vote Type	Opinion	Exchange	Attachment
Content/meaning	Expression of a choice	Trade	Affirmation of subjective identification with a political force
Object/interest	To influence collective policy	Satisfaction of voters' short-term individual interest	Individual interest = class or subcultural collective interest
Channels of communication between voters/parties	Mass media	Direct at election times	Mobilization by subcultural organizations
Social base	High integration within political system	Low integration/periphery	Subcultural integration conflictual/consensual
Vote stability	High volatility	Medium volatility	High stability

Source: Parisi and Pasquino 1977.

important not only to ask "who votes for whom?" but also "who votes for *what?*" They distinguish five aspects of the vote: the content (or the subjective meaning), the object (or interest), the channels of communication between voters and parties, the social base that expresses the vote type, and, finally, voting stability.

The first type is the "opinion vote" (*voto d'opinione*). This type is often referred to in order to explain electoral mobility (i.e., the swing vote). The content of this vote is the expression of a choice among party alternatives. Behind the opinion there obviously is an individual interest, but the vote's object is to influence collective policy. Therefore the subjective interest is obtained through collective action, which the vote will make possible. As to the social base of the opinion vote, it does not refer to individuals' characteristics (though to a certain extent opinion voters are to be found among the rather educated and informed sectors of the electorate) but to the degree of integration within the political system. Opinion voters, therefore, should exhibit a high level of trust in the political system and in its decision-making procedures.

The second vote type is the "exchange" vote (*voto di scambio*). It refers to trading votes for individual rewards. Its object is, then, the satisfaction of voters' short-term, individual interests. While the opinion voter relies on mass media as the means of communication with, and information on, parties, the exchange voter has personal and direct contacts with party members, but only at election times; these kinds of voters are not well integrated in the political system.

The last type is the "vote of attachment," or "belonging" (*voto di appartenenza*). It identifies traditional, subcultural voting. It is the affirmation of voters' subjective identification with a political force that is closely connected with the social group to which the voters belong. For these voters, then, individual and group or class interest tend to coincide. The social base of this vote is to be found among the two major Italian political subcultures, i.e., the Catholic and Socialist/Communist, whose salience and resistance to secularization has been the major source of electoral stability.

The point of departure for the empirical analysis is the hypothesis that economic conditions weigh differently for each voting type: more for the opinion and exchange vote, less for the attachment one. Moreover, the nature of economic concerns varies as well across voting types. Table 3 reports some hypothesized associations between voting types and economic concerns which, following some by now "classic" concepts in the economic voting literature, include several dimensions.

—The distinction between personal and collective (national) economic concerns as the basis of the voters' evaluations. In the first case it is the voter's personal conditions that influence the vote; in the second it is

TABLE 3. Hypothesized Relevance of Economic Voting according to Voting Type

	Opinion	Exchange	Attachment
Economic conditions			
Personal		+	?
Collective	+		?
Attribution of Government			
Responsibility for			
Personal economic conditions		+	
Collective economic conditions	+		+
Voting model			
Retrospective	+	+	+
Prospective	+		
Policy voting	+		+
Incumbency voting	+	+	

the country's economic condition that is assumed to be relevant to voting. Pocketbook or sociotropic orientations (Kinder and Kiewiet 1979 and 1981) may then appeal to different voting types.

—The distinction between simple and mediated impact of economic conditions on the vote. The question is whether it is the simple influence of economic (personal or collective) evaluation or the attribution of government's responsibility for the economic management which is relevant for voting behavior (Fiorina 1981; Lewis-Beck 1988).

—The time-horizon of the voters, that is, whether they rely on past performance or on policy proposals when forming their judgments on the parties. Retrospective versus prospective attitudes (Fiorina 1981; Chappell and Keech 1985) imply different behavioral models to be tested across voting types.

—Finally, the distinction between incumbent and policy voting, which contrasts the traditional hypothesis that economic hardship produces an anti-incumbent vote with the more sophisticated assumption that voters evaluate the economic policy priorities of the parties (Kiewiet 1983).

In view of the previous discussion, the following can be suggested:

—given the opinion voter's aim of influencing collective policy, through which interest satisfaction is attained, collective economic conditions and government responsibility might both matter; the voting model might be retrospective and prospective, therefore allowing both "policy" as well as "incumbency" voting;

—for the exchange voter, the economic influence should be higher for personal concerns, both simple and mediated. This implies incumbency retrospective voting; and

—problems arise with the last voting type, where the hypothesized impact of economic voting should be low. It is therefore hard to choose between personal or collective concerns, or between policy and incumbency voting (which for the attachment voter basically coincide). If economic conditions do exert any influence on these voters, they should belong to the category of mediated retrospective ones.

A general model of economic voting, either prospective or retrospective, sociotropic or pocketbook oriented, is then rejected. Indeed, one can argue that different behavioral voting models need to be employed to explain the degree and direction of economic voting, especially in segmented multiparty political systems. Moreover, the very differences between aggregate results and microlevel (survey) findings may be explained in terms of misspecification of individual voter models (Kiewiet and Rivers 1985). This points to the inadequacy of simple retrospective incumbency economic models to describe the voting behavior of different sectors of the electorate. Finally, the standard incumbency model does not discriminate between economic conditions as an issue whose salience may vary from election to election (such as during an unexpected depression, which may then interact with other vote motives), and evaluations of government economic actions as the general issue that explains both policy and incumbency voting (which thus becomes the sole general vote model).

The best strategy to test the hypotheses above would be to identify empirically the three voting types and examine within each of them the extent of economic voting. Unfortunately Parisi and Pasquino (1977) do not offer any operational definitions for their types. Nor is that easily done, since they refer to the content of the votes, not to the sociobiographical characteristics of the voters. In other words, as Katz (1985, 237) noted, "Although the vote types are mutually exclusive, the individual characteristics associated with them are not." The research strategy adopted will then parallel that of Katz's study on preference voting in Italy. For each vote type a separate model is estimated, including in each equation only those independent economic variables assumed to exert an impact on the vote type. Later, the three (reduced) models will be combined to test whether the different economic variables explain separate portions of the variance of the overall vote.[1]

1. Data employed are from the 1983 Eurobarometer Survey (no. 20). The relevant economic items were ascertained through a project directed by Lewis-Beck, which was supported by a U.S. National Science Foundation grant. Neither he nor the European Commission bears any responsibility for the analysis presented here.

Before moving to the analysis-by-type, it is interesting to observe how the economic variables behave in an equation with some traditional and new controls. The traditional controls are religion, occupation, and ideological identification. The new ones represent an effort to model two features of the voting types described earlier: the first variable is interest in politics, with high and low interest supposedly discriminating between opinion and exchange voting (high vs. low integration within the political system). The variable has been built on the basis of answers to the question: "When you are with your friends, do you talk about politics? Always, sometimes, never" (for the dummy variable coding see table 4). The second variable is party involvement, which is meant to discriminate between attachment voting and the other types. The question employed is: "Is there a party to which you feel closer than others? (if yes) Do you feel very close to this party, close enough, or simply a sympathizer?" Results from a regression analysis are presented in table 4.

TABLE 4. Italian Economic Voting in 1983

	b	p	b	p
Household financial evolution	−.02	.66	−.03	.47
National economic evolution	.08	.06	.05	.21
Government effect on household finances	.05	.30	.04	.39
Government effect on national economy	−.01	.82	−.03	.63
Future government effect on national economy	.16	.00	.16	.00
Anger over government economic rule	.10	.02	.05	.24
Interest in politics				
High			−.11	.02
Medium			−.07	.13
Party involvement				
Very close			−.03	.51
Sympathizer			.01	.75
Household head occupation			.13	.00
Religion			.19	.00
Ideological identification			.18	.00
R^2		.07		.19
N		607		581

Source: Eurobarometer Survey, no. 20.

Note: Entries are OLS standardized regression coefficients.

Definition of variables: Vote: 1 = parties in government (DC, PSI, PRI, PSDI, PLI); 0 = opposition (PCI, MSI, DP, PR). Household financial evolution, national economic evolution: 1 = much worse; 2 = worse; 3 = same; 4 = better; 5 = much better. Government effects on household finances, government effects on national economy: 1 = bad effects; 2 = no effect; 3 = good effects. Future government effects on national economy: 1 = worse; 2 = same; 3 = better. Anger over government economic rule: 1 = always; 2 = often; 3 = sometimes; 4 = seldom; 5 = never. Interest in politics: dummy variables (no interest as reference category). Party involvement: dummy variables (no party as reference category). Household head occupation: 1 = professional, manager, white-collar; 0 = other. Religion: 1 = religious person; 0 = other. Ideological identification: left-right scale coded 1–10.

The economic variables included in the equations are the same as those employed by Lewis-Beck (1986, tables 2 and 3) so as to replicate his findings. Indeed, the replication is quite accurate even with the new controls, since none of the economic items is significant with the exception of the future impact of government economic policy. Among the new controls only the "high interest in politics" dummy variable is significant, shifting the mean vote toward the opposition. It might be added that the regression reported in table 4 explains a significantly lower portion of the variance in the vote (R^2 = .19) compared to Lewis-Beck's specification (R^2 = .48). This appears to be due to the different dependent variable used by Lewis-Beck, who includes only PCI among opposition parties, leaving out the Italian Social Movement (MSI), the Radical party (PR), and the Proletarian Democracy party (DP).

Turning to the opinion voting model we can observe how the economic items from the Eurobarometer Survey, selected according to the hypotheses outlined earlier, behave (see table 5). Bearing in mind that the opinion vote should be specific to voters highly attentive to politics, two interactions between the "high interest in politics" dummy variable and the economic items (leaving aside the affective item) have been inserted in the equations. The

TABLE 5. A Model of Economic Impact on Opinion Voting (interactive specification)

	Full	Reduced
National economic evolution	.03 (1.4)*	.02 (1.3)*
Government effect on national economy	−.03 (−0.81)	
Future government effect on national economy	.09 (3.5)***	.09 (3.5)***
Anger over government economic rule	.03 (1.8)**	.03 (1.7)**
High interest in politics	−.29 (−1.8)**	−.20 (−1.7)**
High interest in politics × national economic evolution	−.01 (−0.26)	
× government effect on national economy	.08 (1.1)	.07 (1.1)
Household head occupation	.12 (2.9)***	.11 (2.9)***
Religion	.23 (4.6)***	.23 (4.6)***
Ideological identification	.03 (4.2)***	.04 (4.5)***
Constant	−.06	−.08
R^2	.18	.17
N	582	599

Note: Entries are OLS unstandardized regression coefficients, *t*-values in parentheses. Codes: interest in politics: 1 = high interest; 0 = other. For other variable coding see table 4.
*$p < .10$.   **$p < .05$.   ***$p < .01$. All significance tests are one-tailed.

results show that prospective evaluations of government economic policy and affective retrospective reactions are positively related to a choice for an incumbent party (both statistically significant at the .05 level, one-tailed). The retrospective mediated evaluation (i.e., government effect on national economy) presents the wrong sign and it is short of significance. However, while its direct effect is inconclusive, its interaction with high interest in politics has the right sign with a better statistical performance. Dropping the insignificant variables presents us with a reduced model that does not, however, change the overall picture.

The results from the exchange voting model appear more promising (table 6). Concern over personal finances does not have any direct effect, while its mediated specification does (i.e., the government effect on household finances, significant at the .10 level, one-tailed). Retrospective personal fear of unemployment shows a direct significant (at the .01 level, one-tailed) effect on the vote, while the collective unemployment item (on neighborhood conditions) is not significant. The most important result, however, lies in the interaction between low interest in politics and fear of losing a job. The statistically significant coefficient (at the .05 level, one-tailed) presents a negative sign. Apparently the lack of fear of losing one's job is associated with a vote for the opposition. On reflection, the meaning of this finding becomes clear: unemployment problems associated with low interest in pol-

TABLE 6.   A Model of Economic Impact on Exchange Voting (interactive specification)

	Full	Reduced
Household financial evolution	−.006 (−0.21)	
Government effect on household finances	.06 (1.5)*	.05 (1.9)**
Fear of losing job	.07 (2.6)***	.09 (3.4)***
Unemployment evolution in neighborhood	.04 (0.98)	
Low interest in politics	.60 (3.0)***	.38 (2.9)***
Low interest in politics		
× fear of losing job	−.09 (−1.6)**	−.11 (−2.3)***
× unemployment evolution in neighborhood	−.88 (−1.3)*	
× government effect on household finances	−.03 (−0.30)	
Household head occupation	.12 (3.1)***	.13 (3.3)***
Religion	.26 (5.2)***	.26 (5.5)***
Ideological identification	.04 (5.1)***	.04 (5.3)***
Constant	−.22	−.19
R^2	.19	.18
N	577	650

Note: Entries are OLS unstandardized regression coefficients; t-values in parentheses. Codes: Fear of losing job: 1 = a lot; 2 = a little; 3 = not at all. Unemployment evolution in neighborhood: 1 = worse; 2 = same; 3 = better. Interest in politics: 1 = low; 0 = other. For other variable coding see table 4.

*$p < .10$.   **$p < .05$.   ***$p < .01$. All significance tests are one-tailed.

itics (i.e., political alienation) "produces" a vote for the incumbent parties. This individual-level finding confirms, then, the aggregate data analyses that linked unemployment to the ruling DC electoral strength, and its power to distribute individual rewards for the vote. Again, dropping the nonsignificant variables gives us a parsimonious reduced model of economic impact on exchange voting that shows the relevance of personal simple and mediated economic concerns.

The last model to be analyzed is that of the attachment vote, where a priori hypotheses on the impact of the economy were not clear. The results (see table 7) show our error in stressing only retrospective evaluations. Both prospective and retrospective collective evaluations are significant. However, the evaluation of the government effect on the national economy changes direction according to whether its direct impact (negative) or its interaction with the dummy variable representing high party involvement (positive sign) is observed. Since both are statistically significant, what is observed here is the strong impact of partisan identification, beyond the control of the ideology variable. In other words, the impact of the evaluation of the government economic policy on the vote depends, for this vote type, on the subcultural identification. For the same reason we can observe that the affective variable,

TABLE 7.   A Model of Economic Impact on Attachment Voting (interactive specification)

	Full	Reduced
Household financial evolution	−.020 (−0.49)	
National economic evolution	.030 (1.2)*	
Government effect on household finances	.020 (0.41)	
Government effect on national economy	−.070 (−1.7)**	−.05 (−1.4)*
Future government effect on national economy	.100 (3.8)***	.11 (4.5)***
Anger over government economic rule	.030 (1.5)*	
Very close to party	−.270 (−1.7)**	−.26 (−2.7)***
Very close to party		
× household financial evolution	.005 (0.10)	
× national economic evolution	−.003 (−0.14)	
× government effect on household finances	.009 (0.14)	
× government effect on national economy	.110 (1.9)**	.11 (2.1)**
Household head occupation	.120 (2.9)***	.11 (2.8)***
Religion	.240 (4.6)***	.22 (4.6)***
Ideological identification	.040 (4.6)***	.04 (5.1)***
Constant	.020	.10
R^2	.19	.17
N	581	604

Note: Entries are OLS unstandardized regression coefficients; t-values in parentheses. Codes: Close to party: 1 = very close; 0 = other. For other variable coding see table 4.

*$p < .10$.   **$p < .05$.   ***$p < .01$. All significance tests are one-tailed.

while significant for the opinion vote, lowers its significance level for the "*voto di appartenenza.*"

As a conclusive test, we can now see whether the three equations are tapping the same variance of the vote by combining them into one (table 8). This does not seem to be the case, since only four out of the twelve economic variables employed (including the interactions) lose significance, and all variables present the same signs as in the original models.

What conclusion can be drawn from the analysis? Both personal and collective economic concerns moderately influence electoral choice in Italy. These major orientations, however, do not exhaust the range of economic concerns.

Evaluations of the government's effect on the national economy, as well as the perception of national economic evolution, are relevant for opinion voters, for whom the vote is an expression of a choice among party alternatives and a means to influence collective policy. Also, personal economic concerns influence party choice, but the direction of the impact depends on the voter's political involvement. This is evident for the exchange voter:

TABLE 8.   An Integrated Model of Economic Voting in Italy (interactive specification)

	Full	Reduced
Fear of losing job	.070 (2.4)***	.08 (2.7)***
National economic evolution	.020 (1.0)	
Government effect on household finances	.005 (0.17)	
Government effect on national economy	−.070 (−1.7)**	−.19 (−1.3)*
Future government effect on national economy	.100 (3.7)***	.12 (4.5)***
Anger over government economic rule	.010 (1.0)	
High interest in politics	−.190 (−1.5)*	−.05 (−.95)
Low interest in politics	.260 (1.8)**	.29 (2.1)**
Very close to party	−.190 (−1.8)**	−.19 (−2.0)**
High interest politics × government effect national economy	.080 (1.2)	
Low interest in politics × fear of losing job	−.080 (−1.6)	−.09 (−1.7)**
Very close to party × government effect national economy	.090 (1.6)	.09 (1.7)**
Household head occupation	.120 (2.8)***	.12 (2.9)***
Religion	.230 (4.5)***	.23 (4.6)***
Ideological identification	.040 (4.6)***	.04 (5.0)***
Constant	−.120	−.12
R^2	.21	.21
N	569	567

Note: Entries are OLS unstandardized regression coefficients; *t*-values in parentheses. For variable coding see table 4.

*$p < .10$.   **$p < .05$.   ***$p < .01$. All significance tests are one-tailed.

personal economic hardship associated with a low integration in the political system produces a "rational" willingness to trade one's vote for economic rewards with ruling parties, while political interest and integration "push" the economically dissatisfied voter to turn to the opposition. Finally, voters with stable loyalties and political identification are not insensitive to economic interests, but their main concern is on the role and efficacy of government economic rule.

A deterministic economic explanation of party support in Italy is then rejected. Economic interests do exert an influence on the vote, but their extent and direction of influence depend on political factors, which affect both the demand and supply of economic outcomes. The ultimate impact of economic concerns upon voting lies, then, in the subjective meaning associated with the vote.

Conclusions

Previous research on economic voting in Italy has shown a weak impact of economic concerns on electoral behavior. This is certainly due to specific systemic characteristics of Italian politics: on the one hand coalition governments blur the identification of ruling parties' responsibilities for the management of the economy; on the other hand the weight of party identification as a major determinant of voting behavior, mirrored in the ideological polarization of the electorate, reduces the general relevance of the economic issue for the vote. Italy could then be interpreted as a deviant case for a rational theory of economic voting in contemporary Western democracies.

This chapter has, however, followed a different strategy: systemic factors were explicitly considered as explanatory variables of economic voting and, therefore, made endogenous to the model. Different economic concerns appear relevant to different sectors of the electorate. Opinion voters react to retrospective and prospective evaluations of the national economic situation and of government management of the economy. Exchange voters are sensitive to retrospective personal economic circumstances, although their behavior—expression of support for ruling parties when faced with employment difficulties—does not follow standard interpretations of rational political action. Voters who are strongly identified with a party show the least reaction to short-term economic evaluations.

The overall electoral impact of economic concerns depends, then, upon the distribution of the three vote types among the electorate. Until recently, the preeminence of stable, ideologically identified voters in Italy has depressed the economic impact on the vote. The current depolarization of Italian voters might increase the relevance of economic issues and, consequently, also affect the parties' political strategies. The analysis of the 1987 national elections has, in fact, shown the electoral relevance of the economic issue for the Socialist party, to which opinion voters also turned in response to its positive management of the economy.

REFERENCES

Alt, James E., and K. Alec Chrystal. 1983. *Political Economics*. Berkeley: University of California Press.
Bellucci, Paolo. 1984. "The Effect of Aggregate Economic Conditions on the Political Preferences of the Italian Electorate." *European Journal of Political Research* 12:387–401.
Bellucci, Paolo. 1985. "Economic Concerns in Italian Electoral Behavior: Toward a Rational Electorate?" In *Economic Conditions and Electoral Outcomes: The United States and Western Europe,* ed. Heinz Eulau and Michael S. Lewis-Beck. New York: Agathon Press.
Calise, Mauro, and Renato Mannheimer. 1982. *Governanti in Italia: Un trentennio repubblicano 1946–1976.* Bologna: Il Mulino.
Chappell, Henry W., and William R. Keech. 1985. "A New View of Political Accountability for Economic Performance." *American Political Science Review* 79:10–27.
Chubb, Judith. 1982. *Patronage, Power, and Poverty in Southern Italy.* Cambridge: Cambridge University Press.
Corbetta, Piergiorgio, Arturo Parisi, and Hans M. A. Schadee. 1988. *Elezioni in Italia: Struttura e tipologia delle consultazioni politiche.* Bologna: Il Mulino.
Downs, Anthony. 1957. *An Economic Theory of Democracy.* New York: Harper and Row.
Eulau, Heinz, and Michael S. Lewis-Beck, eds. 1985. *Economic Conditions and Electoral Outcomes: The United States and Western Europe.* New York: Agathon Press.
Fiorina, Morris P. 1981. *Retrospective Voting in American National Elections.* New Haven, CT: Yale University Press.
Graziano, Luigi. 1984. *Clientelismo e sistema politico: Il caso dell'Italia.* Milano: Franco Angeli Editore.
Hibbs, Douglas A., Jr., Heino Fassbender, with the assistance of R. Douglas Rivers. 1981. *Contemporary Political Economy.* Amsterdam: North-Holland.
Istat. *Annuario Statistico Italiano.* Various Issues. Rome.
Katz, Richard S. 1985. "Preference Voting in Italy: Votes of Opinion, Belonging, or Exchange." *Comparative Political Studies* 18:229–49.
Kiewiet, D. Roderick. 1983. *Macroeconomics and Micropolitics.* Chicago: University of Chicago Press.
Kiewiet, D. Roderick, and Douglas Rivers. 1985. "A Retrospective on Retrospective Voting." In *Economic Conditions and Electoral Outcomes: The United States and Western Europe,* ed. Heinz Eulau and Michael S. Lewis-Beck. New York: Agathon Press.

Kinder, Donald R., and D. Roderick Kiewiet. 1979. "Economic Discontent and Political Behavior: The Role of Personal Grievances and Collective Economic Judgments in Congressional Voting." *American Journal of Political Science* 23:495–527.

Kinder, Donald R., and D. Roderick Kiewiet. 1981. "Sociotropic Politics: The American Case." *British Journal of Political Science* 11:129–41.

Lewis-Beck, Michael S. 1986. "Comparative Economic Voting: Britain, France, Germany, Italy." *American Journal of Political Science* 30:315–46.

Lewis-Beck, Michael S. 1988. *Economics and Elections: The Major Western Democracies*. Ann Arbor, MI: University of Michigan Press.

Lewis-Beck, Michael S., and Paolo Bellucci. 1982. "Economic Influences on Legislative Elections in Multiparty Systems: France and Italy." *Political Behavior* 4:93–107.

Ministro dell'Interno. 1987. *Elezioni della camera dei deputati dell 14 giugno 1987.* Rome.

Paldam, Martin. 1981. "A Preliminary Survey of the Theories and Findings on Vote and Popularity Functions." *European Journal of Political Research* 9:181–99.

Parisi, Arturo, and Gianfranco Pasquino. 1977. "Relazioni partiti-elettori e tipi di voto." In *Continuita' e mutamento elettorale in Italia,* ed. Arturo Parisi and Gianfranco Pasquino. Bologna: Il Mulino.

Pizzorno, Alessandro. 1983. "Sulla razionalita' della scelta democratica." *Stato e mercato* 7:3–46.

Sani, Giacomo, and Giovanni Sartori. 1983. "Polarization, Fragmentation, and Competition in Western Democracies." In *Western European Party Systems: Continuity and Change,* ed. Hans Daalder and Peter Mair. London: Beverly Hills and Sage Publications.

Santagata, Walter. 1981. "Ciclo politico-economico: il caso italiano." *Stato e Mercato* 2:257–99.

Santagata, Walter. 1985. "The Demand Side of Politico-Economic Models and Politicians' Belief: The Italian Case." *European Journal of Political Research* 13:121–34.

Sartori, Giovanni. 1976. *Parties and Party Systems: A Framework for Analysis.* Cambridge: Cambridge University Press.

Unioncamere-Istituto G. Tagliacarne. 1988. *Il reddito prodotto nelle provineie italiane.* Rome.

Whiteley, Paul, ed. 1980. *Models of Political Economy.* Beverly Hills and London: Sage Publications.

Whiteley, Paul, ed. 1986. *Political Control of the Macroeconomy: The Political Economy of Public Policymaking.* Beverly Hills and London: Sage Publications.

Part 2
The Economy and Government Popularity

The Economy and Presidential Approval: An Information Theoretic Perspective

Nathaniel Beck

Why do we need another study estimating a popularity function for American presidents? Compared to other parts of the discipline of political science, the theoretical and econometric standard in this area has been high. For the United States, theoretical developments have been made by Hibbs (1987, chap. 5), Kernell (1978), MacKuen (1984), and Chappell and Keech (1985), among others. Yet there has been little effort by these authors to systematically compare and contrast their theoretical treatments. In this chapter I begin to provide a theoretical treatment of the effect of the economy on presidential popularity based on ideas from the theory of rational choice. While other studies (particularly those of Chappell and Keech) have also used a rational framework, my approach here draws more explicitly on rational choice theory.

How does the study of presidential popularity inform the study of the effect of the economy on elections? The standard answer is that there is a relationship between poll evaluations of presidential popularity and electoral results. This relationship will be strongest if voters are retrospective, so that elections become a referendum on the incumbent. If we think of elections as a principal-agent situation, where voters (principals) are choosing an agent to run the country, then the popularity polls are a measure of whether the principals wish to retain their agent at any given time. This is the perspective I shall take in this chapter and, hence, there is no real dichotomy between the study of elections and the study of presidential popularity.[1]

This chapter was written while I was visiting the Department of Government at Harvard University and owes its existence to my colleague at Harvard, Jim Alt. I would also like to thank Chip Chappell and Bill Keech who, in spite of our disagreements, shared their data as well as their ideas.

1. I use the terms *popularity* and *approval* more or less interchangeably. Poll questions ask whether the respondent approves of the president's performance, but popularity is the term usually applied to the aggregate measure. I try to use approval to indicate an individual-level

Formalizing Presidential Popularity

Most studies of the effect of the economy on governmental popularity regress popularity on measures of the economy (chosen from unemployment, inflation, growth in real per capita income, and rates of change of those variables) and some other variables (war, scandal, honeymoon, or other important events). While most studies find some effect of the economy, the coefficient estimates vary greatly and different studies find different indicators to be important.

It is hard to build a theory relating aggregate economic conditions and presidential popularity. A reasonable theory is going to be based on individuals, and the basic tool we have for modeling individuals is to assume that they are rational. Unfortunately, our best data on popularity and the economy are aggregate time-series data. Before investigating an individually rational model of approval it is necessary to show that such a model can be aggregated in a sensible way so that it can be tested with aggregate data. That is, there must be some relationship between the estimated parameters for the aggregate and the theoretical parameters for individuals.[2]

Fair (1978) has provided a set of conditions that are sufficient for equivalence of individual and aggregate parameters. His conditions are, unfortunately, quite restrictive in that they require all individuals to transform economic variables into political judgments in the same way. If we are willing to have the aggregate parameters reflect the average of the individual parameters, then we can weaken the Fair conditions.

For simplicity, take a model with a single economic indicator related to popularity. Let p_{it} be the ith person's underlying measure of presidential approval at time t as measured on a continuous underlying scale.[3] If X_t is some measure of the economy at time t, we can write

---

response and popularity the national aggregate of approval. The term *president* can presumably be interchanged with chief executive since little of what I say depends on the U.S. context. Empirical work is, however, limited to the postwar United States.

2. Why not work with individual-level survey data? Partly because the surveys lack the richness of economic information available in the time-series data. And partly because, as Kramer (1983) has shown, the individual data can be very misleading. Why not work with time-series constructed for stratified subsamples, as in the work of Hibbs or Chappell and Keech? Because these groups are hardly homogeneous and, in practice, the extra complexity of such stratification has not produced any surprising results. (I refer here to breakdowns by education or income; Hibbs's breakdowns by party have been quite interesting, but for a different set of questions than those asked here.)

3. The Ps are linked to answers to the approve-disapprove question via some measurement equation. Differing assumptions about the error process would lead to either a logit or probit specification. See the threshold model of Kernell and Hibbs (1981).

$$P_{it} = \beta_i X_t + e_{it},$$

assuming that everyone observes the same X_t.

Aggregating over n individuals, the model becomes

$$P_t = \beta X_t + e_t,$$

where the lack of an i subscript indicates averaging. Suppose that b_i and b are ordinary least squares estimates of β_i and β. What is the relationship of b and the b_i?

$$b = \Sigma X_t P_t / \Sigma X_t^2 = (1/n) \Sigma X_t \Sigma P_{it} / \Sigma X_t^2 = (1/n) \Sigma b_i,$$

so the estimated b for the aggregate model is just the average of what the estimated b_is would be for individuals if we had data on the individuals.[4]

The situation becomes more complex if we include variables in the model that are individual-specific (say, perceived unemployment) but some type of averaging more or less holds. In addition, this may not be a problem if we accept Kramer's (1983) argument about the relative merits of aggregate and cross-sectional analysis to study the impact of economic variables. He argued that the aggregate economic indicators may be superior since the individually specific variables contain a lot of what looks like measurement error.

So the estimates for coefficients in aggregate time-series models are, more or less, averages of what the estimates would be over all individuals. Thus we can build a model of aggregate popularity based on individual approval. We are on fairly familiar ground once we decide that we are modeling the behavior of individuals, not collectivities. While there are many types of models of individual behavior, in this chapter I will work only with rationally based models. What can we learn about popularity if we assume that individual approval is rational?

A Monitoring Cost Perspective

Various approval functions contain different economic measures as predictors of presidential popularity.[5] The choice of economic measure in the early

---

4. The "derivation" above is clearly a sketch, at best. But I think it is a sketch that will hold, in general.

5. In this paper, I omit discussion of the effect of noneconomic events on popularity

popularity literature appears to have been somewhat arbitrary. In the cross-sectional literature, much of the debate has been on self-interested versus sociotropic voting, i.e., measures of personal economic well-being versus measures of societal economic well-being. These two models are indistinguishable at the aggregate level and only sociotropic measures are available in the aggregate.

Until recently, popularity functions focused exclusively on the effect of economic outcomes (unemployment, inflation, real per capita income, and/or their growth rates). Chappell and Keech (1985) make the interesting argument that presidents determine policy, not outcomes; hence, intelligent voters should look at policy in determining their attitude toward the president. It would appear as though the Chappell and Keech argument is a real advance; the populace is finally given some credit for intelligence.

Chappell and Keech test their sophisticated popularity model against a naive model where people look only at current outcomes, and find their model superior. While one can take issue with their specific findings, I wish to make a broader argument against their approach, an argument that is grounded in the formal theory of principal-agent relationships (see Ferejohn 1986; Beck 1989).

The critical issue in principal-agent theory is monitoring and information cost, with the agent having an advantage in that arena. The agency perspective emphasizes the monitoring costs of the electorate, and leads to a search for feasible strategies of electoral control. The Chappell-Keech notion of sophistication leads exactly in the opposite direction, toward requiring more information and an increase in the electorate's monitoring costs. It is still an empirical question as to whether the populace behaves in a sophisticated or a naive way, but it is no longer obvious that "sophistication" is theoretically preferable to "naïveté."

It is, unfortunately, more difficult to put policy on the right-hand side of the equation than it is to put outcomes there, since there is no agreed-on measure of policy. Chappell and Keech use Gordon's (1986) measure of the difference between natural GNP and actual GNP as their measure of policy stance, but this means they must assume that voters both care about policy and believe the Gordon model (and have access to the Gordon text to see his data).

Whatever the limitations of the Gordon measures, there is no simple measure of economic policy that macroeconomists agree on. One way out of this thicket is to ask why voters should care about policy. They may care about policy per se, but they are more likely to care about policy because they want to ensure good outcomes for the future; that is, their predictions for the future

(MacKuen 1984 has an excellent treatment of this issue). All empirical work reported here uses a Watergate and a Vietnam variable, both conventionally specified.

affect current evaluations of the president. If one knew that a presidential administration had led to a bad economy and would continue to do so, would it matter if the president were pursuing a "correct" policy?

The answer to this question is not obvious, but the perspective of principal-agent theory can again be of aid. Some argue that voters do not blame a president for bad present and expected outcomes if they are not his "fault." Alt (1985), for example, argues that one should not look for party effects in open economies without first purging the economic outcomes of their international component. Hibbs (1987) subtracts the impact of the OPEC price shocks from his measure of inflation. This logic asks voters to estimate what portion of economic outcomes the president is responsible for. This cuts against the principal-agent perspective of reducing monitoring costs. Moreover, it will lead to campaigns where each side fights about unobservables, namely, what consequences can actually be blamed on the incumbent.[6] Forecasts are not subject to this problem, since here we are simply asking the voters to take future total outcomes into account.[7]

Thus there are a series of possibilities for which economic variables should enter on the right-hand side, ranging from past and present outcomes (as long as they are observable before answering the popularity question), to forecasts of future outcomes, to observations of past and current policy. I rank these alternatives according to monitoring costs. We still have not looked at exactly which economic variables should be selected, nor have we looked at the question of how past economic outcomes should enter the function.

Some economic indicators are easily observable by voters, while others may be politically more relevant, but harder to ascertain. Unemployment is clearly easy to understand, and inflation is widely reported. Real per capita income is more abstract and not so widely reported, with real growth in GNP having similar (but less serious) problems along those lines. There are many measures of inflation, some of which are theoretically superior (GNP price deflator measures) but perhaps less immediately available. Some price measures (such as food prices) are obviously less good measures of inflation but easily ascertainable on a more-or-less continual basis, whereas other series (housing or oil prices) may be more politically relevant but harder to ascer-

---

6. As an example, should either Nixon or Carter have been blamed for the portion of inflation due to the OPEC price increases? They certainly would have shirked responsibility for such price increases, but might not a different international stance have led to a different outcome? Given the difficulties of controlling private economic agents, perhaps the portion of inflation that Nixon and Carter were most responsible for was that due to oil price increases. Alas, we shall never know, and nor shall any voter.

7. The Kramer (1983) critique of the cross-sectional literature on voting and the economy is subject to a similar criticism. He claims that voters should only look at that part of their personal economic situation that can be attributed to the president. This is a difficult quantity for anyone to ascertain.

tain. The agency perspective leads me to believe that the food price series might be the best price measure on the right-hand side.[8]

Do voters look at levels or changes? Theory is of little guide here but, from an information economizing perspective, changes seem more sensible than levels (a constant level is no new information entering the system). On that basis, I would expect that changes in both unemployment and prices (i.e., inflation) are what should enter on the right-hand side, with inflation in food prices being the best candidate for an inflation measure.

Rational and Efficient Use of Information[9]

All but the most primitive popularity studies are dynamic. This means that prior levels of popularity affect current levels, either explicitly or implicitly (Beck 1985). There are a number of different ways that dynamics enter the popularity function, and again it appears that choice among these methods has been somewhat arbitrary.

Using the previous notation (allowing X to be a vector of economic indicators) there are two general ways of writing a dynamic popularity function. One is a distributed lag model with

$$P_t = b_1 X_t + b_2 X_{t-1} + b_3 X_{t-2} + \ldots b_n X_0 + e_t,$$

while the other is a partial adjustment model with

$$P_t = v P_{t-1} + b X_t + e_t.$$

If we assume that the weights in the first model are exponentially declining (so that $b_{k+1} = vb_k$, $-1 < v < 1$), it can be made to look like the partial adjustment model by use of the Koyck transformation. The two formulations are not exactly identical since the Koyck transformation yields a moving average error process whereas the error process in the partial adjustment process is presumably white noise (independent, identically distributed errors).

8. Mosley (1984) makes the argument that price series reported in the newspaper ought to predict popularity better than the official series does. The food price series reported in the *Daily Mirror* is found to outperform the official measure of inflation. He does not test the official food price series against the *Daily Mirror* series.

9. Much of the discussion in this section could go under the heading of "rational expectations." The key insight of rational expectations is that agents use information in the same way they use any other valuable commodity, and that is the insight used here. Rational expectations also contains other insights about macroeconomics (some of which Kirchgässner [1985] has tested for Germany and which I test for the United States) but these move away from the core insight of informational efficiency.

Each model has a different story behind it. The first has voters remembering all past economic outcomes (or decisions) but with exponentially declining impact while the second has only current economic conditions[10] affecting popularity but with popularity only slowly adjusting (or, in other words, prior popularity resembling memory with v indicating the importance of memory).[11]

These specifications are difficult to distinguish empirically. Are any of them preferable on a theoretical basis? The idea of efficient information use may be helpful. P_{t-1} reflects an individual's judgment of the president at time $t-1$. Whatever went into that judgment should be completely summarized by that measure. New information may cause that judgment to be updated, but there is no reason why prior states of the economy should affect that updating. In terms of the algebra of expectations, it ought to be the case that

$$E(P_t/P_{t-1}, X_t) = E(P_t/P_{t-1}, X_t, X_{t-1}, X_{t-2}, \ldots,$$

$$X_{t-n}).$$

As an example, if the Iran affair causes President Reagan's popularity to fall 20 percentage points, that is his level of approval and should form the basis for any future judgments of the president. This need not be what we observe. Events such as Iran might be temporary "shocks" whose impact on popularity is only transient (and, hence, subject to equilibration), but this notion is hard to square with ideas of informational efficiency. Thus the partial adjustment model seems superior to the geometric distributed lag model on theoretical grounds, and I use the partial adjustment model for the empirical work in this chapter.

The idea of informational efficiency can be taken further if we assume that individuals update their evaluations of the president in a Bayesian manner. The popularity measure always used (How good a job do you think the

---

10. I assume that X_t is the most recent observation of the economy before a judgment about P_t is required, so, for example, with monthly data, X_t would correspond to the state of last month's economy. With quarterly data, it is not obvious whether we should look at the current or previous quarter's economic situation.

11. The partial adjustment story looks a bit silly as administrations change, since it claims that popularity in the first month of an administration depends on the (usually low) popularity of the preceding administration. Kernell (1978) deals with this by estimating each administration separately. In all the estimations reported here, I put in a dummy variable marking the start of each new administration (counting Johnson and Ford as new administrations, but not including a dummy variable to mark the start of a second term). This dummy variable effectively breaks the link between administrations. It is not a honeymoon term. All reported estimations use these dummy variables to mark the start of administrations and all formulas should be read to implicitly include these variables if necessary.

president is doing?) is as much a measure of competence as popularity. Presumably there is some relationship between competence and future performance of the economy, that is, individuals have some subjective probability density $f(X_{t+1}/P_t)$. Bayes's Theorem then allows the individual to update P_t to P_{t+1} since the probability density of P_{t+1} given the information available at $t + 1$, $g(P_{t+1}/X_{t+1})$, will be proportional to $f(X_{t+1}/P_t)h(P_t)$ where h represents the prior subjective density of P.[12]

These densities cannot be empirically evaluated with aggregate data. The formula is useful, though, since it shows that the more certain one is about one's judgment at time t, the less importance new information (X_{t+1}) will have for updating P_t to P_{t+1}. The theorem also says that the more unexpected an economic outcome is, given current assessments of competence, the more that assessment of competence will change.

We need proxies for these variables. Presumably the longer a president has been in office, the more certain we are of his competence, so the economy should have its greatest effect on the economy early in a president's term (counting back to his initial election, not the beginning of the current term). If we assume some specific functional form for f, the density of X_{t+1} given P_t, then the impact of X_{t+1} on P_{t+1} should increase with the surprise, $[X_{t+1} - E(X_{t+1}/P_t)]$, where the expectation is with respect to the density f.[13] If we let t represent the number of periods an administration has been in office, and S_t the surprise (relative to prior competence), then the Bayesian updating formula is

$$P_t = w P_{t-1} + e^{-\alpha t} S_t X_t + e_t$$

where the error process is white noise.

Finally, there is the straight rational expectations view of informational efficiency, which assumes that only new (i.e., unforecastable) information should affect popularity (Chrystal and Peel 1986). Much of the current economic situation could have been forecast from the previous observations of the economy and, hence, should have already been incorporated in prior popularity. The only portion of the current observation of the economy that should affect popularity is that part that is unexpected. While this perspective is quite sensible for knowledgeable actors (who have much to gain from their

---

12. The implicit assumption here is that an individual has a probability distribution over the various possible values of popularity or competence, and that this distribution aggregates in some reasonable way.

13. Note that this surprise is different from the rational expectation surprise in X, which is the part of X that cannot be predicted from the past behavior of X.

actions), it might seem less plausible for mass publics asked to make quick judgments of their political leaders.[14]

We now have several theoretical perspectives on presidential popularity. All were set up to be testable with available aggregate data. It is to that task that I now turn. Before doing that, it should be stressed that since each of the models is based on a different theoretical perspective, we cannot judge the models on purely empirical grounds.

Empirical Tests

All reported results are based on either monthly or quarterly models starting with the beginning of the Eisenhower administration and going through the first half of 1986. Estimations are based on the entire sample period, with dummy variables restarting popularity at the beginning of each new presidential administration, so a predecessor's popularity has no impact on the current administration. This is a more efficient procedure than estimating administration by administration, since we can easily force the coefficients to be equal across administrations.

The popularity measure is from the Gallup Opinion Index, while the economic variables are from the Citibase data file. The popularity measure takes only the percent approving the way the president is handling his job, which is standard in the literature. In the monthly analysis the economic variables are entered with a one-month lag, while for the quarterly series contemporaneous values are used. All equations were corrected for both Watergate and the Vietnam war, using the same method as Keech and Chappell.[15]

The basic partial adjustment results (estimated via ordinary least squares) are shown in table 1. These results are sensible; the economy enters with the appropriate sign, and the Watergate and Vietnam variables have the appropriate sign (although they have large standard errors[16]). Lagrange multiplier tests

---

14. I have discussed the theoretical side of rational expectations and popularity in Beck 1989 and the empirical side in Beck 1990. I only summarize the empirical findings in this chapter.

15. The quarterly figures through 1980 were kindly provided by Chappell and Keech. These were updated using the Gallup Opinion Index. The monthly figures were taken directly from the Gallup Opinion Index, using the last survey of the month if necessary.

The Watergate variable is a dummy variable scored 1 for the period July, 1973, through August, 1974, and zero elsewhere. The Vietnam variable is the number of American soldiers killed in Vietnam (divided by 1,000) during the Johnson administration. (See Hibbs 1987 for a justification of including these two variables measured in this way.)

16. Most, but not all, other researchers have found a significant effect of Vietnam and Watergate on popularity. It is important to remember that the effects in table 1 are short-run effects because of the lagged popularity term. Thus, my substantive findings are not all that different from the majority of other researchers. My statistical results on Watergate and Vietnam are

TABLE 1. Basic Regression Results

Variable	Quarterly		Monthly	
	b	SE	b	SE
Popularity lagged	0.84	0.04	0.89	0.02
Change in unemployment	−2.76	0.90	−1.65	0.93
Food inflation	−0.49	0.10	−0.26	0.06
Watergate dummy	−2.64	2.83	−1.85	1.27
Vietnam killed	−0.41	0.48	−1.12	0.74
Constant	10.07	2.41	7.20	1.27
First periods				
Kennedy	14.46	4.51	13.86	4.09
Johnson	18.43	4.48	20.93	4.08
Nixon	18.46	4.67	15.07	4.13
Ford	33.86	4.65	22.90	4.12
Carter	18.15	4.49	17.41	4.07
Reagan	22.17	4.58	15.93	4.12
df	121		388	
R^2	.88		.90	
MSE	4.46		4.07	
SSR	2404.34		6412.76	

Note: The dependent variable is the percentage approving of the president. Unemployment and inflation are lagged one month in the monthly model, contemporaneous in the quarterly model. The sample period in the quarterly model is Second Quarter, 1953, through Second Quarter, 1986; in the monthly model, March, 1953, through June, 1986.

indicate that the error process in the quarterly model is white noise while there is some (small) first-order autocorrelation in the monthly model.[17] Since the small moving average error term did not affect results, I report results based only on the simpler ordinary least squares method. Table 2 and all subsequent tables report only coefficients directly related to the specific issue. Unless otherwise noted, all these coefficients are based on regressions that included the additional variables shown in table 1.

Table 2 presents results about which measure of inflation best predicts popularity (quarterly data only). In specifications 1 and 2 a food inflation measure (from the GNP personal consumption expenditure accounts) is com-

---

similar to those of Chappell and Keech; Hibbs's reported standard errors are incorrect, and so I cannot compare my statistical results to his. In any event there is no question that both Vietnam and Watergate hurt presidential popularity; table 1 shows that it is hard to find a simple model of the dynamics of those effects.

17. A nonlinear least squares reestimate of the monthly equation allowing for an MA1 error process gives a moving average parameter of about −.2 with a standard error of about .05. Substantive estimates change by less than 10 percent from those reported in table 1.

TABLE 2. Test of Which Economic Variables Predict Better

	b	SE
1. Change in unemployment	−2.75	.90
Inflation (food)	−0.41	.12
Inflation (GNP personal consumption)	−0.25	.24
2. Change in unemployment	−2.88	.96
Inflation (food)	−0.45	.13
Inflation (CPI)	−0.14	.19
3. Change in unemployment	−2.74	.95
Inflation (food)	−0.45	.11
Inflation (housing)	−0.42	.22
4. Change in unemployment	−2.80	.95
Inflation (CPI)	−0.51	.16
OPEC oil shock	0.02	.02

Note: The dependent variable is popularity (percentage approve, quarterly data).

pared with two overall inflation indices (the GNP deflator for personal consumption and the Consumer Price Index). In both cases the food inflation measure outperforms the overall inflation measures (by between two and three times). Neither overall measure has a statistically significant coefficient when food inflation is controlled for, whereas controlling for overall inflation still leaves food inflation with a highly statistically significant coefficient. Specification 3 shows that while changes in food prices and housing prices have a similar effect on approval, we can estimate the effect of food prices on approval about twice as accurately as we can estimate the effect of housing prices. Other regressions lead to a similar finding: the prices that best predict presidential popularity are food prices. Voters appear to monitor specific prices that they can easily and directly observe on a continuous basis.

Do voters, as Hibbs (1987) suggested, not penalize the president for economic events beyond his control? Specification 4 shows that a variable measuring the contribution to inflation of the two OPEC oil shocks (the inflation rate in oil prices during the two shock periods) has almost no impact on popularity. The coefficient of this variable is substantively very small, and also small compared with its standard error. Voters appear unwilling or unable to separate that part of the economy that is not under the president's control (or perhaps they correctly perceived that Presidents Nixon and Carter could be blamed as much for the OPEC price shocks as for any other price increase).

As in the Kirchgässner (1985) study, there is no indication that voters respond only to the unexpected component of the economy (table 3, specifications 1 and 2). Here I regressed both the expected and the "surprise" component of economic outcomes on popularity, with the surprise component com-

TABLE 3. Tests of Efficient Use of Information in Approval

	Quarterly		Monthly	
	b	SE	*b*	SE
Impact of Innovations				
1. Change in unemployment	−2.50	.90		
Change in unemployment (innovation)	0.08	.74		
Inflation (food)	−0.70	.13		
Inflation (innovation)	0.31	.15		
2. Change in unemployment	−2.53	.95	−1.35	.94
Inflation (CPI)	−0.60	.15	−0.32	.94
Inflation (innovation)	0.46	.22	0.19	.10
Impact of Forecasts				
3. Change in unemployment	−4.33	2.54	−1.94	1.24
Change in unemployment (1st quarter forecast)	5.73	5.01	1.58	1.60
Change in unemployment (2d quarter forecast)	5.72	4.31	−2.36	2.04
Inflation (food)	−0.56	0.11	−0.24	0.07
Change in inflation (1st quarter forecast)	−0.29	0.26	0.04	0.12
Change in inflation (2d quarter forecast)	−0.51	0.40	−0.16	0.21

Note: The dependent variable is popularity (percentage approve).

puted as the innovation of a recursive vector autoregression.[18] There is simply no indication that the unexpected component predicts popularity, while the total (unexpected plus expected) clearly does.[19] My methodology is a bit different than Kirchgässner's, but our results are identical. The strong form of rational expectations is not upheld. Again, this is consistent with a theoretical view that stresses monitoring costs.

Voters do not seem to take forecasts of the economy into account in evaluating the president. Coefficients on the economic forecasts are weak and quite insignificant (specification 3).[20] It appears that voters evaluate the presi-

18. Innovations were computed using the one-step-ahead forecast errors, using either a univariate or multivariate vector autoregression. Kirchgässner uses only univariate forecasts. The multivariate models include both inflation and unemployment. This general methodology is by now commonplace in empirical work growing out of rational expectations. Innovations were computed based on a regression with a sample period comprising the most recent eight years of data.

19. The results on inflation show a large but wrongly signed coefficient on the innovation term. A 1 point increase in expected inflation leads to a 0.3 point drop in popularity, while a similar increase in unexpected inflation leads only to a 0.1 point drop in popularity.

20. Forecasts were computed using the same methodology as in the analysis of the innovations. A half-year forecast horizon is used.

TABLE 4.   Nested Tests of Chappell-Keech Model

Model	Sum of Squared Residuals
1. Chappell-Keech policy variables	2732.050
2. Unemployment and inflation	2695.250
3. Chappell-Keech policy variables, change in unemployment and inflation	2576.535
4. Chappell-Keech naive (level)	2848.120
5. Chappell-Keech policy variables, Chappell-Keech naive (level)	2601.310
6. Chappell-Keech naive (change)	2615.720
7. Chappell-Keech policy variables, Chappell-Keech naive (change)	2496.660

F-Tests	F	p
Model 1 vs. model 3	3.59	.05
Model 2 vs. model 3	2.74	NS
Model 1 vs. model 5	2.99	NS
Model 4 vs. model 5	5.65	.01
Model 1 vs. model 7	5.60	.01
Model 6 vs. model 7	2.84	NS

Note: All F-tests have 2 and 119 degrees of freedom. All tests include Vietnam, Watergate, and administration start dummies. NS = not significant.

dent based on the state of the current economy. It is possible that a better forecasting scheme would obtain better results, but as of now it appears that voters are highly sensitive to monitoring costs (or distrustful of theoretical concepts, preferring to base their evaluations on observable indicators).

Do voters look at outcomes or policy? The results reported by Chappell and Keech show that both the sophisticated and naive models perform similarly with regard to standard errors of the regression (with the sophisticated model often, but not always, doing a bit better).[21] They do not provide a test of the two models. In table 4 I test the two alternatives in the context of the partial adjustment model. To do this, I nest both specifications inside a large specification and then do F-tests on whether either the sophisticated or naive variables can be excluded from the big model.[22]

The Chappell-Keech sophisticated model outperforms a naive model

---

21. Data are from Gordon 1986 which differ from the Gordon data used by Chappell and Keech.

22. This is a computationally simple variant of the Cox 1961 procedure for testing non-nested hypotheses. The variant has been in use for a long time, but was first justified in Quandt (1974).

TABLE 5.   Impact of Past Information on Current Approval

	Quarterly		Monthly	
	b	SE	b	SE
Tests for Longer Lags				
1. Inflation (food)	−0.49	0.10	−0.25	.06
Change in unemployment	−2.72	1.16	−1.32	.95
Change in unemployment (lag 1)	−0.05	1.18	−1.13	.94
2. Change in unemployment	−2.47	0.90	−1.54	.93
Inflation (food)	−0.39	0.11	−0.20	.15
Inflation (lag 1)	−0.31	0.13	−0.05	.16
Inflation (lag 2)	0.14	0.13	—	—
3. Popularity (lag 1)	0.87	0.06	0.84	.04
Popularity (lag 2)	−0.03	0.06	0.05	.04
Test of Bayesian Learning				
4. Change in unemployment	−3.31	1.63	−2.85	2.17
α (U)	−0.58	1.46	−1.78	3.11
Inflation (food)	−0.54	0.16	−0.25	0.09
α (I)	−0.25	0.76	0.13	0.79

Note: The dependent variable is popularity (percentage approve).

using inflation and the level of the output ratio as the "naive" indicators. All my estimations, however, are based on voters monitoring changes in the unemployment rate (which is conceptually similar to the output ratio). When the naive model is estimated using either a change in the output ratio or the change in unemployment rate, the naive model outperforms the sophisticated model. In fact, we can reject the Chappell-Keech sophisticated variable in favor of either set of naive variables that are based on changes, not level, in output or unemployment. It is easier for voters to monitor outputs than to monitor policy, and they appear to use the informationally simpler strategy.[23]

Does popularity summarize all the available information at any given time? Chrystal and Peel show that a model that includes popularity lagged one period need not include any other lagged terms. This finding is basically upheld here. Table 5, specification 1 shows that lagged unemployment never

---

23. This finding should be taken as quite preliminary. I have shown the superiority of the naive model by trying alternative specifications of the naive variables leaving the sophisticated variables unchanged. Presumably one could improve the performance of the sophisticated model also. But at present there is no very strong evidence in favor of the sophisticated model. (It should also be noted that my partial adjustment model is different than the Chappell-Keech exponentially distributed lag model, and that my sample period is six years longer. On the other hand, their own reported results do not strongly favor the sophisticated model.)

predicts current popularity, but specification 2 shows that lagged inflation predicts current popularity in the quarterly model. Given the number of different specifications tested, it is hard to know whether to take this one finding contrary to a rational model very seriously. In any event, higher-order lagged economic variables never affect current popularity, so there is little evidence that the past economy affects current popularity other than through past popularity.

With Kirchgässner and Chrystal and Peel, I find that one lagged popularity variable adequately summarized past popularity. Specification 3 shows that second-order lagged popularities do not affect current popularity; other tests give similar results for higher-order lags. In the quarterly model, there is no evidence that the residuals are subject to any form of autocorrelation[24] so there is no evidence of either equilibration or long-term memory. The monthly data tell a different story. A Lagrange multiplier test shows that there is first- (but no higher) order autocorrelation. I cannot tell whether this is via a moving average or an autoregressive process. The coefficient of the moving average process shown is about $-.2$, so previous shocks to popularity are (somewhat) offset.

Measurement error alone would imply a moving average error process, so it is unclear whether there is equilibration over and above that due to measurement error. In Beck 1990, I reestimate the model of table 5 in state-space form, which allows for separation of measurement error from substantive error. The moving average error is not due only to measurement error, and hence the rational expectations hypothesis proposed by Chrystal and Peel is not upheld.

The Bayesian updating scheme proved not to work at all (table 5, specification 4). There is no indication whatsoever that voters use economic information differently over the course of a presidential term (and rather strong evidence that this use is constant over the term). The αs reported in the table indicate the level of exponential decline in the importance of new economic information over time (in line with the Bayesian updating equation). While three of the four coefficients have the right sign, none are close to being statistically different from zero, and all indicate (at best) modest effects over a presidential term.

Other indicators of the importance of new information also fail to support the Bayesian updating equation. Economic information is no more important when popularity is changing rapidly; it is no more important when the population is divided in its opinion of the president; it is no more important when economic outcomes are surprising, given the level of prior popularity. I am quite disappointed by this failure. I have tried hard to make the Bayesian

---

24. Lagrange multiplier tests for autocorrelation up to one year all proved insignificant.

updating scheme work, but it appears that voters use expected and unexpected information at all time periods in more or less the same way.[25]

Conclusion

Voters appear to use an informationally efficient strategy. They cue on easy-to-obtain indicators of changes in the state of the economy. They do not attempt to separate the forecastable component of those indicators; they do not attempt to discount the politically irrelevant component of those indicators; they do not look at forecasts and they do not look at policy.

The American populace does not, however, seem to use this information in a strongly rational manner. The main rational expectations hypothesis is not upheld, although several subsidiary hypotheses do hold. The Bayesian updating scheme does not appear to work. We need further inquiry on how and why voters process the simple information they do process.

REFERENCES

Alt, James. 1985. "Political Parties, World Demand and Unemployment: Domestic and International Sources of Economic Activity." *American Political Science Review* 79:1016–40.

Beck, Nathaniel. 1985. "Estimating Dynamic Models Is Not Merely a Matter of Technique." *Political Methodology* 11:71–90.

Beck, Nathaniel. 1989. "Presidents, the Economy and Elections: A Principal-Agent Perspective." In *The Presidency in American Politics,* ed. Paul Brace, Christine Harrington, and Gary King. New York: New York University Press.

Beck, Nathaniel. 1990. "Estimating Dynamic Models Using Kalman Filtering." *Political Analysis,* vol. 1. Ann Arbor: University of Michigan Press.

Chappell, Henry, and William Keech. 1985. "A New View of Political Accountability for Economic Performance." *American Political Science Review* 79:10–27.

Chrystal, Alec, and David Peel. 1986. "What Can Economists Learn from Political Science and Vice Versa?" *American Economic Review* 76(2): 62–65.

Cox, Donald. 1961. "Tests of Separate Families of Hypotheses." *Proceedings of the Fourth Berkeley Symposium,* vol. 1. Berkeley: University of California Press.

Fair, Ray. 1978. "The Effect of Economic Events on Votes for the President." *Review of Economics and Statistics* 60:159–73.

Ferejohn, John. 1986. "Incumbent Performance and Electoral Control." *Public Choice* 50:5–25.

Gordon, Robert. 1986. *Macroeconomics.* Boston: Little, Brown.

---

25. My current research gives more support to the Bayesian updating scheme in the context of an error-correcting model, but these findings have not yet been published.

Hibbs, Douglas. 1987. *The American Political Economy: Macroeconomics and Electoral Politics in the United States*. Cambridge, MA: Harvard University Press.

Kernell, Samuel. 1978. "Explaining Presidential Popularity." *American Political Science Review* 72:506–22.

Kernell, Samuel, and Douglas Hibbs. 1981. "A Critical Threshold Model of Presidential Popularity." In *Contemporary Political Economy,* ed. Douglas Hibbs and Heino Fassbender. Amsterdam: North-Holland.

Kirchgässner, Gebhard. 1985. "Rationality, Causality, and the Relationship between Economic Conditions and the Popularity of Parties." *European Economic Review* 28:243–68.

Kramer, Gerald. 1983. "The Ecological Fallacy Revisited: Aggregate- versus Individual-Level Findings on Economics and Elections, and Sociotropic Voting." *American Political Science Review* 77:92–111.

MacKuen, Michael. 1984. "Political Drama, Economic Conditions, and the Dynamics of Presidential Popularity." *American Journal of Political Science* 28:164–92.

Mosley, Paul. 1984. "'Popularity Functions' and the Role of the Media: A Pilot Study of the Popular Press." *British Journal of Political Science* 24:117–33.

Quandt, Richard. 1974. "A Comparison of Methods for Testing Non-nested Hypotheses." *Review of Economics and Statistics* 56:92–99.

Economic Conditions and the Popularity of West German Parties: Before and after the 1982 Government Change

Gebhard Kirchgässner

1. Introduction

In October, 1982, the social-liberal coalition under Chancellor Helmut Schmidt lost power in the Federal Republic of Germany and a new coalition of Christian Democrats and Free Democrats came into office. This so-called *Wende* took place under general economic conditions that were much worse than those during earlier changes in government in 1966 or 1969. The seasonally adjusted unemployment rate was above 8.0 percent, and it was still increasing. It had never been as high since the first half of the 1950s. The inflation rate was declining, but at 4.8 percent it was still relatively high. Real disposable income had fallen about 3.7 percent since the fourth quarter of 1981. This economic crisis and the conflict between the two coalition parties on how to solve it led to the fall of the Schmidt government.[1]

The impact of the economic decline could also be seen in the results of opinion polls. The perception of the general economic situation, as regularly investigated by Infratest since 1971, reached its historical low in January, 1983: only 11 percent of the electorate rated the general economic situation as "good" or "very good." About two years before, in September, 1980, just before the last general election, 65 percent of the electorate had rated it this way. During the second half of 1982, the popularity of the leading party in government, the SPD, sometimes was below 30 percent, as Allensbach and Infratest data showed. The popularity of the FDP, the SPD's partner in government, was even below 5 percent, a crucial limit in West German elections.

The data used in this research were made available by the West German Press and Information Office, Bonn, the Institut für Demoskopie, Allensbach, and Infratest GmbH, Munich. I also thank Helmut Norpoth for helpful comments and Anna Rushing-Jungeilges for English editing.

1. Source of the economic data: Statistische Beihefte zu den Monatsberichten der Deutschen Bundesbank, Reihe 4; Saisonbereinigte Wirtschaftszahlen, various volumes.

Therefore, it seems to be clear that economic conditions influenced the behavior of the electorate and thereby political conditions too.[2]

There are several studies showing that during the period of the "social-liberal coalition," which lasted from October, 1969, to October, 1982, economic conditions had a significant impact on the behavior of the electorate as measured by polls.[3] This chapter examines whether, under the worsened economic conditions of the 1980s, the familiar economic variables, namely unemployment, inflation, and real income, had the same effect on the voting intentions of the electorate as they did during the comparatively less rough 1970s. Furthermore, there are several studies estimating popularity functions with a change of the (leading) party in government taking place during the estimation period.[4] This implies that, despite possible effects on the constant term, the influence of economic conditions on the popularity of the party (parties) in government may not depend on which party is in office. This is a very strong assumption that has rarely been tested.[5] The data available for the Federal Republic of Germany permit a test of this assumption.

I will proceed as follows: In the next section, I outline the theoretical model on which the empirical results are based. Then, I present popularity functions for the period of the SPD/FDP government from 1971 to 1982 (sec. 3). Contrary to earlier estimates, I use not only the unemployment and inflation rates as indicators of economic development, but also the growth rate of real disposable income. It is shown that the economic indicators as well as the perception of the general economic situation had a significant influence on the popularity of both major German parties during this time. In section 4, I perform the same estimates for the period of the CDU/CSU-FDP government after 1982. These estimates provide much less evidence for an influence of economic conditions on voting behavior. However, tests for structural stability performed in section 5 do not permit a rejection of the null hypothesis of no structural change between the two periods.

All the empirical estimates that are presented in this paper, as well as the theoretical model, are based on the idea of rational voter behavior. However,

---

2. Source of the political data: (1) Popularity of the CDU/CSU and the SPD: Noelle-Neumann (ed.), *Jahrbuch der öffentlichen Meinung*, Allensbach, different volumes; (2) Perception of the general economic situation: Infratest Politik Barometer, 1971–86. The popularity of a party is defined as the share of those who intend to vote for this party when asked "If there were a general election next Sunday, which party would you vote for?" Don't knows are excluded. The perception of the economic situation is defined as the share of those who evaluate the economic situation as "good" or "very good." Don't knows are again excluded.

3. See, e.g., Kirchgässner 1985a and 1985b or the survey in Kirchgässner 1986a.

4. See, e.g., Frey and Schneider 1978 for the United Kingdom and Frey and Schneider 1979 for the Federal Republic of Germany.

5. This holds although Frey and Garbers (1972) distinguished different reaction schemes of British voters depending on which party was in government.

the concept of rationality can be defined very broadly, including the idea of "bounded rationality" in the sense of Simon 1955 and of "rational expectations" in the sense of Muth 1961. The latter version is widely employed in macroeconomics. Therefore, it is interesting to see whether the behavior of the German electorate, as reflected in polls, is compatible with this concept. Corresponding tests are presented in section 6.

2. The Theoretical Model of the Popularity Function

According to the theory of Downs (1957) and its further development by Davis, Hinich, and Ordeshook (1970), I assume that the individual voters make voting decisions so as to maximize their utility. Each voter has an optimal position in the n-dimensional politico-economic space $\mathbf{R}^n$, each party also has such a position. The individual voter evaluates the positions of the different parties and calculates the expected utilities if these positions are realized. If there are significant differences between the expected utilities, he or she decides to vote and then votes for the party whose position maximizes his or her expected utility.

The voter has two different sources of information about the positions of the different parties:

1. The actual record of the government during the current parliamentary term, for estimating the position(s) of the party (parties) in power.
2. Concepts, programs, and promises (and possibly the record of earlier legislative periods) of all parties, government as well as opposition.

If the government is held responsible for the performance of the economy, whereas the opposition is not held responsible, then the evaluation of the position of the party in power depends on the current economic situation, whereas the evaluation of the opposition's position is independent of it.

The election period goes from $t = 0$ to $t = T$. The state of the (politico-) economic system at time t is described by the n-dimensional vector

$$x(t), \ x \in \mathbf{R}^n, \ \forall \ t \in (0,T). \tag{1}$$

The individual voter has the evaluation function

$$F[x(t),t]: \ \mathbf{R}^{n+1} \to \mathbf{R}, \tag{2}$$

which estimates the utility he or she derives if position $x(t)$ is realized at time t. Looking back at the election date T, the utility he or she derived during the electoral term is given by

$$J(T) = \int_0^T F[x(t), t] \exp[\mu(t - T)] \, dt, \tag{3}$$

where $\mu \geq 0$ and μ is the (backward looking) political discount rate.[6] Holding the position of the opposition constant, the voter votes for the government (one of the parties in government) if the utility $J(T)$ is greater than some upper benchmark $\bar{J}$, votes for the opposition (one of the opposition parties) if it is smaller than some lower benchmark $\underline{J}$; and abstains if it is between the two boundaries. Thus, we have two switchpoints, one where the voter switches from abstention to voting and one where he or she switches from abstention to voting for the opposition (and vice versa). Assuming that all voters have the same evaluation function (2) and the same political discount rate μ, and employing a sufficient set of assumptions for aggregation, as, e.g., proposed by Fair (1978) or Borooah and van der Ploeg (1982), we end up with the collective voting function

$$GP(T) = GP(0) \exp(-\mu T) + \int_0^T g\{F[x(t),t]\} \exp[\mu(t - T)] \, dt, \tag{4}$$

where $GP(T)$ is the vote share the government receives in the current election, and $GP(0)$ is its share in the previous election. Equation 4 shows that the vote share (record) of the government on election date T depends on its discounted share (record) in the previous election and on the political and economic development during the electoral term. Because the values of the vector $x(t)$ are not continuously measured, we have to switch from equation 4 to a discrete formulation of the voting function. Thus, we get:

$$GP_T = GP_0 \, \lambda^T + (1 - \lambda) \sum_{t=1} \{g(F(x_t,t)] \, \lambda^{T-t}\}, \tag{5}$$

where $\lambda = \exp(-\mu)$. For time periods between elections, i.e., for $t = 1$, . . . , $T - 1$, we can get the voting attitude, as measured by the polls, as

$$GP_t = GP_0 \, \lambda^t + (1 - \lambda) \sum_{\tau=1}^{t} g[F(x_t,t) \, \lambda^{t-\tau}]. \tag{6}$$

Using the Koyck transformation, this can be simplified to

$$GP_t = \lambda \, GP_{t-1} + (1 - \lambda) \, g[F(X_t,t)], \tag{7}$$

which is the generally used form of a popularity function for the government.

---

6. See Nordhaus 1975, 182.

As a first-order approximation, one can obtain the linear regression model

$$GP_t = \beta_0 + \lambda \, GP_{t-1} + \sum_{i=1}^{n} \beta_i \, x_{i,t} + u_t, \tag{8}$$

where x_{it} is the ith component of the vector x_t at time t, and u_t is a stochastic disturbance term. In a two-party system, the vote share of the opposition (as measured in percent) is given by

$$OP_t = \beta_0' + \lambda \, OP_{t-1} - \sum_{i=1}^{n} \beta_i \, x_{i,t} - u_t, \tag{9}$$

where $\beta_0' = 100 \, (1 - \lambda) - \beta_0$,

because the government's and the opposition's popularity add up to 100 percent. Therefore, in a two-party system it is sufficient to estimate only the equation of the government's popularity. However, such "pure" cases of two-party systems rarely exist, and the Federal Republic of Germany certainly does not have such a system, because beneath the two major parties, the Christian Democrats (CDU/CSU) and the Social Democrats (SPD), there are other small parties like the Free Democrats (FDP) that play an important role in West German politics. In a multi-party system with k parties ($k > 2$) and Pop_j being the popularity of party j, instead of equations 8 and 9 we get the systems of equations

$$Pop_{j,t} = \beta_{j,0} + \lambda \, Pop_{j,t-1} + \sum_{j=1}^{n} \beta_{j,i} \, x_{it} + u_{j,t} \tag{10}$$

where $j = 1, \ldots, k$, for which the restrictions hold:

$$\sum_{j=1}^{k} \beta_{j,0} = 100 \, (1 - \lambda), \tag{11a}$$

$$\sum_{j=1}^{k} \beta_{j,i} = 0, \tag{11b}$$

where $i = 1, \ldots, n$, and

$$\sum_{j=1}^{k} u_{j,t} = 0, \tag{11c}$$

where $t = 1, \ldots, T$. If we restrict the parameter of the lagged endogenous variable, λ, to be the same in all equations, the restrictions in equations 11a–11c are fulfilled automatically. Therefore, one can drop one equation and estimate only the $k - 1$ remaining equations.

3. Popularity Functions for the Period from 1971 to 1982

I will now examine the popularity of the two major German parties, the Social Democrats (SPD), who headed the government, and the Christian Democrats (CDU/CSU), the opposition party during the period of the "social-liberal" coalition from October, 1969, to September, 1982. Since it is unreasonable to assume that a new government is held responsible by the electorate for the economic condition just after it has been elected, and since Infratest data are available only from 1971 onward, I dropped the first year of this coalition and used as the observation period February, 1971, to September, 1982.

Because income data are not available on a monthly basis for the Federal Republic of Germany, the economic variables usually employed for estimating (monthly) popularity functions are the rates of unemployment (UR) and inflation (IR). However, as preliminary investigations with quarterly data showed, the growth rate of real disposable income (YVR) seems to be an important variable influencing German voting behavior. Therefore, I assumed that nominal disposable income in the mean month of each quarter is one third of its quarterly value, and constructed the missing observations by linear interpolation. Thus, we are able to employ all three economic variables in monthly estimates. Using Allensbach popularity data and under the cross-equation constraint mentioned above, we get the following "Full Information Maximum Likelihood" (FML) estimates:[7]

$$SPD_t = 14.365 + 0.682\ SPD_{t-1} - 0.383\ UR_t$$
$$(5.91)\quad (15.84)\phantom{\ SPD_{t-1}}\quad (-2.44)$$

$$- 0.171\ IR_t + 0.318\ YVR_t + \hat{u}_{1,t},$$
$$(-0.92)\quad (2.50) \tag{12a}$$

$$R^2 = 0.853,\ SE = 1.838,\ \hat{h} = 0.13,\ df = 135.$$

---

7. The numbers in parentheses are the $\hat{t}$-values of the estimated parameters. SE is the standard error of regression, h the value of the Durbin $\hat{h}$ test, and df the number of degrees of freedom for the T-test. Estimations are performed on the CDC of the computer center of the ETH Zürich using TSP, version 3.5. The popularity figures of CDU include the popularity of its Bavarian sister party, the CSU.

$$CDU_t = 15.214 + 0.682\ CDU_{t-1} + 0.206\ UR_t$$
$$(6.16)\quad (15.84)\qquad\qquad (1.50)$$

$$-\ 0.016\ IR_t\ -\ 0.184\ YVR_t + \hat{u}_{2,t},$$
$$(-0.11)\qquad (-1.74)$$
(12b)

$$R^2 = 0.724,\ SE = 1.623,\ \hat{h} = -0.38,\ df = 135.$$
Logarithm of the Likelihood Function: -499.820.

Contrary to earlier estimates, as presented, e.g., in Kirchgässner 1985a, inflation has no significant effect on the popularity of the two parties except that it reduces real income.[8] Therefore, if we drop the inflation rate we get the following results:

$$SPD_t = 12.379 + 0.697\ SPD_{t-1}\ -\ 0.282\ UR_t$$
$$(6.49)\quad (16.10)\qquad\qquad (-2.45)$$

$$+0.375\ YVR_t + \hat{u}_{1,t},$$
$$(3.89)$$
(13a)

$$R^2 = 0.852,\ SE = 1.839,\ \hat{h} = 0.04,\ df = 136.$$

$$CDU_t = 14.421 + 0.697\ CDU_{t-1} + 0.201\ UR_t$$
$$(6.98)\quad (16.10)\qquad\qquad (1.77)$$

$$-\ 0.174\ YVR_t + \hat{u}_{2t},$$
$$(-2.09)$$
(13b)

$$R^2 = 0.725,\ SE = 1.605,\ \hat{h} = -0.61,\ df = 136.$$
Logarithm of the Likelihood Function: -501.207.

Now, all coefficients of the economic variables are significantly different from zero, at least at the 10 percent level. If we compare the two systems, 12 and 13, using a likelihood ratio test, the null hypothesis that the rate of inflation has no significant influence cannot be rejected at any conventional significance level. On the other hand, if we compare system 13 with a purely autoregressive system to check whether the economic variables altogether have a significant impact, we get $\hat{\chi}^2 = 27.990$. Thus, the null hypothesis of no influence can be rejected even at the 0.1 percent significance level.

---

8. Of course, a significant coefficient could be produced using the growth rate of nominal, instead of real, income.

System 13 implies that, in the long run, an increase of the unemployment rate of 1.00 percentage point leads to a loss of the SPD popularity of nearly 1.00 percentage point and to a gain of the CDU of 0.66 percentage points. An increase in the rate of real disposable income of about 1.00 percentage point leads to a gain of the SPD of about 1.20 percentage points and a loss of the CDU of nearly 0.60 percentage points. The differences are mainly gains or losses of the FDP.

If we use the perception of the general economic situation (*GES*) instead of the objective economic indicators as explanatory variable, we get:

$$\text{SPD}_t = 6.461 + 0.788 \text{ SPD}_{t-1} + 0.047 \text{ GES}_t$$
$$(5.56) \quad (23.45) \qquad \qquad (3.67)$$

$$+ \hat{u}_{1,t}, \tag{14a}$$

$$R^2 = 0.840, \text{ SE} = 1.908, \hat{h} = 0.11, df = 137.$$

$$\text{CDU}_t = 11.962 + 0.788 \text{ CDU}_{t-1} - 0.036 \text{ GES}_t$$
$$(6.50) \quad (23.45) \qquad \qquad (-3.98)$$

$$+ \hat{u}_{1,t}, \tag{14b}$$

$$R^2 = 0.727, \text{ SE} = 1.592, \hat{h} = -1.89, df = 137.$$
Logarithm of the Likelihood Function: -507.083.

Four out of eighteen voters, whose perception of the general economic situation is improved, change their voting intention in favor of the SPD. Three of these come from the Christian Democrats (and one from the Free Democrats). If we compare these estimates with those of equation 2, the equation of the SPD performs somewhat worse and the one of the CDU somewhat better. Altogether, as measured by the value of the likelihood function, the system employing the objective economic variables, equation 2, performs somewhat better than the one using the (subjective) perceptions.

However, what are the main determinants of the perception variable? If we employ all three economic variables, we get the following result:

$$\text{GES}_t = 11.906 + 1.121 \text{ GES}_{t-1} - 0.222 \text{ GES}_{t-2}$$
$$(2.87) \quad (13.22) \qquad \qquad (-2.68)$$

$$- 0.550 \text{ UR}_t - 1.095 \text{ IR}_t + 0.045 \text{ YVR}_t + \hat{u}_t, \tag{15}$$
$$(-1.70) \qquad (-2.90) \qquad (0.20)$$

$$R^2 = 0.942, \text{SE} = 3.906, \hat{h} = 8.33, df = 133.$$

These results seem to be very astonishing. On the one hand, the variable with the strongest influence on the popularity of the two parties, the rate of growth of real income, has no impact at all on the perception of the economic situation. On the other hand, the inflation rate, which has no significant influence on the popularity of the two parties, is the economic variable having the most important impact on the perception of the general economic situation. It is approximately twice that of unemployment. A change of the inflation rate by one percentage point in the long run gives rise to a revision of the perception of the economic situation of about 11 percent of the electorate, whereas a one percentage point change of the unemployment rate influences only about 6 percent of the voters. With respect to their evaluation of the economic situation, German voters seem to react more strongly to inflation than unemployment, but not with respect to their voting intention (and not with respect to their evaluation of the government's record).

The reason for this apparent contradiction is probably that only a small part of the electorate is crucial to electoral outcomes: the "floating voters." Their decisions are mainly based on real income and unemployment, not inflation. Yet, when it comes to the general economic situation, not only do the opinions of the floating voters count, but also those of the numerically much stronger groups of traditional government and opposition voters. They base their economic perception largely on the inflation rate. However, as it is not only inflation that counts, but also unemployment, and as the latter is relevant to the voting decision, the perception of the general economic situation also has a significant impact on the popularity of the two parties. Thus, what seems to be a contradiction is actually the result of the different weights that different groups of voters have when answering different questions at the polls.[9]

4. Popularity Functions for the Period after the *Wende*

For the Kohl government, which came to office in October, 1982, I again assume that it was not held responsible by the electorate for the economic situation during its first year in office. Since I only have data until October, 1986, I can only use the time span from October, 1983, to October, 1986,

---

9. See Kirchgässner 1990 for an extensive discussion of this point.

i.e., 37 observations.[10] Again, employing all three economic variables, we get the following FIML estimates:

$$CDU_t = 77.757 + 0.531\ CDU_{t-1} - 5.850\ UR_t$$
$$\quad\ (2.79)\quad (5.20)\qquad\qquad (-2.12)$$

$$- 0.271\ IR_t - 0.700\ YVR_t + \hat{u}_{1,t},$$
$$(-0.38)\qquad (-1.23)$$

$$\tag{16a}$$

$$R^2 = 0.555,\ SE = 1.276,\ \hat{h} = -2.16,\ df = 32.$$

$$SPD_t = -41.112 + 0.531\ SPD_{t-1} + 6.174\ UR_t$$
$$\quad\ (-1.59)\quad (5.20)\qquad\qquad (2.30)$$

$$+ 0.733\ IR_t + 1.619\ YVR_t + \hat{u}_{2,t},$$
$$(0.82)\qquad (1.62)$$

$$\tag{16b}$$

$$R^2 = 0.556,\ SE = 1.580,\ \hat{h} = 0.82,\ df = 32.$$
Logarithm of the Likelihood Function: -119.561.

Once more, the coefficients of the inflation rate have the expected sign but are not significantly different from zero. The coefficients of the unemployment rate have the expected signs and are both significantly different from zero at the 5 percent significance level; however, they are incredibly high. According to these estimates, a reduction of the unemployment rate by one percentage point leads to a popularity gain by the Christian Democrats of approximately 6 percent and to a corresponding loss by the Social Democrats. On the other hand, the dominating economic variable during the 1970s, the growth rate of real income, is not significantly different from zero but has the wrong sign in both equations. This could reflect the recent German experience that reasonable growth rates of real income are compatible with no or, at most, very small reductions of unemployment, which might have shifted the attention of floating voters from real income to unemployment. In addition, it seems as if the success of the new government in fighting inflation could not be converted into votes for the Christian Democrats, which is consistent with the suggestion mentioned above that floating voters are not reacting to changes in the inflation rate.

10. According to information from Dieter Roth (Forschungsgruppe Wahlen, Mannheim), one can assume that from autumn 1983 onward, German voters held the new government of CDU/CSU and FDP responsible in the same way for the economic development as the old government of SPD and FDP before October, 1982.

If we use the perception of the economic situation instead of the objective indicators, we get:

$$CDU_t = 18.050 + 0.620\ CDU_{t-1} - 0.003\ GES_t$$
$$ (4.07) \quad (6.96) \quad\quad\quad (-0.14)$$

$$+\ \hat{u}_{1,t}, \tag{17a}$$

$$R^2 = 0.458,\ SE = 1.366,\ \hat{h} = -0.77,\ df = 34.$$

$$SPD_t = 15.645 + 0.620\ SPD_{t-1} - 0.002\ GES_t$$
$$ (4.21) \quad (6.96) \quad\quad\quad (-0.07)$$

$$+\ \hat{u}_{2,t}, \tag{17b}$$

$$R^2 = 0.500,\ SE = 1.625,\ \hat{h} = 0.79,\ df = 34.$$
$$\text{Logarithm of the Likelihood Function: } -123.959.$$

There is no indication at all that the perception of the economic situation had any influence on the voting intentions during this period.

If we ask for the factors influencing the perception of the economic situation during this period, we get:[11]

$$GES_t = -0.38 + 1.003\ GES_{t-1} - 0.249\ GES_{t-2}$$
$$ (-0.02) \quad (6.34) \quad\quad\quad (-1.53)$$

$$+\ 1.707\ UR_t - 2.465\ IR_t - 0.077\ YVR_t$$
$$ (0.68) \quad\quad (-1.26) \quad\quad (-0.09)$$

$$+\ \hat{u}_t, \tag{18}$$

$$R^2 = 0.956,\ SE = 3.270,\ DW = 1.99,\ df = 44.$$

Again, real income has no influence whatsoever on the perception of the economic situation. But unemployment also seems to have absolutely no influence on the perception of the economic situation: the corresponding

---

11. There is no reason, in this instance, to exclude the data at the beginning of the new government. Therefore, we use the whole observation period from October, 1982, to October, 1986, and have forty-nine observations. Because $n \cdot \text{var}(\beta_1) > 1$, the Durbin h-statistic cannot be computed. Moreover, as we included two lags of the endogenous variable, the Durbin h-test is not appropriate in this case. Thus, we only present the Durbin-Watson statistic.

coefficient is in no way significantly different from zero. The only relevant variable seems to be the inflation rate, but its (negative) coefficient is also not significantly different from zero.[12] This could indicate that the meaning of the term *general economic situation* has changed; voters put up with high unemployment and are mainly concerned with changes in the rate of inflation (and the corresponding losses of real income). However, in such a situation it seems even more astonishing that the growth rate of real income itself has no significant impact, as equation 18 shows. On the other hand, if—according to the estimates in equation 17—voters are mainly interested in reductions of unemployment, equation 18 can explain why the perception of the economic situation no longer influences the popularity of the two parties: improvements of the general economic situation due solely to reductions of inflation might not help the government gain votes.

However, these considerations are somewhat speculative; their empirical basis is rather weak. Three years, or thirty-seven monthly data, are not enough to draw strong conclusions. At the 5 percent level, only the estimated coefficients of the unemployment rate in the popularity functions are significantly different from zero. Moreover, during the period considered, the time-series of the (seasonally adjusted) unemployment rate showed only very little variance, while the variables with important variation proved not to have had significant impact.

5. Tests of Structural Change between the Periods before and after 1982

The question remains whether there was a structural change between the period of the SPD/FDP coalition before October, 1982, and the period of the CDU/CSU-FDP coalition after October, 1982. Even if the regression results for the second period are not very conclusive, it is possible to test whether the behavior of the electorate changed from the first to the second period. In particular, was there a significant change with respect to the influence of the economic situation on the popularity of the leading party in government (GP) and of the leading opposition party (OP)?

First, two new series had to be constructed using the popularity series of the Christian Democrats and the Social Democrats. Again, for the same reason cited above, I dropped the data from October, 1982, to September, 1983. Second, I introduced a dummy variable, *DCDU*, that takes on the value 1.0 during the time of the CDU/CSU-FDP government after October, 1982, and zero elsewhere. To check whether the coefficients of the economic vari-

---

12. Contrary to unemployment, it becomes significantly different from zero at least on the 10 percent level once unemployment is excluded from this equation.

ables during the second period are different from those during the first period, I performed likelihood ratio tests.[13]

Including only the unemployment rate and the growth rate of real income, under the null hypothesis of structural stability we get the following estimates:

$$GP_t = \underset{(7.49)}{12.534} + \underset{(4.47)}{3.725}\ DCDU_t + \underset{(18.51)}{0.698}\ GP_{t-1}$$

$$\underset{(-3.02)}{-\ 0.309}\ UR_t + \underset{(4.04)}{0.335}\ YVR_t + \hat{u}_{1,t}, \tag{19a}$$

$$R^2 = 0.881,\ SE = 1.751,\ \hat{h} = -0.20,\ df = 172.$$

$$OP_t = \underset{(7.86)}{14.277} - \underset{(-4.41)}{3.484}\ DCDU_t + \underset{(18.51)}{0.698}\ OP_{t-1}$$

$$+ \underset{(1.95)}{0.214}\ UR_t - \underset{(-2.03)}{0.159}\ YVR_t + \hat{u}_{2,t}, \tag{19b}$$

$$R^2 = 0.856,\ SE = 1.596,\ \hat{h} = -0.52,\ df = 172.$$
Logarithm of the Likelihood Function: -629.403.

These estimates are very similar to those for the period of the "social liberal" coalition until 1982. The development after 1982 does not seem to have changed the situation. If we allow the four coefficients of the economic variables to take different values for the two time-periods, we get -626.568 for the logarithm of the likelihood function. The test statistic for the likelihood ratio test is $\hat{\chi}^2 = 5.670$. Thus, with 4 degrees of freedom the null hypothesis of structural stability cannot be rejected even at the 10 percent significance level. However, the highly significant coefficient of the dummy variable shows that the popular support for the Christian Democrats is, ceteris paribus, several percentage points higher than it is for the Social Democrats, regardless of whether they are in government or in opposition.

If we use the perception of the general economic situation as the explanatory variable for party support, we get:

$$GP_t = \underset{(6.35)}{6.593} + \underset{(3.32)}{1.492}\ DCDU_t + \underset{(26.97)}{0.792}\ GP_{t-1}$$

---

13. This is a generalization of the Chow test. See, e.g., Dhrymes 1978, 62.

$$+ 0.040 \ GES_t + \hat{u}_{1,t},$$
$$(3.72)$$

$(20a)$

$$R^2 = 0.871, \ SE = 1.817, \ \hat{h} = -0.26, \ df = 173.$$

$$OP_t = 11.568 - 1.683 \ DCDU_t + 0.792 \ OP_{t-1}$$
$$(7.26) \ (-4.39) \qquad (26.97)$$

$$- 0.032 \ GES_t + \hat{u}_{2,t},$$
$$(-3.89)$$

$(20b)$

$$R^2 = 0.856, \ SE = 1.594, \ \hat{h} = -1.75, \ df = 173.$$
Logarithm of the Likelihood Function: -637.581.

The test for structural stability yields $\hat{\chi}^2 = 2.818$. Thus, the null hypothesis cannot be rejected at any conventional significance level. According to these estimates, the advantage of the CDU/CSU over the SPD is several percentage points in government as well as in opposition. Rated by the logarithm of the likelihood function, the equations using the objective economic variables, 19, perform clearly better than those employing the subjective perception variable, 20.

However, the "advantage" of the CDU/CSU over the SPD implied by these estimates is not "structural" in the sense that generally, ceteris paribus, the Christian Democrats could get so many more votes than the Social Democrats. We have to consider that the economic situation at the beginning of the CDU/CSU-FDP government in 1982 was much worse than the situation when the SPD/FDP coalition started in 1969. If voters judge the record of a government's economic policy comparing the actual development with the situation at the beginning of this government and not with a fictitious "optimal" situation,[14] this will influence the size and significance of the dummy variable's coefficients. To exclude such effects, I employed intervention analysis in the sense of Box and Tiao (1975) and estimated the following purely autoregressive model:

$$GP_t = 6.074 + 1.026 \ DCDU_t + 0.849 \ GP_{t-1} + \hat{u}_{1,t},$$
$$(5.70) \quad (2.15) \qquad (32.82)$$

$(21a)$

$$R^2 = 0.863, \ SE = 1.867, \ \hat{h} = -0.34, \ df = 174.$$

$$OP_t = 7.361 - 1.184 \ DCDU_t + 0.849 \ OP_{t-1} + \hat{u}_{2,t},$$
$$(5.84) \ (-2.98) \qquad (32.82)$$

$(21b)$

---

14. See, for such considerations, Hibbs and Vasilatos 1981.

$$R^2 = 0.843, \text{SE} = 1.658, \hat{h} = -1.43, df = 174.$$
Logarithm of the Likelihood Function: -646.266.

These estimates show a "structural" advantage for the Christian Democrats over the Social Democrats as well, in government and opposition. Both coefficients are, at least at the 5 percent level, significantly different from zero.

The estimates of equation 21 can also be used to check whether the combined economic variables or the perception of the economic situation have a significant impact on the popularity of both parties. Employing a likelihood ratio test to compare systems 19 and 21, we get $\hat{\chi}^2 = 33.726$. Thus, with 4 degrees of freedom the null hypothesis of no influence can be rejected even at the 0.01 percent significance level. The same holds if we compare systems 20 and 21. There, we get $\hat{\chi}^2 = 17.370$, with 2 degrees of freedom.

Finally, we want to check whether the influence of the objective economic indicators on the perception of the economic situation changed between the two periods. As the growth rate of real income was not significant during the first or during the second period, I exclude it from the estimations and use only the unemployment and inflation rates. For the whole observation period from March, 1971, to October, 1986 (188 observations), the results are:

$$GES_t = 12.820 + 1.112 \, GES_{t-1} - 0.221 \, GES_{t-2}$$
$$(4.21) \quad (15.18) \qquad\qquad (-3.12)$$

$$- 0.062 \, DCDU_t - 0.612 \, UR_t - 1.127 \, IR_t$$
$$(-0.05) \qquad\qquad (-2.70) \qquad (-3.97)$$

$$+ \hat{u}_t, \tag{22}$$

$$R^2 = 0.947, \text{SE} = 3.723, \text{DW} = 1.96, df = 182.$$

Employing an F-test to check whether there was a significant change in the coefficients of the unemployment and inflation rate before and after October, 1982, we obtain $\hat{F} = 0.635$. Thus, with F (2, 180) the null hypothesis of no structural change cannot be rejected at any conventional significance level. Moreover, as the $\hat{t}$-value of the dummy variable shows, there is also no significant change of the constant term.[15]

Thus, leaving aside the "structural" advantage of the Christian Democrats over the Social Democrats, there is no indication at all for a structural change between the two periods. This holds although the separate estimates for the two periods looked quite different.

---

15. This also holds if the period from October, 1982, to September, 1983, is excluded.

6. Testing the Rational Expectations Hypothesis Using Popularity Data

As mentioned in the introduction, I am interested in seeing whether the behavior of German voters is consistent with rational expectations in the sense of Muth (1961). In Kirchgässner 1985b and 1986a, I have shown how popularity data can be used to test (implications of) this hypothesis. Using German data from 1971 to 1982, this hypothesis had to be rejected. First, estimates showing that unemployment has a significant effect on the government's popularity are hardly compatible with the Lucas-Sargent proposition, as rational voters who know the inability of the government to influence unemployment in a systematic manner should not punish the government for high unemployment rates.[16] Second and more important, even if voters hold the government responsible for the performance of the economy, only unexpected changes of the economic variables should change the record of the government in their eyes.

If only unexpected developments of the economic variables matter, the popularity of the parties should follow a random walk.[17] At the same time, it must be noted that the popularity series is affected by measurement error. Let $\overline{POP}_t$ be the true popularity and POP_t be the measured popularity at time t. Then, we get the model

$$POP_t = \overline{POP}_t + \epsilon_t, \tag{23a}$$

$$\overline{POP}_t = \overline{POP}_{t-1} + \eta_{t'} \tag{23b}$$

where ϵ and η are independent white-noise error processes. Taking first differences, we get

$$(1 - L)POP_t = \epsilon_t + (1 - L)\eta_t = (1 - \gamma L)\zeta_t, \tag{24}$$

where $|\zeta| < 1$, i.e, equation 24 can be written as an ARIMA(0,1,1) model, where ζ is again white noise. Thus, one possible test procedure is to estimate the ARMA(1,1) model,

$$(1 - \delta L)POP_t = (1 - \gamma L)\zeta_t, \tag{25}$$

and to check whether $\hat{\delta}$ is significantly different from one.

When I estimate such models for both parties and for both subperiods

---

16. This holds at least as long as demand management policy (monetary policy) is considered. They might, however, punish the government for high unemployment resulting from bad supply-side policies.

17. This argument is analogous to the one developed by Hall (1978) with respect to consumption.

separately, I never find that $\hat{\delta}$ is significantly different from one. This seems to be in line with the rational expectations hypothesis. However, the picture changes when these models are estimated over the whole period from 1971 to 1986:[18]

$$\text{CDU}_t = \begin{array}{l} 9.093 + 0.812\ \text{CDU}_{t-1} + \zeta_{1,\,t} \\ (3.39)\quad (14.64) \end{array}$$

$$\begin{array}{l} - 0.130\ \zeta_{1,\,t-1}, \\ (-1.35) \end{array} \tag{26a}$$

$$R^2 = 0.664,\ \text{SE} = 1.663,\ \hat{Q}(9) = 11.234.$$

$$\text{SPD}_t = \begin{array}{l} 4.384 + 0.891\ \text{SPD}_{t-1} + \zeta_{2,\,t} \\ (2.96)\quad (24.67) \end{array}$$

$$\begin{array}{l} - 0.051\ \zeta_{2,\,t-1}, \\ (-0.61) \end{array} \tag{26b}$$

$$R^2 = 0.805,\ \text{SE} = 1.881,\ \hat{Q}(9) = 9.766.$$

One can test whether the coefficients of the lagged endogenous variables are significantly different from one by using the Dickey-Fuller procedure and comparing the estimated t-statistics with the critical values ($\hat{\tau}_\mu$) presented by Fuller (1976, 373, table 8.5.2). The result is the rejection of the null hypothesis in both cases at the 5 percent level. Thus, the hypothesis of rational expectations has to be rejected. These results are much more clear-cut than the corresponding results in Kirchgässner (1985b and 1986b).[19]

Since the second period is too short and most of the coefficients that have been estimated for the economic variables in this period are not significantly different from zero, it does not seem to be meaningful to apply the other procedures proposed in Kirchgässner (1985b) to our data for the second period. However, for the first period these tests showed unambiguously that the rational expectations hypothesis had to be rejected. Thus, German voters make vote decisions that may be rational in the sense of Simon (1955), but not in the sense of Muth (1961).

---

18. For these estimates, I have used MICRO-TSP, version 5, for the IBM PC-AT. As this program provides no possibility of estimating systems of equations that include MA terms, I had to estimate the two equations separately and could not impose the cross-equation constraint. $\hat{Q}(k)$ denotes the value of the Box-Pierce Q-statistic with k degrees of freedom.

19. These results seem to contradict those of Chrystal and Peel (1986). However, those authors only look at the Box-Pierce Q-statistics, and according to this criterion we are also not able to reject the null hypothesis of the ARIMA (0,1,1) model.

7. Summary and Conclusions

Let me summarize: Contrary to the time before 1982, for the period after the *Wende* there is no strong evidence that economic performance influences the vote intentions of the German electorate. This holds whether I use objective economic indicators like unemployment, inflation, and the growth of real income or subjective perceptions of the general economic situation. On the other hand, if structural changes between the two periods are tested, I can find no evidence of such changes. Therefore, I have a puzzle that can be solved only by additional data that are not yet available.

Concerning the specific economic variables influencing the voters' decisions, it seems clear that for the period of the "social-liberal" government (1969–1982), unemployment and real income were the determining factors, whereas for the time after 1982 only unemployment proved to be significant. In both periods, inflation seemed to have no influence. On the other hand, inflation seems to be the most important factor determining the perception of the general economic situation both before and after the *Wende*. The solution to this puzzle might rest in the fact that traditional government and opposition voters give more weight to inflation, whereas floating voters give more weight to unemployment and income when evaluating economic performance. A closer investigation of this relation is, however, the topic of another paper.

Besides the small number of observations available, another reason why I cannot draw strong conclusions with respect to the second period is that the variation of the (seasonally adjusted) unemployment rate was rather small during this time. Thus, we have to wait not only for more observations, but also for larger changes—hopefully a decline—in the unemployment rate.

If we ask whether the popularity data follow a random walk, which would fit the rational expectations hypothesis popular today in macroeconomics, the answer is no. Thus, confirming earlier results for the first period, the popularity data are compatible with rational behavior in the sense of Simon (1955), but not in the sense of Muth (1961). Since "wrong" political decisions do not impose costs on the individual voter, there are no strong incentives to behave in the way described by Muth when voters are asked about their intentions. Where such incentives exist, e.g., in auction markets, economic agents might behave according to that concept of rationality.

REFERENCES

Borooah, Vani, and Rick van der Ploeg. 1982. "The Changing Criteria of Economic Success: Performance and Popularity in British Politics." *The Manchester School*, 61–78.

Box, George E. P., and George C. Tiao. 1975. "Intervention Analysis with Applications to Economic and Environmental Problems." *Journal of the American Statistical Association* 70:70–79.

Chrystal, K. Alec, and David P. Peel. 1986. "What Can Economists Learn from Political Science and Vice Versa?" *American Economic Review* 76(2): 62–65.

Davis, Otto A., Melvin J. Hinich, and Peter C. Ordeshook. 1970. "An Expository Development of a Mathematical Model of the Electoral Process." *American Political Science Review* 64:426–48.

Downs, Anthony. 1957. *An Economic Theory of Democracy*. New York: Harper and Row.

Dhrymes, Phoebus J. 1978. *Introductory Econometrics*. New York: Springer.

Fair, Ray C. 1978. "The Effect of Economic Events on Votes for President." *Review of Economics and Statistics* 60:159–73.

Frey, Bruno S., and Hermann Garbers. 1972. "Der Einfluß wirtschaftlicher Variabler auf die Popularität der Regierung." *Jahrbücher für Nationalökonomie und Statistik* 186:281–320.

Frey, Bruno S., and Friedrich Schneider. 1978. "A Politico-Economic Model of the United Kingdom." *Economic Journal* 88:243–53.

Frey, Bruno S., and Freidrich Schneider. 1979. "An Econometric Model with an Endogenous Government Sector." *Public Choice* 34:29–43.

Fuller, Wayne A. 1976. *Introduction to Statistical Time Series*. New York: Wiley.

Hall, Robert E. 1978. "Stochastic Implications of the Lifecycle-Permanent Income Hypothesis: Theory and Evidence." *Journal of Political Economy* 86:971–88.

Hibbs, Douglas A., and Nicholas Vasilatos. 1981. "Macroeconomic Performance and Mass Political Support in the United States and Great Britain." In *Contemporary Political Economy*, ed. Douglas A. Hibbs and Heino Fassbender, 31–47. Amsterdam: North-Holland.

Kirchgässner, Gebhard. 1985a. "Causality Testing of the Popularity Function: An Empirical Investigation for the Federal Republic of Germany, 1971–1982." *Public Choice* 45:155–73.

Kirchgässner, Gebhard. 1985b. "Rationality, Causality, and the Relation between Economic Conditions and the Popularity of Parties: An Empirical Investigation for the Federal Republic of Germany, 1971–1982." *European Economic Review* 28:243–68.

Kirchgässner, Gebhard. 1986a. "Economic Conditions and the Popularity of West German Parties: A Survey." *European Journal of Political Research* 14:421–39.

Kirchgässner, Gebhard. 1986b. "Überprüfung der Hypothese rationaler Erwartungen anhand von Popularitätsdaten: Eine Untersuchung für die Bundesrepublik Deutschland, 1971–1982." *Zeitschrift für Wirtschafts- und Sozialwissenschaften* 106:363–86.

Kirchgässner, Gebhard. 1990. "Zur gegenseitigen Abhängigkeit von Parteipräferenz und Wirtschaftslage: Eine empirische Untersuchung für die Bundesrepublik Deutschland, 1971–1986." In *Wahlen, Parteieliten, Politische Einstellungen*, ed. Karl Schmitt. Frankfurt: Peter Lang.

Muth, John F. 1961. "Rational Expectations and the Theory of Price Movements." *Econometrica* 29:315–35.

Nordhaus, William D. 1975. "The Political Business Cycle." *Review of Economic Studies* 42:169–90.

Simon, Herbert A. 1955. "A Behavioral Model of Rational Choice." *Quarterly Journal of Economics* 69:99–118.

Political Dyarchy and Popularity Functions: Lessons from the 1986 French Experience

Jean-Dominique Lafay

Popularity and vote functions have the advantage of fulfilling many of the necessary (and sufficient) conditions for scientific success: they concern a subject with a high mythic content for the nonscientific population, i.e., explaining and predicting political success and failure; they occupy a strategic theoretical position, as a link between economics and politics; their formulation and estimation raise interesting technical problems, for political scientists as well as for economists; and the data necessary for at least a partial empirical verification are now abundant and easily available. Furthermore, the current economic situation, with a large variance in economic variables, is particularly well-suited for econometric tests.

Consequently, the number of studies concerning this question has grown at an impressive rate. So much has been said that the subject may now appear to be an overplowed field. New sources for research may come from three main directions: development of more general theories (notably the theory of choice), progress in econometric techniques (but with the risk of seeing the debate degenerate into a mere race for sophistication), and using original data. The present study tries to take advantage only of the last kind of research stimulus, utilizing a neglected data set, the Figaro-Sofrès monthly surveys.

The March, 1986, French general elections gave rise to a very original situation, called "cohabitation": The president of the Republic, François Mitterrand, who was elected in 1981 by a majority of Socialist and Communist voters, had to share power with Jacques Chirac, a right-wing prime minister supported by a new Conservative majority in Parliament. How did citizens assess the responsibilities of each for the political situation? What were the

I would like to thank Joanne Gerber, New York University, and Michael S. Lewis-Beck for their help in editing the English version of this text.

effects of political successes or failures of each member of this "dyarchical" leadership on the popularity of the other?

Though he no longer had any effective responsibility for economic policy, Mitterrand still had a popularity index. In other words, we witness a kind of laboratory experiment where the influences of economic and political variables on political support are institutionally isolated.

Moreover, though he had been in charge for five years, Mitterrand benefited, as well as Chirac, from a sizable "honeymoon effect," a phenomenon that somewhat contradicts the existing theory regarding this effect. What are the possible a priori explanations of this paradox and how do they conform to the data?

Section 1 gives some highlights of French politics since the beginning of the Fifth Republic (1958). It aims to offer a better understanding of the specifics of the complex political situation. Section 2 presents the theoretical basis of the popularity functions that will be used for the empirical tests. There is no attempt to discuss the literature exhaustively. The analysis will concentrate instead on the points that are essential for this study. Section 3 shows the empirical results obtained from monthly data (December, 1978, through April, 1987), using the Figaro-Sofrès political "Barometer" and INSEE (Institut National de la Statistique et des Etudes Economiques) economic series. Section 4 summarizes major conclusions.

1. President and Prime Minister in the French System

From 1946 to 1958, during the Fourth Republic, French governments were highly unstable and under permanent pressure from the party coalitions in parliament. The military revolt in Algeria (May, 1958) ended that situation. General de Gaulle was called back as prime minister (June, 1958). A referendum was organized (September, 1958) for the approval of the constitution of the new Fifth Republic. A new parliament was elected (November), with a strong Gaullist party (but not a majority). De Gaulle was elected as president of the Republic (December, 1958), under the then prevailing restricted suffrage regime (i.e., by about 80,000 *grands électeurs*).

In October, 1962, a major change in the constitution was approved by referendum: the election of the president of the Republic by universal—and no longer restricted—suffrage. The new system was based on two rounds: the top two candidates from the first balloting would compete against each other in the second. De Gaulle was reelected under this regime in 1965 (December). After his resignation, in 1969, a new election took place and the former Gaullist prime minister, Georges Pompidou, succeeded him.

The election of "liberal" Valéry Giscard d'Estaing (May, 1974), after the death of Pompidou, though a victory of the right-wing coalition, was a major political change.[1] The Gaullist party lost the presidency when their candidate, Jacques Chaban-Delmas, was defeated in the first balloting. Despite that, the Gaullist party remained dominant within the right-wing coalition in parliament. Giscard d'Estaing was never able to change this state of affairs throughout the whole period of his mandate.

The choice of Giscard d'Estaing in the wake of the first oil crisis was perhaps the first indication of the desire of a majority of the voters to change the ruling elite in the face of economic difficulties (the desire was for a limited change, however; the voters wanted to reform the ruling coalition, not to overthrow it). The election of Mitterrand (May, 1981), less than two years after the second oil shock, may be seen as an evolution of the preceding trend: the desire for reform within the governing coalition had become a desire to change coalitions altogether.

Despite the profound ideological differences between the old and new governing coalitions, the French political system worked in the same manner from October, 1962 (referendum on universal suffrage for the presidential election), to March, 1986. The president still commanded a majority in parliament and the prime minister, appointed by him, had no other alternative than to follow him or to resign.[2]

When a president lacked sufficient control over the Parliament, he obtained it either by dissolution (de Gaulle in 1962 and 1968, Mitterrand in 1981) or by an implicit or explicit threat of dissolution (Giscard d'Estaing between 1979 and 1981 with the Gaullist party).

The system worked hierarchically, with a president managing the "reserved domain," i.e., foreign policy and defense, and defining the "broad lines" for the other policies; and a prime minister in charge of the details of domestic policies and protecting the president from the negative fluctuations of public opinion (a "screen effect" or "scapegoat role").

All presidents have had, however, problems with their prime ministers. The well-known falling-out between de Gaulle and Pompidou, during the 1968 crisis, led to the replacement of the latter after the June, 1968, electoral victory (cf. Viansson-Ponté 1971; Roussel 1984). De Gaulle's successors have had to change their prime minister for similar reasons two or three years after their election.

A candidate needs allies to be elected president. His choice of his first

---

1. "Liberal" is used here according to the French meaning, i.e., closer to U.S. Republicans or English Conservatives, less interventionist (at least during that period) and nationalist than the Gaullist party.

2. Four months before his own resignation, Chirac said prophetically: "In our institutions, there can be no shadow of disagreement between the President and Prime Minister. If there is disagreement, the Prime Minister must give way" (April 12, 1976, in a meeting with the *Association de la Presse Ministérielle*).

prime minister is generally a reward, though not necessarily preagreed, for support given during elections. This means that the prime minister has an autonomous political base. The sources of discord tend to accumulate with time. For example, the prime minister may become more popular than the president (Chaban-Delmas with Pompidou), or he may have to defend the interests of his own party (Chirac with Giscard) or he may not share the president's ideological shifts (Mauroy with Mitterrand). Presidents generally reacted to the resulting conflicts with their prime minister by choosing replacements who were less well-known and more ideologically compatible (Pierre Messmer, Raymond Barre or Laurent Fabius).

The above system was swept away in March, 1986, in a single electoral night. The left-wing president no longer had control over the new right-wing assembly and could not hope to change the situation through dissolution, at least not before the 1988 presidential elections. The president then chose the solution of "cohabitation": appointing a right-wing prime minister and hoping to exploit the power granted to the presidency by the constitution. Ironically, Mitterrand was the first president obliged to accept the "famous dyarchy of power" which he referred to in 1974 as a potential defect of the constitution of the Fifth Republic.

According to the text of the constitution, the president only appoints the prime minister (Art. 8). It is the government that "determines and conducts the policy of the nation" (Art. 20). The president retains an independent role in foreign policy (Arts. 14 and 52), in defense policy (as "chief of the Armies," Art. 15), and in the appointment of high officials. But even here there are serious difficulties because the prime minister also has important constitutional responsibilities in these domains (Arts. 20 and 21). Before March, 1986, foreign and defense policies were, in practice, a "reserved domain" for the president. Since then, because of the ambiguities in the constitution, there has been a need for at least some consensus between the president and the prime minister.

As the roles of the president and of the prime minister have been so deeply modified, one might think that the determinants of their respective popular support would be similarly changed. The empirical analysis in section 3 will try to examine to what extent this assertion is true. But it is necessary to develop, first, a formal model representing this situation.

2. A Formal Model of Popularity Fluctuations

As a consequence of V. O. Key's analysis, several models of political behavior have been based on the idea that electors are jurors in a formal (elections) or informal (popularity surveys) lawsuit against the government (Peffley 1985). To pronounce their verdict, they have to assess responsibilities and to examine facts retrospectively. This idea is surely interesting for social-psychological analysis but, on a priori grounds, it is not directly compatible with what economists define as "rational choice." From this perspective, it is now well-recognized that votes or political support are decided on the basis of opportunity costs (see Fiorina 1981 or Chappell and Keech 1985).

An individual will support the government if it is expected to bring him or her more utility than any other alternative (i.e., the opposition in a two-party system).

$U[(Y - Y^*), (X - X^*), (Z - Z^*)]$ is the utility function of a given individual. To simplify, one assumes a one-period horizon and perfect foresight (i.e., actualization and behavior toward risk problems will not be formally introduced).

U is supposed to depend on:

—a vector Y of "public" objective variables, which the individual regards as indirectly controlled by the state;
—a vector X of instruments directly controlled by the state;
—a vector Z of predetermined variables (i.e., not under direct or indirect state control).

Y^*, X^*, Z^* are vectors of "ideal" values for the elements of Y, X, Z (corresponding to unconstrained maximization of U).

The individual takes into account a set of *perceived* constraints for the whole social system: $F(Y,X,Z) = 0$. For Z°, a given value of Z, the individual is able to calculate:

—the level of utility, U', corresponding to his or her own optimal policy $U[(Y' - Y^*), (X' - X^*), (Z^\circ - Z^*)] = \text{Max } U$ under F (this policy depends partly on the distributional advantages expected by the individual);
—the level of utility expected from the present government $Ug[(Y_g - Y^*), (X_g - X^*), (Z^\circ - Z^*)]$ Y_g is not independent of X_g: the expectations must be consistent with F. As a consequence, the expected utility of governmental policies depends only on the expected values of its instruments (for $Z = Z^\circ$); and
—the level of utility expected from the opposition if it wins the elections (for voting behavior) or if it were in charge of power (for popularity indexes) $U_o[(Y_o - Y^*), (X_o - X^*), (Z^\circ - Z^*)]$ (the same remark as above, concerning the dependence upon X_o of Y_o can be made).

The government is supported (voted for) if $(U_g - U') - (U_o - U') > 0$.

In the above analysis, the crucial elements are the perceived social model

(F) and the predicted values of *instruments*. Per se, the observed values of Y are unimportant because they cannot be the source of differences between U', U_g, and U_o.[3]

Politico-economic analysis often supposes, however, that individuals are "rationally ignorant." Unless voters have a strong distributive interest, the information costs are so high that they do not invest much for a better knowledge of the "true" social structure (i.e., F[Y,X,Z]). To form their expectations, they prefer to use low-cost information: "experts' reports" offered by the media and, more important, observed *results* regarding the objective variables for the government or for the opposition when it was in power (as in Hibbs 1982). In the context of the principal/agent relationship existing between the electorate and the government, the result-based behavior also has a strategic interest. This specific application of the caveat venditor principle conveys important information to the government: the government knows that if it makes bad policy it will be punished, because this policy will lead to bad results. Indeed, the reverse is not true: bad results do not imply bad policy. But a rational, nonexpert voter prefers to risk voting against a good government than to retain a possibly bad one in power, because of the incentives the latter behavior could create for future government.

Recent studies have analyzed the consequences of the rational expectation theory. For Chrystal and Peel (1986, 62), it is "relevant to the formation of expectations of the performance of political parties." If this definition means only that individuals "apply the principle of rational behavior to the acquisition and processing of (costly) information and to the formation of expectations" (Maddock and Carter 1982, 41), no conflict appears with the "rational ignorance" idea. However, if it implies the Lucas-Sargent "impotence result" for economic policy, based on low information and adjustment costs, the conflict seems unsolvable. Knowing "about this inability of the government, why should rational voters hold the government responsible for cyclical fluctuations?" (Kirchgässner 1985, 244). As the argument can be extended to all government policies, not only to economic ones, popularity will follow a random walk. The final question would then perhaps be this: Why a government at all?

Finding that, for the popularity and voting functions, there is "strong evidence against this strong version of the theory of rational expectations," Kirchgässner (1985) tried to test a weak version, i.e., the idea that "only unanticipated changes of the economic situation should affect the voting deci-

---

3. Except indirectly, if F contains reaction functions and if these include elements that differentiate between the government and the opposition. This corresponds, for example, to the idea that people prefer left-wing parties to fight unemployment and right-wing parties to fight inflation.

sion." However, his tests do not concern policy instruments but objective variables (unemployment and inflation). What is then the rationality of "punishing" a government for all changes, even those that are due to purely exogenous shocks? Is it not simply because the government is thought to have failed to stabilize the economy?

As a consequence of the preceding discussion, the individual support decision will be represented by the "rational ignorance" model, based on results for objective variables. We suppose that linearization is possible as follows:

$$DU_t = a_o + \sum_j a_j (EF_{gjt} - EF_{ojt}),$$

where

> DU_t is the utility differential,
> EF_{gjt} is the governmental "efficiency" for objective variable j
> $(EF_{gjt} = |y'_{jt} - y_{jt}*|/|y_{gjt} - y_{jt}*|)$, and
> EF_{ojt} is the potential "efficiency" of the opposition for the objective variable j $(EF_{ojt} = |y'_{jt} - y_{jt}*|/|y_{ojt} - y_{jt}*|)$.

Aggregation for all the individuals is possible, either directly (i.e., by calculating the proportion of persons with a $DU > 0$ for given values of y_g, y', and y_o) or on the basis of a "critical threshold" model (Kernell and Hibbs 1981), after having introduced the adequate probabilistic elements. The resulting popularity function is then as follows:

$$POP_t = a_o + \sum_j a_j (EF_{gjt} - EF_{ojt}).$$

For a given government, t is the time since its election. The expected efficiency of the opposition depends on its former performance and on ideological beliefs. The following formulation of EF_{ojt} corresponds to these ideas:

$$EF_{ojt} = k_j - \mu^t (1 - EF_{ojo}),$$

where $1 - EF_{ojo}$ is the observed inefficiency of the opposition at the end of its term; $\mu = 1/(1 + \delta)$ is a parameter, between 0 and 1, saying that the electors forget the previous inefficiency of the opposition at a rate δ; and k is an ideological constant, between 0 and 1. As time goes by, the expected performance of the opposition is based less and less on its previous historical record and more and more on ideology.

Substituting EF_{ojt} by its value in POP_t and subtracting $\mu \cdot POP_{t-1}$ from POP_t gives, for $t > 0$:

$$POP_t - \mu\,POP_{t-1} = (a_o - \sum_j a_j\,k_j)\,(1 - \mu) + \sum_j a_j(EF_{gjt} - \mu\,EF_{gjt-1}).$$

POP_t can then be determined without an explicit knowledge of the expected efficiency of the opposition.[4]

Empirically speaking, the above analysis says that:

—the popularity of the government depends on the observed judgments on its "efficiency" for the pertinent objective variables, on the one-period lagged values of these variables, on the lagged endogenous variable, and on specific dummies, with value 1 at the moment of a governmental change and zero elsewhere;

—the "efficiency" judgments for the government are based on the observed results for objective variables, i.e., present and lagged values used to derive y_{gjt}, and on the absolute standard (y'_{jt}) retained by the electorate. Efficiency judgments can then be explained econometrically if the y'_{jt} are either constant or linked, like y_{gjt}, to the observed results for the objective variables.

3. Empirical Analysis of the French Case

The analysis covers the period from December, 1978, to April, 1987. It corresponds to Giscard d'Estaing's presidency up to May, 1981, and to Mitterrand's thereafter. Barre was prime minister until May, 1981, Mauroy from June, 1981, to August, 1984, Fabius from September, 1984, to March, 1986, and Chirac since April, 1986.

The popularity function for the prime ministers (table 1) was obtained by regressing (OLS) the Figaro-Sofrès "reliance" index (PM) on the "efficiency" indexes concerning income growth (EF_y), inflation (EF_i) and employment (EF_u). When significant (i.e., for inflation and unemployment), the lagged values for these variables have been retained in the final equation. The lagged endogenous variable and dummies for specific quarters, with value 1 at the period of a governmental change, are also introduced. Note that specific dummies for the governing period of a given prime minister (with value 1 on all that period) are not significant and do not appear here: consequently, there

---

4. The only problem is for $t = 0$, when a new government is appointed: POP_{t-1} and the EF_{gjt-1} concern the previous government. However, POP_t is obtained directly, knowing a_o and the a_{js}, because EF_{ojo} is then the last—and observed—judgment on the efficiency of the just-defeated government.

TABLE 1. Dependent Variable: Popularity of the Prime Minister (PM_t), December, 1978–April, 1987

Variables	Constant	EFy_t	EFp_t	EFp_{t-1}	EFu_t	EFu_{t-1}	D81.06	D84.09	D86.04	PM_{t-1}
Coefficients	2.60	0.16	0.30	-0.32	0.26	-0.35	37.25	28.89	19.40	0.90
(t-value)	(1.7)	(1.4)	(2.7)	(2.6)	(1.8)	(2.5)	(9.7)	(9.1)	(4.4)	(23.5)

$R^2 = 0.93$ F = 139.37   DW = 2.23   SE = 3.07   h = -1.34   df = 91

Note: See appendix for the definition of variables.

are no long-term differences between prime ministers, based on their own personality or on their ideological affiliations. They simply benefit from a large "honeymoon effect" when they are appointed (the coefficients of D81.06, D84.09, D86.04 in table 1 are high and significant).

This first equation shows that the popularity of the prime ministers is clearly linked to their perceived performance concerning inflation and unemployment. The results concerning income growth are less satisfying (maybe because of multicollinearity). The high value of the lagged endogenous variable shows that the electors have a high μ, i.e., they forget only gradually (with a mean lag of 10.3 months) the performance of the former government. The coefficients of the lagged exogenous variables are not significantly different from their theoretical values, μa_i ($0.902 \times 0.305 = 0.275$ for inflation, $0.902 \times 0.256 = 0.232$ for unemployment, and $0.902 \times 0.157 = 0.142$ for income growth).

I have tried to introduce variables corresponding to efficiency judgments regarding foreign policy or social peace maintenance but they are not significant. The above result remains true even when the period falling within "cohabitation," i.e., from April, 1986, to April, 1987, is considered separately. The introduction of $Fsv \times D86.04-87.04$ or $ISfr \times D86.04-87.04$ as supplementary independent variables in table 1 does not lead to statistically significant coefficients. Contrary to what one might have thought, public opinion did not assign the Chirac government partial responsibility for the "reserved domain" of the president.[5]

Tables 2, 3, and 4 show how judgments about the "efficiency" of inflation, unemployment, and income growth policies are linked to the observed results concerning these respective variables. It is clear that an adaptive expectation model, based on observed results for the objective variables, provides, in all cases, a satisfying explanation of all these "efficiency" judgments.

As $EF_{it} = |y'_{it} - y_{it}*|/|y_{igt} - y_{it}*|$ and $y_{it}*$ is probably a constant, this implies that $y_{igt} = \varphi_g(y_{it}, y_{it-1}, \ldots, y_{it-n})$ and/or $y'_{it} = \varphi'(y_{it}, y_{it-1}, \ldots, y_{it-n})$. In fact, it is logical to think that the individual will determine his or her own standard of performance on the basis of the same information as for the expected performance of the government, plus an ideological or personality bias (see Berdot and Lafay 1986 for a detailed analysis of these ideological or personality biases in the case of inflation). In the three functions, the personality or ideological bias appears under two forms:

—a temporary prejudgment, measured by a dummy variable with a value 1 when a new government is appointed,

5. The number of data points concerning the "cohabitation" period—thirteen—may not be sufficient, however, to prove such an effect.

TABLE 2. Dependent Variable: Efficiency of Growth Policy (EFy_t), December, 1978–April, 1987

Variables	Constant	$y12_{t-1}$	D81.06	D86.04	EFy_{t-1}	D81.06–86.03
Coefficients	1.89	0.45	8.76	3.91	0.74	1.45
(t-value)	(3.3)	(3.2)	(3.8)	(1.7)	(13.6)	(3.2)

$R^2 = 0.80$ $F = 79.76$ DW $= 2.48$ SE $= 2.31$ $h = -2.89$ $df = 95$
Cochrane-Orcutt correction: rho $= -0.23$

Note: See appendix for the definition of variables.

TABLE 3. Dependent Variable: Efficiency of Anti-Inflation Policy (EFp_t), December, 1978–April, 1987

Variables	Constant	$p3_{t-1}$	D84.09	D86.04	EFp_{t-1}	D81.06–86.03
Coefficients	5.82	−0.33	−6.72	−21.14	0.84	1.22
(t-value)	(3.8)	(4.4)	(2.5)	(7.2)	(16.4)	(2.6)

$R^2 = 0.86$ $F = 124.44$ DW $= 2.66$ SE $= 2.75$ $h = -4.10$ $df = 95$
Cochrane-Orcutt correction: rho $= -0.34$

Note: See appendix for the definition of variables.

TABLE 4. Dependent Variable: Efficiency of Employment Policy (EFu_t), December, 1978–April, 1987

Variables	Constant	u_{t-1}	D81.06	EFu_{t-1}	D81.06–86.03	D86.04–87.04
Coefficients	15.29	−1.79	8.77	0.61	7.57	9.68
(t-value)	(3.9)	(3.7)	(3.2)	(7.0)	(3.9)	(3.7)

$R^2 = 0.77$ $F = 66.26$ DW $= 2.57$ SE $= 2.27$ $h = -5.94$ $df = 95$
Cochrane-Orcutt correction: rho $= -0.28$

Note: See appendix for the definition of variables.

—a permanent bias, measured by a difference in the intercept for each government (a possibility allowed by our theoretical model through the values of k_j).

The two left-wing governments benefited from a permanent ideological advantage for all the policy domains. This advantage was particularly important in regard to unemployment policy. The temporary ideological prejudgment was also a sizeable advantage for them for unemployment and income growth policy, but not for inflation policy. All in all, a look at the significant dummies in the three functions reveals that a new government faces, ceteris paribus, an unfavorable evaluation in the domains where the policies of its predecessor were considered successful (Fabius and Chirac on inflation policy) and conversely (Mauroy and Chirac on income growth and unemployment).

The variables explaining the popularity of the prime minister appear to be essentially economic: except for the "cohabitation" period, this was a result of the French institutional division of political labor. As table 5 shows, up to March, 1986, the global popularity of the prime minister is a basic variable to explain the popular judgment on the "reliability" of the president for *economic* policy. This may be considered as a supplementary and indirect test of the strong economic content of the prime minister's popularity.

Contrary to the prime minister, the president is in charge of primarily political problems, particularly at the level of foreign policy and "general management of institutions." What were the respective weights of these policies before April, 1986? Table 6 shows how the global popularity of the president can be explained, prior to March, 1986, by its popularity in the three main specialized domains.

The estimated weight of judgments on economic policy is 0.51, a figure to compare with the 40 percent attributed to economic factors by Paldam (1981). Reliance upon the president for the management of institutions, a variable closely linked to the "fear of social conflicts," has a coefficient of 0.36, and "judgments on foreign policy" is far from being negligible (contrary to a common opinion), with a coefficient of 0.27.

The function of table 6, however, raises two problems:

—the question concerning confidence in the president for economic policy was discontinued in April, 1986, because it was assumed that a socialist president could not be considered responsible for the actions of a right-wing government;

—the causal link between global popularity and specialized popularity may be partially in the opposite direction: for example, the president may be popular for the management of the institutions simply because he is popular in the other domains.

TABLE 5.   Dependent Variable: "Reliability" of the President for Economic Policy (*PRe*), December, 1978–March, 1986

Variables	Constant	PM_t	D81.06	D84.09	PRe_{t-1}	PM_{t-1}
Coefficients	4.21	0.51	8.47	−12.98	0.88	−0.49
(*t*-value)	(3.1)	(5.9)	(1.8)	(3.7)	(23.1)	(5.6)

$R^2 = 0.91$ $F = 186.85$ DW = 2.23   SE = 2.48 $h = -1.2$ $df = 82$

Note: See appendix for the definition of variables.

TABLE 6. Dependent Variable: President's Popularity (PR_t), December, 1978–March, 1986

Variables	Constant	PRf_t	PRe_t	PRi_t
Coefficients	−3.83	0.27	0.51	0.36
(*t*-value)	(2.3)	(5.1)	(9.3)	(5.2)
$R^2 = 0.98$	$F = 1224.99$	DW = 1.24	SE = 1.33	
$df = 84$	Cochrane-Orcutt correction: rho = 0.32			

Note: See appendix for the definition of variables.

As a solution to the first problem, the popularity index of the prime minister has been introduced instead of the specialized judgments on economic policy in the popularity function of the president (table 7, variables 4, 5, 6, and 7). The second problem has been solved by using responses to questions that are less dependent on the dependent variable. For foreign policy efficiency, responses to the question "do you find that the role of France in the world is stronger (weaker)?" have been used. For the "management of the institutions" variable, we retained responses to the question "do you think that the social problems during the next months will be solved by violence and protest or by negotiation?" (This last question is clearly linked to opinions regarding the role of arbitrator attributed to the president.)

The estimation in table 7 confirms the independent influence of foreign policy factors (variable 2) and fear of social conflict factors (variable 3). The cohabitation period has seen a significant reduction in the impact of prime ministerial popularity on presidential popularity (variables 6 and 7). However, the real surprise is that it is still significant at all (0.54 − 0.18 = 0.36 for the contemporaneous variable and −0.43 + 0.22 = −0.21 for the lagged one). As the president and the prime minister were both potential candidates for the 1988 presidential election, this complementarity of their situations raised a complex strategic problem.

No specific "honeymoon" dummy is significant in this function. When the popularity of the prime minister is introduced, Mauroy's own "honeymoon" explains Mitterrand's in June, 1981. In contrast and very logically, Mitterrand did not benefit from the "honeymoon" of his second prime minister, Fabius, in the precohabitation period. Thus, we were obliged to "purge" the prime minister popularity series from this phenomenon (thanks to variables 9 and 10 in table 7).

As any new ruler, Chirac benefited from a strong "honeymoon" in the post–April, 1986, period. Rather surprisingly, Mitterrand benefited also from a similar upsurge in its popularity, so that no similar correction, as for the Fabius period, was necessary (Chirac's "honeymoon" in PM_t "explains"

TABLE 7. Dependent Variable: President's Popularity (PR_t), December, 1978–April, 1987

Variables	(1) Constant	(2) $ISfr_t$	(3) Fsv_t	(4) PM_t	(5) PM_{t-1}	(6) CPM_t	(7) CPM_{t-1}	(8) PR_{t-1}	(9) D84.09	(10) D84.09–86.03
Coefficients	12.23	0.25	-0.09	0.54	-0.43	-0.18	0.22	0.63	-11.51	-4.24
(t-value)	(4.4)	(4.8)	(2.3)	(12.2)	(8.8)	(1.8)	(2.1)	(10.8)	(4.5)	(4.0)

$R^2 = 0.94$ $F = 180.01$ $DW = 2.13$ $SE = 2.07$ $h = -0.84$ $df = 91$

Notes: CPM_t is a dummy variable equal to $PM_t \times$ D86.04–87.04. It accounts for a change in the impact of PM_t on the dependent variable (PR_t) during the cohabitation period. The dummy variable CPM_{t-1}, equal to $PM_{t-1} \times$ D86.04–87.04, has the same function for PM_{t-1}. See appendix for the definition of variables.

Mitterrand's "honeymoon," just as much as in Mauroy's case). How is it that a president in office for five years obtained a "honeymoon" after the electoral defeat of his supporters? There are at least two explanations for this. First, the president kept the domains of responsibility where he was the most popular (foreign policy and management of the institutional system) and lost most of those where he was unpopular. Second, the radical change in the president's responsibilities made it seem that he was entering a new office. For this new office, the president's economic record, a major cause of the electoral defeat of the Socialist party, was no longer a relevant factor in the formation of "efficiency" expectations.

4. Conclusions

The period of cohabitation in France between a Socialist president and a right-wing prime minister presents the following new characteristics concerning popularity functions:

—the popularity function for the prime minister does not seem to have changed much. Economic variables still played a major role. Moreover, there were no surprises in the observed "honeymoon" effects, in the popularity function or in the functions linking economic variables to basic "efficiency judgments";

—the popularity of the president has changed much more. If the impact of the variables representing "efficiency judgments" about foreign policy or preservation of social peace is still the same, the link between the popularity of the prime minister and presidential popularity is, as expected, much weaker. But the real surprise is that a significant relationship remains. A second surprise is the "honeymoon" that Mitterrand enjoyed after the electoral defeat of his party in the March, 1986, elections. This paradox can be explained by the fact that the institutional changes brought by cohabitation had profoundly altered the nature of the presidency. This new presidency excluded from its domain precisely those policy areas in which the Socialist government had fared poorly. Thus, the very policies that led to the Socialist defeat in 1986 were no longer needed to form "efficiency" expectations.

5. Postscript

The "cohabitation period" ended in 1988, with the reelection of Mitterrand as president, the appointment of Socialist Michel Rocard as prime minister, the dissolution of Parliament, and the (relative) victory of the Socialists in the parliamentary elections in June, 1988. The French Fifth Republic functions again as it did before April, 1986. There is an important difference, however. The Socialist party does not have an absolute majority in Parliament; mathematically, a coalition of Communists and right-wing parties could command a majority against the government. Indeed, for that reason, the cohabitation period does not lose its interest. It represents an exceptional kind of laboratory experiment.

APPENDIX: LIST OF VARIABLES

1. *EFp:* percentage of persons finding the government efficient against inflation.
2. *EFu:* percentage of persons finding the government efficient against unemployment.
3. *EFy:* percentage of persons thinking conditions will improve in the near future (understood as equivalent to efficiency judgments on the government income growth policy—see Fontaine 1986, 7, n. 1 for a justification of this choice).
4. D, *XX.XX–YY.YY:* Dummy variable, taking the value 1 between the specified dates and zero elsewhere.
5. *Fsv:* percentage of persons fearing social violence in the near future (taken as an inverse indicator of the achievement of the goal of good management of the institutional system).
6. *ISfr:* percentage of persons thinking that the international strength of France is higher than before (understood as an indicator of the efficiency of foreign policy).
7. *pij:* growth rate of consumer price index, lagged i, computed on j periods.
8. *PM:* percentage of persons finding the prime minister reliable in general.
9. *PR:* percentage of persons finding the president reliable in general.
10. *PRe:* percentage of persons finding the president reliable on economic policy.
11. *PRf:* percentage of persons finding the president reliable on foreign policy.
12. *PRi:* percentage of persons finding the president reliable on the management of political institutions.
13. *U:* unemployment rate (*demandes d'emploi non satisfaites,* corrected for seasonal fluctuations, as a percentage of active population, monthly interpolation).
14. *yij:* real disposable income of consumers (nominal monthly data interpolated from INSEE quarterly series on the basis of the monthly wage rate of workers and corrected for price inflation with the consumer price index).

Sources: Figaro-Sofrès monthly survey for variables 1, 2, 3, 5, 6, 8, 9, 10, 11, and 12. INSEE (Institut National de la Statistique et des Etudes Economiques) for variables 7, 13, and 14.

REFERENCES

Berdot, J. P., and J. D. Lafay. 1986. "Political Biases in Popular Judgments on Economic Policy: The Case of Inflation (France 1977.02–1985.12)." IRAPE, University of Poitiers. Mimeo.

Chappell, H., and W. Keech. 1985. "A New View of Political Accountability for Economic Performance." *American Political Science Review* 79(1):10–27.

Chrystal, K., and D. Peel. 1986. "What Can Economics Learn from Political Science and Vice Versa?" *American Economic Review* 76(2):62–65.

Fiorina, M. 1981. "Short- and Long-Term Effects of Economic Conditions on Individual Voting Decisions." In *Contemporary Political Economy*, ed. Douglas Hibbs and Heino Fassbender, 73–100. Amsterdam: North-Holland.

Fontaine, C. 1986. "Conjoncture sociale: Eclaircie et échéances électorales." *Chroniques d'actualités SEDEIS* 34(1):14–25.

Godechot, J., ed. 1979. *Les constitutions de la France depuis 1789*. Paris: Garnier Flammarion.

Hibbs, D. 1982. "The Dynamics of Political Support for American Presidents among Occupational Classes: A Dynamic Analysis." *American Political Science Review* 76:259–79.

Kernell, S., and D. Hibbs. 1981. "A Critical Threshold Model of Presidential Popularity." In *Contemporary Political Economy*, ed. Douglas Hibbs and Heino Fassbender, 49–71. Amsterdam: North-Holland.

Kirchgässner, G. 1985. "Rationality, Causality, and the Relation between Economic Conditions and the Popularity of Parties." *European Economic Review* 28(1–2):243–68.

Le Monde. 1986. *L'histoire au jour le jour*. Vols. 1–4. Paris: Le Monde.

Maddock, R., and M. Carter. 1982. "A Child's Guide to Rational Expectations." *Journal of Economic Literature* 20:39–51.

Paldam, M. 1981. "A Preliminary Survey of the Theories and Findings of Vote and Popularity Functions." *European Journal of Political Research* 9:181–99.

Petfley, M. 1985. "The Voter as Juror. Attributing Responsibility for Economic Conditions." In *Economic Conditions and Electoral Outcomes*, ed. Heinz Eulau and Michael Lewis-Beck, 187–206. New York: Agathon Press.

Roussel, E. 1984. *Georges Pompidou—Le Président de la crise*. Paris: Editions J. C. Lattès.

Viansson-Ponté, P. 1971. *Histoire de la République Gaullienne*, May 1958–April 1969. Paris: Arthème Fayard.

The Popularity of the Thatcher Government: A Matter of War and Economy

Helmut Norpoth

British Prime Minister Harold Wilson was neither the first nor the last to observe, as he put it, that "the standing of the government and its ability to hold the confidence of the electorate at a General Election depend on the success of its economic policy" (Watt 1968). But he was certainly someone who should know, having led his party to victory in four elections, and wisely bowing out before testing his proposition one more time.

Margaret Thatcher, who came to office in the election foregone by Harold Wilson, has also led her party to electoral victory several times. Because of the success of her economic policy? It does strain credulity to argue that, especially, her first government (1979–83) was an economic success story. During that time, Britain experienced the worst recession since the 1930s. Economic analysts noted ominous "parallels with the Great Depression" and went as far as to voice fears that "the prospects for a thirties-style recovery [were] not good" in the 1980s (Buiter and Miller 1983, 307–9). The 1981 budget was condemned in a letter to the *Times* (1981) signed by no fewer than 364 economists: "Present policies will deepen the depression, erode the industrial base of our economy, and threaten its social and political stability" (for a contrary view, see Walters 1986; and for an overview, Maynard 1988).

Yet the Thatcher government remained unmoved by those warnings and persisted with its austerity policy. How did it manage to retain enough popular support to secure electoral victory in 1983, and again in 1987? The question has ignited a spirited debate that goes to the heart of economic voting and the calculus of government support in the mass public.

The Meanings of Economic Success

Admittedly, something like the "success of economic policy" is no easy matter to define. In the end, what matters for the popular standing of the government is whether people *perceive* it as a success or not. So the question is, by what criteria voters arrive at judgments that proclaim an economic policy to be successful. Needless to say, the ordinary voter is no economist and pays limited attention to political as well as economic news. He or she may be totally in the dark about the premises and outlines of a government's economic policy. There can be little doubt that the general public is attuned to economic outcomes rather than the minutiae of fiscal and monetary policy (Butler and Stokes 1969).

Even with attention limited to economic outcomes, what constitutes success? To take a concrete example, does the combination of a 10 percent inflation rate and 1.3 million unemployed spell success? Any more or any less than the combination of a 4 percent inflation rate and 3.0 million unemployed? Prime Minister Callaghan, Harold Wilson's luckless successor, lost the 1979 election with the first combination of economic outcomes; Mrs. Thatcher, in turn, won the 1983 election (as well as the one in 1987) with the second combination of unemployment and inflation.

The contrast of 1979 and 1983 suggests the possibility that in their evaluations of the economy the British public keyed on the one goal that Mrs. Thatcher's government had staked out as its primary one: inflation. On this issue, the scourge of the 1970s that had bedeviled her predecessors, some measure of success had been achieved by 1983. Were British voters, therefore, willing to set aside the painful recession of 1980–81 as well as the horrendous climb of unemployment and turn in a positive verdict because of the decline of inflation? If so, it would tell us a lot about the government's ability to set the agenda of public debate and frame the issues in a light favorable to its cause. Or perhaps, the public had begun to appreciate the necessary trade-off between unemployment and inflation, accepting high unemployment as the price to pay for low inflation.

One might also suspect that as the economy recovered from the recession, good feelings about the recovery displaced ill feelings about the recession that preceded it. Sooner or later something like that is bound to happen. Much depends on the time frame of popular evaluations and on the speed at which evaluations of the economy adjust.

It is also conceivable that the public takes a forward-looking perspective (Fiorina 1981) and, despite a bleak present situation, is confident that a given government will be delivering a rosier economic future. This may hold especially at moments when discontent with economic performance has accumulated for some time and a new government comes to office with the promise of putting things right. The public may suppress its critical instinct and give the new government the benefit of the doubt.

Optimistic expectations about the economy ahead play a key part in a provocative study of the standing of the Thatcher government. Sanders et al. (1987) claim that such expectations shored up popular support for her government enough to assure electoral victory in 1983. Their analysis goes on to show that the much-touted Falklands factor played a minimal role in the Conservative recovery. The Thatcher government, accordingly, was not threatened with electoral disaster over the results of its economic policy from which a timely war, or fratricide in the opposition, had to save it. Thus, be it by way of the salience of inflation, the perception of economic recovery, or expectations about the future, the "success of its economic policy" may still hold the key to the success of the Thatcher Government at and in the polls.

The Economy versus the Electoral Cycle

Economic success, to be sure, is a heavily traded stock in the government popularity exchange. But it is not the only one. Another one is the cyclical nature of such popularity. Practitioners of politics as well as observers in the media and academe are familiar with that stock. For as long as people have chosen political leaders through some form of election, it has been noted, almost like a law of politics, that popularity diminishes with time in office. "No man will ever bring out of the Presidency the reputation which carries him into it," remarked Thomas Jefferson (Kenski 1980, 68). In Britain, the governing party feels the sting of that "rule" with every seat lost in a by-election. Polls of the British electorate usually confirm that such losses are not simply local aberrations but signal dwindling popularity across the land (Mughan 1986).

At the same time, governing parties have also learned to take by-election defeats and popularity troughs in stride. The approach of the next general election generally reverses the sagging popularity curve and the governing party often recovers enough ground to triumph over an opposition that was encouraged to think it would win the election just a few months before. This decline-recovery cycle repeats itself with such regularity that it poses a serious rival to the economy as an explanation of government popularity.

Goodhart and Bhansali (1970) were the first to put these rival hypotheses to the statistical test with data from 1947 to 1968, at about the same time as Mueller (1973) did for the popularity of American presidents from Truman to Johnson. Goodhart and Bhansali show that two measures of economic performance, unemployment and the rate of inflation, significantly influence the popularity of British parties. Even though the hypothesis of a regular interelection swing is also confirmed, their study heavily stresses the economic explanation. "Indeed, the apparent sensitivity of political popularity to economic conditions, as shown by the equations, seems almost too much to credit" (1970, 86).

In a challenge to Goodhart and Bansali's study, Miller and Mackie (1973, 279) shift the attention to the cyclical nature of government popularity:

"When the electoral cyclical component is removed from the government popularity series, none of our performance measures added much to the prediction of popularity." However measured, economic variables register only slight effects on popularity once time has taken its toll and handed out its benefits to the governing party. Miller and Mackie warn against viewing politics as a struggle between "competing teams of economic managers" in which the electorate makes its choices largely on economic grounds.

In extending the popularity function into the 1970s, Alt (1979) finds that inflation appears to cost the governing party in Britain far less in popularity than the effects estimated during the 1950s and 1960s would lead one to predict. The key reason, according to Alt, is that as inflation accelerated in the late 1960s and 1970s, the public's standard of an acceptable rate of inflation adjusted upward as well. People judge economic performance not by some fixed standard, but in light of recent experience. "Government popularity is diminished by inflation when inflation is high relative to recent experience" (Alt 1979, 120). An inflation rate of 10 percent, for example, would cause the government harm when recent inflation was 8 percent, but not when it was 12 percent.

People, in other words, get used to economic conditions and constantly adapt their expectations of acceptable performance. A rise of the inflation rate from 5 percent to 10 percent becomes acceptable after some time, as will a rise from 10 percent to 20 percent. According to Alt's analysis, which measures "critical rates" of inflation by way of three-year moving averages, the adaptation to a higher level would take three years at most. Treated in this form, inflation registers a marginally significant effect on popularity in the 1970s (while it has no effect when expectations are ignored).

In a similar vein, while employing a longer frame for past experience (seven-year moving averages), Mosley (1984) examines the effects of unemployment and prices. His findings confirm Alt's in showing that only when it is above crisis levels does inflation affect government popularity; yet autocorrelation casts a pall over the all too modest significance of economic effects. In all fairness, Mosley makes no strong claim for the influence of the economy on government popularity.

In contrast to almost all previous studies of the popularity function, Hibbs (1982) posits a model of cumulative effects. Past performance serves not so much as a benchmark for appraising current performance but as a key element in the decision calculus. The popularity of the governing party at any given time derives from current performance as well as geometrically discounted past performance. The more recent the performance, the heavier the weight. In addition, Hibbs allows for comparisons between the current government and previous ones. This is especially significant at the beginning of a newly elected government, which has no record of its own. At that time, the model postulates that the worse the performance of prior governments, the higher will be the new government's initial support; and vice versa.

While not matching the emphasis Hibbs places on the economy, several other studies of government popularity in Britain also present strong evidence (Frey and Schneider 1978; Pissarides 1980). Most employ a basic reward-and-punishment model, although some put heavier stress on the punishment side. The British popularity function has even survived several ARIMA tests (Whiteley, 1986; Mishler, Hoskin, and Fitzgerald 1988). Individual-level studies have shown economic perceptions to make a significant contribution to electoral choices in Britain (Butler and Stokes 1969, chap. 18; Lewis-Beck 1988). Still, the specification of economic performance, the judgmental rules employed by voters to relate such performance to government popularity, and the role of noneconomic influences remain bones of contention.

A Model of British Government Popularity

This study focuses on the approval ratings of the prime minister as the measure of government popularity. While British popularity studies generally do not focus on the prime minister (for an exception, see Hudson 1984), Mrs. Thatcher unquestionably deserves to be singled out in such an analysis. Mrs. Thatcher has been a highly salient political figure in Britain during the 1980s. Her policies and style of government have already earned her an "ism." Few believe that British politics, or even the politics of her party, would have been the same under another prime minister. Mrs. Thatcher's approval ratings (the percentage saying that they are "satisfied with the way [she] is doing her job as prime minister") is charted in figure 1.

However unique the reactions Mrs. Thatcher may provoke in the British

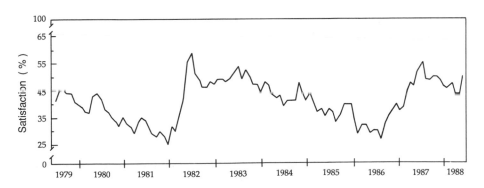

Fig. 1. Satisfaction with Mrs. Thatcher as prime minister (data from MORI surveys [monthly])

public, her ratings are not unrelated to a respondent's partisanship. For many individuals, the judgment of a prime minister's performance is not the result of a comprehensive search but a reflex of long-term attitudes. It will surprise no one to learn that someone with a Conservative party loyalty is highly likely to express approval of Mrs. Thatcher as prime minister, whereas a Labour loyalist is highly unlikely to do so.

The Long-Term Component of Popularity

Although this pattern should not be surprising it is surprising how little recognition it usually receives in aggregate studies of government support. Long-term partisan attitudes account, by far, for the lion's share of popularity judgments recorded at any given time. When such judgments, in the aggregate, are tracked over time, one does not find that they exhaust the full range of variation possible, from 0 to 100 percent. Instead, they fluctuate within a fairly narrow range. Mrs. Thatcher's job ratings from 1979 to 1988 averaged 41 percent with a standard deviation of 7.4. In other words, she rarely fell below 26 percent or topped 56 percent. While she could count on a hard core of loyalists at the gloomiest moments, she could not sway close to half at the most glorious ones. Long-term partisanship both serves to cushion the fall and to brake the surge of popularity that performance judgments could generate.

However important for individual behavior, long-term partisanship can be treated as a constant in aggregate time-series studies of government popularity so long as it remains stable throughout the time period under study. That may be safely assumed in this case. The 1979–88 period did not witness significant shifts in Conservative party identification. The British Election Studies report a Conservative share of 38 percent for 1979, 36 percent for 1983, and 37 percent for 1987. Whatever partisan dealignment may have occurred in British politics, the Conservative party was not its victim in the 1980s; nor, in all fairness, did it score a major advance in long-term partisan support. As a result, such support will not enter as a variable into the popularity function, but as a constant. It defines the baseline around which government popularity happens to oscillate over time.

Short-Term Memory

To a considerable extent, these oscillations follow a dynamic of their own. That is to say, they do not move abruptly from one moment to the next one, but at a sluggish pace instead. If the popularity rating in a given month lies above the baseline, it very likely will do so the next month as well. That suggests that the individual judgments being aggregated to a popularity measure each month have a memory that influences current behavior. Chances are that an individual voter who expressed support for the governing party yesterday will do so today as well, aside from the effect of long-term partisan attachments. People do not, as a rule, make popularity judgments by flipping a coin.

What kind of memory process drives them can be examined with ARIMA models (Box and Jenkins 1976). For the series of Mrs. Thatcher's approval rating, the estimation yields a first-order autoregressive process with a parameter equal to .90 (and a standard error of .04). Such an estimate lies dangerously close to the limit of 1.0, hinting at the possibility of the popularity series not being stationary. But the approval series exhibits no overall trend or random walk type of behavior, which would call for differencing the series in order to make it stationary. To a great extent, the autoregressive (AR) parameter is so high because it is the only one in the popularity function at this point. It is expected to fall to a more moderate level once economic performance and political events are brought to bear on government popularity.

Economic Performance

The performance of the economy is measured by three indicators: inflation (the percentage change of the price index over the last twelve months), unemployment (actual numbers, seasonally adjusted) and economic growth (the percentage change of the gross domestic product over the last four quarters). Unemployment and inflation have dominated the issue agenda in public opinion polls for most of the last quarter century, with unemployment the preeminent one in the 1980s, as polls by Market and Opinion Research International (MORI) and other institutes have shown.

Both unemployment and inflation denote negative valence issues, that is, conditions to be avoided. As a result, their salience in public opinion is by itself an indication of dissatisfaction. People do not say inflation is important when they are satisfied with the rate at which prices are rising; and the same goes for unemployment. Inflation and unemployment can only help the governing party by not showing up conspicuously on the list of important issues cited by the general public. Economic growth is a different kind of issue—with a positive valence—that rarely, if ever, shows up in opinion polls. Yet that is not to say that the public does not desire the achievement of that goal, especially after a painful recession.

It is assumed that the public perceives economic performance largely by what it learns about it from the reporting of economic news in the media. Since reports of unemployment figures and inflation rates are always published for the preceding month, these two indicators will be entered with a one-month lag into the popularity function; the quarterly reports of economic growth are entered with a four-month lag.

No matter how those reports penetrate the awareness of the general public, they do not supply an evaluation by themselves. Is unemployment of one million a good or bad performance? Or 10 percent inflation? Some, like Alt (1979) and Mosley (1984), maintain that the public alters its critical standards fairly rapidly in response to changing performance. Yet, as the British Election Studies show, unemployment was as big an issue in 1987 as in 1983; the governing party got as poor a rating for its handling of unemployment in 1987 as in 1983. There seems to be no evidence that the British public gradually adopted a more tolerant standard for unemployment in the 1980s. As for inflation, this issue virtually disappeared from the salience screen in 1983 when inflation settled at the rate of 4 percent. That might suggest that the standard for an acceptable inflation rate is perhaps quite firm in the medium term. It seems to take a sustained surge above that critical rate to trigger public concern and an equally sustained return below it to defuse it. It is assumed, therefore, that during the period of interest here, the British public evaluated economic performance against a standard that did not substantially shift. Experiments with a large number of variable standards (including twelve-month changes as used by Norpoth 1987a) did not produce results that provided a better fit than the model positing a fixed standard.

The Falklands War

While economics is a steady companion of the daily lives of ordinary citizens, most other issues are either too remote or do not pay regular calls. Yet when some of them do, their impact may be jarring. In 1982, Britain went to war with Argentina over the Falkland Islands (Sunday Times 1982; Hastings and Jenkins 1983). This was not a war over great strategic or economic stakes. Some dismissed it as theater of the absurd. Jorge Luis Borges likened it to "two bald men fighting over a comb" (Theroux 1984, 47). On the other hand, the war was brief, lasting barely ten weeks, aroused considerable national passion on both sides, and ended victoriously for the government whose popularity is being examined here.

> This war came and went like something from the Victorian stage: a simple plot, a small but well-defined cast of characters, a story in three acts with a clear beginning, middle, and end, and a straightforward conclusion which everybody could understand. (Freedman 1988, 1)

War is said to rally popular support around the government; to elicit support from segments of the public that would not normally approve of its performance. International crises are known to spark such "rallies 'round the flag" in the U.S. public (Mueller 1973), although the rally-induced popularity gains prove fleeting. Moreover, once military actions taken in response to a crisis ensnarl the country in a prolonged war, popular support typically erodes. War then sparks more public jeering than cheering. Short of revolution, the discontent over the war may explode at election time, if it does not already register in falling popularity ratings of the government in office (Mueller 1973; Kernell 1978; Norpoth 1984). The Falklands War most likely ended before any of this had a chance to unfold.

Being a rare event, something like the Falklands War cannot be expected to affect the public in the same way as the steady trickle of economic news. For the Falklands, there is no standard of comparison, no past experience to draw on for most voters. The crisis arrives suddenly, the government acts swiftly, and the public reacts to the event and the way the government is handling the situation. When the crisis is over, voters may simply return to their status quo ante ratings of government performance and to their concerns with such matters as unemployment over 10 percent. On the other hand, their impressions about the government's handling of the crisis may linger. The end of the war need not signal the end of the popularity rally, especially so when the government is perceived as having achieved a widely acclaimed goal.

To capture what the Falklands War did to government popularity I rely on an intervention model that allows for both shifts in popularity during the war months and a regular, though nonlinear, decline of the accumulated gain afterward (Box and Tiao 1975; McCleary and Hay 1980; Norpoth 1987b). The two basic parameters of that model are denoted omega (ω) and delta (δ).

$$Y_t = \frac{\omega_0 + \omega_1 B + \omega_2 B^2}{1 - \delta B} \; I_t^*$$

where

1. ω_j (B) are step changes in Y at various time points produced by the intervention,
2. δ is the rate of decay of those step changes,
3. B is the backshift operator such that $BY_t = Y_{t-1}$, and
4. I_t^* is an intervention variable with values of 0 for t before and after the intervention, and a value of 1 at the intervention.

Technically, this is a "gradual-temporary" model. The omega parameters measure the changes of popularity associated with the three months of the war (April through June) while the delta parameter denotes the rate at which those changes are maintained afterward. A delta equal to zero would imply that none of the popularity changes survived the war. It was a rally of the briefest possible kind. Whatever effect the Falklands may have had was so temporary that it did not persist for even one month afterward. On the other hand, a delta equal to 1.0 would indicate that the change remain fully in effect forever (in the time frame examined); the intervention effect would be permanent, in other words.

Electoral Campaigns

In addition to international events, some domestic events may also be expected to spark rallies, of some sort, in popular support for the incumbent government. Since coming to power in 1979, Mrs. Thatcher has led her party through two further election campaigns. What international crises and military campaigns may do inadvertently, electoral campaigns are meant to achieve: raise popular support for the government. In particular, the incumbent leader hopes to swing back those voters with long-term attachments to his or her party who have drifted away, and to sway most nonpartisans to his or her side. The opposition will try its best to persuade these voters to vote their misgivings.

As the campaign gets underway, the opposition emerges from the relative obscurity in which it has lingered. The voters will be bombarded with information as to the kind of record the opposition offered when last in power and with the kind of record it might offer if victorious. As that happens, the record of the governing party invites comparisons not just with a standard of satisfaction, but also with the expected record of the opposition. That shift in the public's frame of reference may raise the prime minister's rating and drive some voters who joined the chorus of government disapproval back into the arms of the governing party, especially those with an attachment to that party.

Election victory is expected to confirm the raised standing of the governing party and the prime minister, but then the accumulated gain is likely to erode as the drudgery of governing replaces the excitement of the campaign. Like the Falklands War, the campaign-cum-election interventions enter the popularity function with a gradual-temporary effect. For reasons of economy, in the sense of parsimony, however, only one omega parameter is used instead of four.

The hypothesis of a campaign-election effect is in the tradition of Goodhart and Bhansali (1970), with their notions of "backswing" and "continual trend." At the same time, what they tried to capture by means of linear functions of time, my analysis aims to do by means of a nonlinear process. Moreover, instead of separating surge and decline, the intervention model connects the two; only the part of government popularity that is gained from the campaign is subject to the process of decline afterward. For analytical purposes, the campaign-election interventions are scored 1 for the month of the election, the two months before, and the first month afterward. In other words, the campaigns are said to commence by the time the public has compelling clues that an election will be called. I consider the presentation of the budget in the election years as having conveyed that signal to the general public.

Government Turnover

The move of the opposition leader into 10 Downing Street as Britain's new prime minister after a general election victory is often thought to bestow a special measure of popularity to the newly governing party and its leader. Voters without attachments to either the old or the new governing party would seem most likely to contribute to this "euphoria" (Goodhart and Bhansali 1970) or "honeymoon" effect. It can be seen as giving the benefit of the doubt to a new government, which has not had enough time yet to establish a record of its own.

Obviously, whatever good or, more likely, harm the economy and other conditions did to the popularity of the preceding government should not afflict the new government at the beginning of its term; it bears no responsibility for them. Or, to put it differently, the effect of such things as economic performance is overridden for the time being. As a result, the new regime typically takes office amidst a sense of euphoria that is bound to wear off like the rallies associated with the Falklands and the election campaigns of successful governing parties.

However, it is one of the remarkable features of the Conservative victory in 1979 that it did not spark a measurable euphoria for the new prime minister. Mrs. Thatcher's initial job rating of 41 percent in Gallup Polls barely topped the final rating of 39 percent for Mr. Callaghan. Nor did it measurably exceed her rating as a "good leader of the Conservative party" prior to the election, which averaged 40 percent from 1975 to 1978 (Crewe 1981, 274). Mrs. Thatcher's initial rating in 1979 turns out to be no higher than her average during the next nine years and barely rises above the share of long-term Conservative support in the British electorate. Throwing out the rascals in 1979 did little or nothing to brighten the public mood. No rousing welcome greeted the new regime. Expectations for the future were nothing but gloomy. Preliminary attempts to fit a "euphoria" term to Mrs. Thatcher's popularity equation yielded no significant results. None was therefore included in the model presented in table 1.

The Economy and Mrs. Thatcher's Standing

The estimates of Mrs. Thatcher's popularity function (table 1) indicate that unemployment makes a substantial and significant difference. By contrast, the

**TABLE 1.   Estimates for a Model
of Mrs. Thatcher's Popularity,
June, 1979–June, 1988**

Variables	Parameter	SE
Constant	30.80	2.30
Memory (AR1)	0.53	0.09
Unemployment $(t - 1)$	−0.66	0.18
Inflation $(t - 1)$	0.05	0.29
Growth of GDP $(t - 4)$	0.12	0.29
Falklands War		
April, 1982	7.40	2.90
May, 1982	16.30	2.90
June, 1982	3.80	3.00
Rate of Decay	0.94	0.01
1983 Election		
March-June	2.60	1.10
Rate of Decay	0.98	0.01
1987 election		
March-June	4.60	0.90
Rate of Decay	0.94	0.03
N	108	
R^2	.89	
LBQ/df	36/19	

Sources: MORI surveys 1979–88; Monthly Digest of Statistics.

Note: Model estimates obtained with BMDP2T.

contribution of inflation proves negligible as well as statistically insignificant; and so does economic growth. To gauge how substantial the estimate for the unemployment coefficient is, consider that it translates the 3.0 million number into an expected popularity loss of twenty points. That calculation, of course, takes zero unemployment as the baseline. Using the more realistic baseline of roughly 1.3 million, which prevailed at the beginning of Mrs. Thatcher's term of office, one would estimate an expected loss of popularity equal to eleven percentage points. This is still a staggering amount, especially so since Mrs. Thatcher did not commence her term with a lot of popularity to spare.

Whatever cushion she could rely on is denoted by the estimate for the constant: approximately 31 percent. To be sure, that falls short of the Conservative share of party identification, averaging around 37 percent. In other words, not every self-identified Conservative partisan in the British electorate thus approved of Mrs. Thatcher at the average level of economic performance during her tenure and in the absence of such events as the Falklands War or other helpful events. She could count on only those with fairly strong party attachments.

As the memory parameter (0.53) suggests, the short-term fluctuations of Mrs. Thatcher's popularity are guided by considerable, though not excessive, inertia. Past experience carries over to the present but is discounted, for all practical purposes, after a few months unless its retention is explicitly provided through an intervention model. Current information, even if it is no different from last month's information, has an excellent opportunity to influence popularity judgments. One way of interpreting this finding is to say that voters are quite myopic. But there is another way as well, namely that the general public shows little tendency to get used to bad performance like 3 million or so unemployed. Reports of such figures retain a certain freshness even after the umpteenth month. Long after crossing the 3 million mark, unemployment remained the most important issue on the public's agenda.

Turning from unemployment to the other economic indicators, it is puzzling to see inflation making no substantial impression on Mrs. Thatcher's popular standing. After all, this is the issue that she took head-on and where she achieved some measure of success. Was it not true that early in her first term when inflation rose above 20 percent, her popularity began to buckle? And did it not recover as inflation was tamed? Indeed, the simple correlation between inflation and Thatcher's approval rating happens to be significant and pointing in the right (negative) direction.

This relationship does not survive in the full popularity model. At first glance, unemployment might rate as a prime suspect, given the high correlation between monthly unemployment and inflation ($-.86$) for the Thatcher years. But since both unemployment and inflation are thought to affect popularity with the same (negative) sign, the negative correlation between the two predictors should not diminish the effect of either one. In other words, the inclusion of unemployment in the popularity model should not rob inflation of the effect that it appears to have with unemployment omitted.

What makes it even more vexing to account for the vanishing of the apparent inflation effect is that individual-level studies do reveal a significant effect for the government's handling of this issue (Whiteley 1985, 70–71; Lewis-Beck 1988, 90). The British public gave the Thatcher Government a highly favorable rating on its inflation performance in 1983 and 1987, as shown by the British Election Studies. And these ratings helped the standing of Mrs. Thatcher. Then how is it possible that there is no evidence for an inflation effect in the time-series analysis?

To be sure, what is measured there is the actual inflation rate, not the *perception* of voters of how the Thatcher Government had handled inflation. Were those perceptions mistaken? Certainly not in the sense that the inflation rate was considerably lower in 1983 than it had been in 1979. Whatever the inflation perceptions, they were not the only ones that mattered; so did perceptions of unemployment. And they proved highly unfavorable for the Thatcher

Government. Survey analysis of the British Election Studies shows that unemployment perceptions hurt the government's standing more than inflation perceptions helped (Whiteley 1985, 72; Lewis-Beck 1988, 90). On balance, the unemployment effect prevailed.

If that is true time after time, then over time, in the aggregate, only the dominant issue of the two rival ones is likely to emerge as significant. The findings of the time-series analysis of Thatcher popularity tell us that the benefits from (low) inflation were not able to offset losses from (high) unemployment, not necessarily that the government's inflation performance paid no popularity dividends whatsoever. In all likelihood, unemployment would have cost the Thatcher government even more dearly in popular support had it not been for its inflation performance.

This kind of caution should also apply to the interpretation of the economic growth variable, as measured by the growth of the gross domestic product (GDP). It, too, does not register a significant effect on the popularity series. The GDP, of course, is not as visible and publicized an indicator of economic performance as are unemployment and inflation. It rarely shows up as an issue in public concerns. Still, lack of a contribution of economic growth to aggregate government popularity suggests that, in addition to inflation, another favorable aspect of Britain's economic performance, at least since 1981, failed to pay popular rewards large enough to offset the penalty for the unfavorable aspect, unemployment.

Evidence is mounting that, in the manner of Gresham's law, bad economic news (on unemployment) may be driving out good news (on prices and growth) in their competition to influence executive popularity. What one takes away, the other does not give back. When simultaneously confronted with good and bad news about the economy, the public does not weigh those two kinds of news equally. This finding confirms the general hypothesis that bad economic times do more to hurt the incumbent government in its standing with the public than good times do to help. As the authors of *The American Voter* conclude:

> . . . changes in the party balance are induced primarily by negative rather than positive attitudes toward the party controlling the executive branch of the federal government. . . . A party already in power is rewarded much less for good times than it is punished for bad times. (Campbell et al. 1960, 554–55)

This asymmetry has been documented for the popularity of U.S. presidents (Mueller 1973; Lanoue 1988) as well as congressional elections (Bloom and Price 1975; Kernell 1977). The public apparently heeds bad news more than good news, because often good news is no news. One takes good performance for granted and takes issue with bad performance. This is not to say, however, that governments are doomed, being denied credit for good performance by an ungrateful public. First off, good performance keeps the partisans in the electorate in line. They see no reason to defect, and that should assure the governing party of its normal level of popular support. Moreover, there are circumstances in which good economic performance may become salient. That is when bad performance has driven a government from office and the new government is on the spot to do a better job.

In the event that the new government is able to handle the problem(s) that dogged its predecessor, the new government may reap handsome rewards for a while. At that point, good news *is* news. Viewed in this light, one may well have expected that Mrs. Thatcher's public stock should have risen as the result of declining inflation. For that was the problem that had bedeviled her predecessors. Yet it appears that, before this good news could sink in and impress the British public, the unemployment escalation buried the good news on inflation.

Another widely used indicator of economic performance, real disposable income, was included in an alternative specification of Thatcher's popularity but also failed to register a significant effect. Real income declined or stagnated throughout Mrs. Thatcher's first term, but inched upward in her second term. Her popularity neither suffered first from the fitful income development nor did it later benefit from the hopeful turn.

The Falklands, Elections, and Mrs. Thatcher's Standing

With economic performance cutting deeply into Mrs. Thatcher's popularity, how did she survive as prime minister? The buoy of partisanship may have saved her popularity from sinking to the bottom, but it could not be expected to lift her out of an unfriendly element. Good news on prices and economic growth provided little or no relief. What restored her standing with the British public, as can be seen in table 1, was the Falklands War. It sparked a spectacular rally that offset much of the economic damage for months to come after the end of the war.

According to those estimates, Mrs. Thatcher's popularity rose seven points in April of 1982, the first month of the war, and sixteen further points in May of 1982; the rise of nearly four more points in June, the final month of the war, is not statistically significant. Altogether these gains represent one of the most remarkable surges in the ratings of British prime ministers. What is also noteworthy is that the Falklands surge by no means subsided as quickly as it materialized. With a rate of decay estimated to be 0.94, Mrs. Thatcher maintained much of the gains from the Falklands War for quite some time. Given the slow pace of decay, and even ignoring the June effect of dubious significance, Mrs. Thatcher still retained almost half of her Falklands gain one year later, as table 2 shows. That was enough, even then, to make up almost in full for what high unemployment had taken from her popular standing.

These bare-bones findings on the Falklands effect can be fleshed out with a rich supply of survey results. From the very beginning of the conflict, opinion polls conducted by MORI, among others, revealed a public taste for military action and little patience with diplomatic face-saving schemes. The sending of the naval task force was greeted with almost unanimous applause; but it was not enough. In a mid-April poll, two-thirds expressed support for the landing of troops in the Falklands, a proportion that grew to near unanimity by late May; the share of those supporting the sinking of ships rose from 50 percent to 80 percent; and a handful even called for the use of nuclear weapons (Worcester and Jenkins 1982, 54).

With the task force steaming toward a showdown, the initial sense of embarrassment and humiliation caused by the Argentinian invasion lifted. By mid-April, already, 60 percent expressed satisfaction with the Thatcher government's handling of the conflict. Satisfaction climbed above 80 percent in late May, as the government pursued its course of retaking the islands by force, if necessary. Along with this trend, Mrs. Thatcher's approval ratings also grew more favorable. It seems safe to conclude that she did not so much reap a windfall from a crisis sewn elsewhere as earn a reward for her conduct. People did not simply rally 'round her with misty-eyed patriotism but registered clear-headed approval once steps were taken to achieve a strongly desired goal.

Even so, by no means everyone joined in the chorus of prime ministerial approval, not even all those who supported her government's actions. One suspects that not a few Labour partisans refrained from giving a favorable rating to someone who, after all, was the leader of the opposite party, however much they might applaud the actions taken by her government (Norpoth n.d.). Most likely the Falklands helped Mrs. Thatcher recover support among Con-

TABLE 2. A Cost-Benefit Ledger of Mrs. Thatcher's Popularity

	Falklands Benefit	Unemployment Cost[a]
May, 1982	21.8	−10.6
May, 1983	10.4	−11.2
May, 1984	4.9	−11.2
May, 1985	2.3	−12.5

[a]The popularity cost of the latest unemployment level compared with unemployment at the beginning of Mrs. Thatcher's term (1.3 million in May, 1979).

servative partisans and gain a strong foothold among nonaligned voters. Admittedly, those gains were not permanent, but they relieved for almost two years the pressure felt from an unfavorable economic performance.

In addition, Mrs. Thatcher managed to improve her standing at moments when it counted the most, namely at election time. As table 1 shows, both the 1983 campaign and the one in 1987 raised her popularity sharply. The cumulative shift from the 1983 campaign (plus electoral victory), according to our estimate, was 10 percent, and the one from 1987 an even more astounding 17 percent. These are staggering gains, which materialize even with the three measures of economic performance and the Falklands factor held constant.

Those gains hint at a unique potential of incumbent leaders to improve their fortunes when they face voters at the polls, not just respondents in polls. Some considerations that may not weigh much on the general public, day in and day out, apparently take on a decisive significance as election day approaches. In both years, Mrs. Thatcher may have benefited from the comparison with Labour leaders whose popular ratings fell short of hers. And especially in 1987, after six straight years of economic expansion, perceptions of economic growth may have raised her standing at election time in a way not found between elections. Perhaps it takes an election campaign for the prime minister to take advantage of good news.

Discussion

While squaring with the results of several other studies (e.g., Dunleavy and Husbands 1985; Clarke, Stewart, and Zuk 1986), the finding of a robust Falklands effect clashes sharply with that offered by Sanders et al. (1987 and in this volume). In a nutshell, the Sanders study maintains that improvements of the British economy felt by the public in 1982–83 sparked a recovery of government popularity that secured reelection in 1983; the Falklands made only a negligible contribution. The economy held all the cards, in other words, for the standing of the Thatcher government.

The Sanders study raises numerous issues of model specification and estimation discussed in detail by Clarke, Mishler, and Whiteley (1990). The linchpin of its popularity function is "personal economic expectation," which is found to correlate strongly with government popularity during the period examined (1979–83). But does that prove that personal economic expectations determine government popularity?

For one thing, purely "personal" economic attitudes of the pocketbook variety rarely impinge with much force on political choices (Kinder and Kiewiet 1981), unless a clear connection is made between government action and one's personal situation (Lewis-Beck 1988, 56). The same applies to future personal expectations as well. Moreover, in the case at hand there are strong signs that economic expectations are subject to noneconomic forces. In April–June of 1982, for example, expectations surged dramatically and then receded again. What triggered the sudden brightening of a gloomy economic outlook? Is it not conceivable that the displacement of the economy as the key issue and the surge in government popularity at that very time, namely during the Falklands War, boosted both the government's standing and, along with that or as a result, economic optimism as well? It is difficult to imagine what kind of economic performance could spark such rallies in popular expectations, especially if they quickly subside again.

Except for that brief moment and another one—the 1983 election campaign—the British public was mostly pessimistic about the economy until the mid-1980s. No rosy view of the future distracted attention from unpalatable current news. Neither subdued inflation nor revived economic growth offset the losses inflicted on Mrs. Thatcher's popularity by unemployment. During her first term as prime minister she managed to hold the confidence of the electorate in spite of, not because of, the results of her economic policy.

REFERENCES

Alt, James E. 1979. *The Politics of Economic Decline*. Cambridge: Cambridge University Press.
Box, George E. P., and Gwilym M. Jenkins. 1976. *Time Series Analysis*. Rev. ed. San Francisco: Holden-Day.
Box, George E. P., and G. C. Tiao. 1975. "Intervention Analysis with Applications to Economic and Environmental Problems." *Journal of the American Statistical Association* 79:70–79.
Bloom, Howard S., and H. Douglas Price. 1975. "Voter Response to Short-Run Economic Conditions: The Asymmetric Effect of Prosperity and Recession." *American Political Science Review* 69:1240–54.
Buiter, Willem H., and Marcus H. Miller. 1983. "Changing the Rules: Economic Consequences of the Thatcher Regime." *Brookings Papers on Economic Activity*, 305–65.
Butler, David, and Donald Stokes. 1969. *Political Change in Britain*. New York: St. Martin's.
Campbell, Angus, Philip E. Converse, Warren E. Miller, and Donald E. Stokes. 1960. *The American Voter*. New York: Wiley.
Clarke, Harold D., William Mishler, and Paul Whiteley. 1990. "Recapturing the Falklands—Models of Conservative Popularity." *British Journal of Political Science* 20:63–81.
Clarke, Harold D., Marianne C. Stewart, and Gary Zuk. 1986. "Politics, Economics, and Party Popularity in Britian, 1979–1983." *Electoral Studies* 5:123–41.

Crewe, Ivor. 1981. "Why the Conservatives Won?" In *Britain at the Polls, 1979,* ed. Howard Penniman, chap. 9. Washington, DC: American Enterprise Institute.

Dunleavy, Patrick, and Christopher T. Husbands. 1985. *British Democracy at the Crossroads.* Boston: Allen and Unwin.

Freedman, Lawrence. 1988. *Britain and the Falklands War.* New York: Basil Blackwell.

Fiorina, Morris P. 1981. *Retrospective Voting in American Elections.* New Haven, CT: Yale University Press.

Frey, Bruno S., and Friedrich Schneider. 1978. "A Politico-Economic Model of the United Kingdom." *Economic Journal* 88:243–53.

Goodhart, C. A. E., and R. J. Bhansali. 1970. "Political Economy." *Political Studies* 18:43–106.

Hastings, Max, and Simon Jenkins. 1983. *The Battle for the Falklands.* New York: Norton.

Hibbs, Douglas A., Jr. 1982. "On the Demand for Economic Outcomes: Macroeconomic Performance and Mass Political Support in the United States, Great Britain, and Germany." *Journal of Politics* 43:426–62.

Hudson, John. 1984. "Prime Ministerial Popularity in the UK: 1960–81." *Political Studies* 32:86–97.

Kenski, Henry. 1980. "Economic Perception and Presidential Popularity." *Journal of Politics* 42:68–75.

Kernell, Samuel. 1977. "Presidential Popularity and Negative Voting." *American Political Science Review* 71:44–66.

Kernell, Samuel. 1978. "Explaining Presidential Popularity." *American Political Science Review* 72:506–22.

Kinder, Donald R., and D. Roderick Kiewiet. 1981 "Sociotropic Politics: The American Case." *British Journal of Political Science* 11:129–61.

Lanoue, David. 1988. *From Camelot to the Teflon President: Economics and Presidential Popularity since 1960.* New York: Greenwood.

Lewis-Beck, Michael S. 1988. *Economics and Elections: The Major Western Democracies.* Ann Arbor, MI: University of Michigan Press.

Maynard, Geoffrey. 1988. *The Economy under Mrs. Thatcher.* New York: Basil Blackwell.

McCleary, Richard, and Richard A. Hay, Jr. 1980. *Applied Time Series Analysis.* Beverly Hills: Sage.

Miller, W. L., and M. Mackie. 1973. "The Electoral Cycle and the Asymmetry of Government and Opposition Popularity." *Political Studies* 21:263–79.

Mishler, William, Marilyn Hoskin, and Roy Fitzgerald. 1988. "British Parties in the Balance: A Time-Series Analysis of Long-Term Trends in Labour and Conservative Support." *British Journal of Political Science* 19:211–36.

Mosley, Paul. 1984. *The Making of Economic Policy: Theory and Evidence from Britain and the United States since 1945.* New York: St. Martin's.

Mueller, John. 1973. *War, Presidents, and Public Opinion.* New York: Wiley.

Mughan, Anthony. 1986. "Toward a Political Explanation of Government Vote Losses in Midterm By-Elections." *American Political Science Review* 80:761–76.

Norpoth, Helmut. 1984. "Economics, Politics and the Cycle of Presidential Popularity." *Political Behavior* 6:253–73.

Norpoth, Helmut. 1987a. "Guns and Butter and Government Popularity in Britain." *American Political Science Review* 81:949–59.

Norpoth, Helmut. 1987b. "The Falklands War and Government Popularity in Britain: Rally without Consequence or Surge without Decline?" *Electoral Studies* 6:3–16.

Norpoth, Helmut. N.d. "The Falklands War and British Public Opinion." In *International Crisis and Domestic Politics,* ed. James W. Lamare. New York: Praeger. Forthcoming.

Pissarides, C. A. 1980. "British Government Popularity and Economic Performance." *Economic Journal* 90:569–81.

Sanders, David, Hugh Ward, David Marsh, and Tony Fletcher. 1987. "Government Popularity and the Falklands War: A Reassessment." *British Journal of Political Science* 17:281–313.

Sunday Times of London Insight Team. 1982. *War in the Falklands.* New York: Harper and Row.

Theroux, Paul. 1984. *The Kingdom by the Sea.* New York: Washington Square Press.

Times (London). 1981. "Letters to the Editor." March 31.

Walters, Alan. 1986. *Britain's Economic Renaissance: Margaret Thatcher's Reforms, 1979–1984.* New York: Oxford University Press.

Watt, David. 1968. "Labour's Hard Road to Recovery." *Financial Times,* March 8.

Whiteley, Paul. 1985. "Perceptions of Economic Performance and Voting Behavior in the 1983 General Election in Britain." In *Economic Conditions and Electoral Outcomes,* ed. Heinz Eulau and Michael S. Lewis-Beck, 62–77. New York: Agathon Press.

Whiteley, Paul. 1986. "Macroeconomic Performance and Government Popularity in Britain: The Short-Run Dynamics." *European Journal of Political Research* 14:45–61.

Worcester, Robert, and Simon Jenkins. 1982. "Britain Rallies 'round the Prime Minister." *Public Opinion* 5:53–55.

Macroeconomics, the Falklands War, and the Popularity of the Thatcher Government: A Contrary View

David Sanders, Hugh Ward, and David Marsh

For students of British political history, one of the more intriguing episodes of recent years was the revival in political fortunes experienced by the Thatcher government during the course of 1982. In popular discourse, the favored explanation for this transformation has centered on the domestic political effects of the Falklands War. Crewe, for example, while recognizing that there were signs of an economic upturn in early 1982, argues that the impact of macroeconomic forces was minimal in comparison with the powerful effects on popularity of the Falklands campaign. He notes that between the time of the Argentinian invasion on March 31, 1982, and the British occupation of Port Stanley on June 14, Conservative support in the opinion polls increased by some fifteen percentage points. "In the space of three months," he concludes, "public opinion and party politics had been transformed" (Crewe 1985, 159).

In this chapter we review the existing evidence that has been presented in support of the "Falklands factor" interpretation of Mrs. Thatcher's political resurgence. We then offer some alternative evidence that casts a rather more ambiguous light on the events of 1982. By our account, the renewed popularity enjoyed by the Thatcher government from the spring of 1982 onward was largely the result of intelligent (or, perhaps, cynical or even fortuitous) macroeconomic management. We certainly do not deny that there was a massive increase in government popularity at the time of the Falklands War. In our view, however, the importance of the Falklands factor in the genesis of the increase has been substantially overestimated.

The authors are indebted to Mark Franklin, Helmut Norpoth, Martin Paldam, Paul Whiteley, Harold Clarke, and William Mishler for their helpful comments on an earlier draft of this chapter.

161

The Existing Evidence for the Falklands Effect

Quantitative studies of government popularity in Britain enjoy a long pedigree. Goodhart and Bhansali's seminal study from the early 1970s has subsequently been supplemented by contributions from a variety of other writers.[1] Most of these studies take as their dependent variable the month-by-month variations in the percentage of Gallup (or other) poll respondents who say they would vote for the incumbent government "if there were to be a general election tomorrow." They then attempt to model these variations in terms of movements in various aggregate-level political and economic variables. Three recent studies have concentrated exclusively on the Thatcher years: Dunleavy and Husbands's analysis of the 1983 general election (Dunleavy and Husbands 1985); Clark, Stewart, and Zuk's (1986) application of Box-Jenkins techniques to a variety of political and economic indices over the period 1979–83; and Norpoth's (1987) attempt to model the decay factor in the Falklands effect using Box-Jenkins and Box-Tiao techniques.

Dunleavy and Husbands's (1985) study provides clear empirical corroboration for the popular orthodoxy that the Falklands War substantially bolstered public support for the Thatcher government. After "extensive experiment" with various models, they present a predictive equation that (1) accounts for some 87 percent of the variance in government popularity between September, 1979, and April, 1983, and (2) contains only two predictor variables: the percentage rate of unemployment (lagged four months) and a "Falklands dummy" variable. On the basis of this model, Dunleavy and Husbands (1985, 153–54) estimate that the Falklands War led to a long-term increase in government popularity of over sixteen percentage points.

A somewhat more conservative estimate of the effects of the Falklands campaign is reported by Clarke, Stewart, and Zuk (1986), who argue that most econometric models of party popularity fail to control adequately for specific political events. By including various macroeconomic measures in their models (notably inflation and unemployment statistics), together with political event variables such as the occurrence of by-elections, Clarke, Stewart, and Zuk conclude that the Falklands affair still produced a sustained and significant increase in Conservative popularity of over seven percentage points. Although the magnitude of the Falklands factor is, on this estimate, only half that suggested by Dunleavy and Husbands (1985), it is nonetheless highly significant.

The analyses considered so far assume that the Falklands War had an "abrupt-permanent" effect on domestic British politics: government popu-

---

1. For review, see Paldam 1981 and Whitely 1984. Particularly important work on Britain includes: Frey and Schneider 1978, Mosley 1978 and 1984, Alt 1979, and Hibbs 1982.

larity jumped between April and May, 1982, and this effect appears to have persisted right through to the 1983 election. On both theoretical and empirical grounds, Norpoth doubts the adequacy of this characterization. He suggests, instead, that the war produced a fairly rapid buildup in support for Mrs. Thatcher followed by a *gradual* decline in the ensuing months: what he describes as a "gradual-temporary" model.[2] Controlling for inflation (which he finds to be nonsignificant) and unemployment, Norpoth concludes that the Falklands War produced a gradual-temporary increase in party support of eleven percentage points during May and June of 1982 but that this Falklands effect decayed at a rate of just under 0.07 per month thereafter. According to this model, the Falklands factor was still worth five percentage points by May, 1983, and may have been crucial to the Conservatives' landslide victory.

Conceptualizing Macroeconomic Effects: The Problem of Misspecification

All three of the studies referred to above are cogently argued and, as far as they go, methodologically sound. Equally—and this is a general complaint that can be leveled at most quantitative research—they are all open to the criticism that the models that they develop are misspecified because some potentially relevant independent variable(s) has (have) been omitted from them. "If only Z had been included in the appropriate equation," observes the carping critic, "then X might not have been found to exert such a significant influence on Y." We obviously do not wish to be unnecessarily critical in this regard, but in our view the studies we have reviewed all fail adequately to conceptualize the role of the macroeconomy in the determination of government popularity. To be sure, all three studies emphasize the two macroeconomic phenomena (unemployment and inflation) that opinion surveys have repeatedly shown to be of major concern to electors. However, we would argue that an exclusive focus on these two phenomena during the early Thatcher years captures only a part of the potential effects of the macroeconomy on the political process. Such a restrictive focus is inadequate both theoretically and empirically.

From a theoretical point of view, as discussed subsequently, it ignores both the particular problems that the Thatcherite economic strategy faced during 1979–81 and the resultant policy efforts that were made during 1982

---

2. It should be noted that in contrast to the other studies referred to above, Norpoth follows the North American convention of modeling support for the *leader* of the government rather than for the government as a whole. This means that his dependent variable is slightly different from that analyzed in other studies, but since Mrs. Thatcher's personal rating and that of the government as a whole are highly correlated ($R = .91$), his findings are of considerable relevance to our discussion.

and 1983 to secure the government's reelection. Empirically, it fails to explain why government popularity experienced a marked recovery from December, 1981, onward: four months before the Argentine invasion and five months before the May, 1982, "Falklands effect" was supposedly observed in the opinion polls. This explanatory failure can be clearly seen in figure 1 which plots movements in popularity against the predictions made by the Dunleavy-Husbands "unemployment-plus-Falklands-factor" model.[3] (Dunleavy and Husbands, like all other researchers of this problem, found the effects of inflation to be nonsignificant.) Although the Dunleavy-Husbands equation is extremely attractive—it is highly parsimonious and explains some 88 percent of the variance in popularity—it clearly fails to model the decisive "turning point" in the popularity series that occurred during the winter of 1981–82. We consider this to be a serious deficiency. Popularity was already increasing rapidly *before* the outbreak of the Falklands War. Moreover, as we argue below, there is good reason to believe not only that this initial recovery was generated primarily by economic factors but also that these same factors would in all probability have continued to strengthen the government's electoral position even if the Falklands War had not interposed itself during the course of 1982.

But if an exclusive reliance on unemployment and inflation as macroeconomic indicators is unsatisfactory, how should macroeconomic effects be conceptualized? We hypothesize that the effects of the macroeconomy upon government popularity operate through two distinct, if related, mechanisms. The first can be characterized as primarily *instrumental*. It is concerned with the elector-as-consumer, with the extent to which changes in the macroeconomy either advance or retard the personal self-interests of the elector and her or his immediate family. Quite simply, if governments are successful in advancing the self-interests of a sufficient number of people, then they are likely to be reelected; if not, then the chances of electoral defeat increase.[4] We would argue that the best indicator of how well people feel they

---

3. The model upon which the predicted values in figure 1 are based is:

	Estimate	t-value
Unemployment $(t - 4)$	-2.22	11.23
Falklands dummy (May, 1982, to June, 1983)	17.46	17.59
Constant	48.05	36.76

$$R^2 = .88 \qquad F = 160.59 \qquad DW = 1.35$$

4. These instrumental effects were particularly important during the Thatcher years as a direct result of Thatcherism's emphasis on individual responsibility and personal advancement. In Mrs. Thatcher's Britain, rising living standards were to result only from greater individual

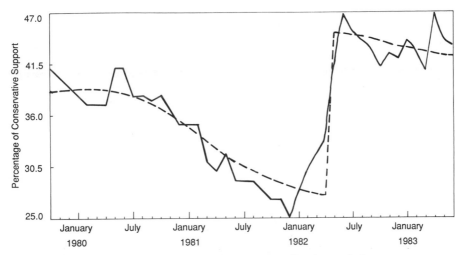

Fig. 1. Dunleavy-Husbands observed and predicted popularity scores. Solid line: observed Conservative support (%): average of major monthly polls (Gallup, MORI, NOP, Marplan, and Harris). Dashed line: predicted Conservative support (%) from Dunleavy-Husbands's "Unemployment-plus-Falklands" model.

are doing now is their degree of confidence about their personal economic prospects for the future. Indeed, we hypothesize that the more optimistic people become about the economic future of their immediate family, the more likely they are to offer their instrumental support to the incumbent government in order to sustain the very conditions that have produced their optimism in the first place. Other things being equal, therefore, we would expect to find that government popularity rose and fell in response to upward or downward movements in aggregate economic expectations. This is not to suggest, of course, that economic expectations had to rise among all voters for government popularity to increase; merely that popularity could be given an important boost if a significant proportion of electors believed that their personal economic prospects were improving.

Our preferred method of measuring aggregate personal expectations is based on the regular Gallup poll questions concerned with whether or not respondents think that their "own household's financial situation" will improve over the next twelve months. Our month-by-month measure of personal

---

efficient and effort; given that, according to the prime minister herself, there was "no such thing as society," the individual head of household was to take far more responsibility for the well-being of her or his immediate family. In these circumstances, Thatcherism's ability to convince voters that it was, indeed, capable of rewarding personal merit was crucial to its subsequent electoral success.

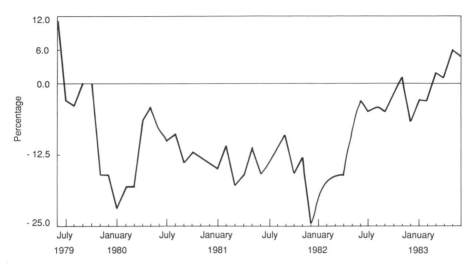

Fig. 2. Personal Expectations Index, June, 1979–June, 1983. The expectations index is constructed from Gallup's regular monthly question: "How do you think the financial situation of your household will change over the next twelve months?" The figures shown are derived by subtracting the percentage who think things will get worse from the percentage thinking things will get better.

expectations is obtained by subtracting the percentage of respondents who think that their household's economic position will worsen from the percentage who think it will get better. Figure 2 outlines the movements in the resultant expectations index over the 1979–83 period. We regard it as no coincidence that the index follows a similar decline-recovery pattern as that shown in the popularity series shown in figure 1, though more on this later.

A second mechanism that connects macroeconomic changes with movements in government popularity is primarily *evaluative*. Evaluative effects are concerned with how far electors take a positive view of government economic performance: to the extent that the government's macroeconomic policy is regarded as being "successful," it can expect to reap some sort of electoral reward; failure, on the other hand, is likely to elicit a commensurate electoral punishment. Four macroeconomic indicators seem to us to be of potential relevance in this context: two that are of "general" importance (unemployment and inflation) and two that are of special significance to the political economy of the early Thatcher years (the exchange rate and the Public Sector Borrowing Requirement or PSBR).

As we have noted, it is standard procedure in quantitative analyses of government popularity to apply statistical controls for unemployment and inflation. Although the precise form of operationalization varies from study to study, it is generally understood that since both phenomena are so patently undesirable as far as most electors are concerned, adverse movements in either indicator are likely to be punished by a loss of governmental support, even if favorable movements fail to bring a corresponding electoral reward. As also noted, various efforts (including our own) to model the effects of inflation during the first Thatcher term have, in fact, all met with failure: the Thatcher government's defeat of inflation in 1980–82 seems to have left its popularity entirely unaffected. In these circumstances, unemployment has, in effect, been regarded as the only major "evaluative" macroeconomic influence on government popularity during the 1979–83 period.

Unfortunately, this convenient conclusion, because it ignores two vitally important features of the political economy of early Thatcherism, cannot be sustained. The first of these features was the external value of sterling. It is widely acknowledged that the protracted overvaluation of the £ during 1979–80 was primarily responsible for the massive shakeout of British industry that occurred in the early 1980s: the loss of competitiveness in export markets that accompanied the overvaluation was so severe that, notwithstanding the extremely vocal complaints of the Confederation of British Industry, between October, 1979, and May, 1981, the British economy lost some 20 percent of its manufacturing base. However, from its high point (of £1 = $2.40) in October, 1980, the exchange rate was gradually reduced by progressive adjustments to interest rates. By September, 1981, the exchange rate had fallen to $1.80, giving a considerable boost to export competitiveness, a much needed tonic for the country's beleaguered exporters. In our view, it seems highly unlikely that these exchange rate shifts were unrelated to the govern-

TABLE 1. Effect of Lagged Exchange Rate (£ vs. $) on Index of Industrial Production, June, 1979–June, 1987 (*t*-statistics in parentheses)

	Index of Industrial Production, OLS	Index of Industrial Production Maximum Likelihood	Change in Index of Industrial Production, OLS[a]
Constant	120.03	119.0	−0.02
	(60.37)	(26.42)	(0.18)
Exchange rate	−9.23	−9.03	−7.26[b]
(lagged 8 months)	(8.28)	(3.62)	(2.62)
R^2	.42	.94	.07
DW	0.09	2.06	2.12
AR(1)		.93	
		(28.7)	

[a]No AR(n) or MA(n) process in error term.
[b]Change in exchange rate (lagged 8 months).

ment's popularity. As table 1 shows, exchange movements—with a lag of about eight months—seem to be consistently associated with changes in industrial output; a dollar increase (or decrease) in the pound's external value eliciting a nine-point fall (rise) in the official index of industrial production over the period 1979–87. What this in effect means is that during the 1980s, exchange rate movements were intimately bound up with changes in the overall level of economic activity: a substantial rise in the exchange rate being associated, ceteris paribus, with a fall in economic activity; a decline in the rate with increased activity. As discussed below, it seems reasonable to argue that, during the early Thatcher years, these exchange rate–generated variations in economic activity were in turn related to variations in government popularity, especially in view of the considerable media attention that was devoted to them in the early 1980s.

The second macroeconomic factor specific to the first Thatcher government that needs to be considered is the public sector borrowing requirement (PSBR): the amount that the government has to borrow from private investors in order to finance its current spending program. From June, 1979, onward one of the major goals of the new Conservative government was a reduction in the overall level of state spending—and especially that financed through state borrowing—an objective which was to be achieved through rigid budgetary controls. The main target for the new policy in the early years was PSBR. Indeed, the need to reduce PSBR became a central feature of Conservative rhetoric. While it is obviously the case that the average voter pays little attention to such remote macroeconomic intangibles as PSBR, we would argue that, in terms of the popular political discourse of the early 1980s, movements in PSBR were of considerable significance for the credibility of the Thatcher government's economic strategy.[5] Reductions in PSBR were regarded as evidence that the government's economic strategy was successful, that it was achieving one of its own publicly stated and much emphasized goals; conversely, increases in PSBR were interpreted as evidence that it was experiencing difficulties.

The question that obviously follows from the preceding discussion is *how* movements in macroeconomic phenomena such as unemployment, the exchange rate and PSBR are translated into variations in government popularity. Although we cannot demonstrate it here, we consider the role of the mass media to be crucial in this context: we would argue that their speculative endeavors were of fundamental importance in determining the way in which changes in macroeconomic indicators were interpreted and, therefore, evalu-

---

5. Our current research, as yet incomplete, undertakes a content analysis of a representative sample of British newspapers. Preliminary indications suggest that PSBR was, indeed, accorded a considerable amount of press attention during the period in question.

ated by electors. While it seems unlikely that the average voter can make a sophisticated judgment about the relevance of recent changes in either unemployment, the exchange rate or PSBR, we would argue that electors are readily susceptible to the sort of "more good news" or "more bad news" messages that the British media—and particularly the press—consistently seek to convey.[6] Viewed in this light, the translation of higher unemployment (or a higher exchange rate or a higher PSBR) into a fall in support for the government becomes rather less tortuous: if the news regarding unemployment (or the exchange rate or PSBR) has been "good" for the past few months, then the electorate is more likely to make a positive evaluation of the incumbent government; if the news has been consistently "bad," then evaluations are more likely to be negative. It is, of course, extraordinarily difficult to specify the precise length of time required before an objective macroeconomic change can be processed by the media and evaluated by the electorate. However, given Dunleavy and Husbands's (1985) findings cited earlier that unemployment (lagged four months) seemed to correlate most strongly with the downward movements in popularity between 1979 and 1983, it seems reasonable to suppose that, during this time period at least, the "translation" process did indeed take something on the order of four months. Assuming that the translation takes the same length of time for each evaluative macroeconomic variable, we accordingly hypothesize that unemployment and PSBR (via the intervening but unmeasured effects of the mass media) should each exert a negative influence on popularity with a lag of four months; the exchange rate (since its objective effects on industrial output, as noted above, work through with a lag of eight months) should exert a negative influence on popularity with a lag of eight months (objective lag) plus four months (translation lag), or twelve months in total. These hypothesized evaluative effects, together with the instrumental effects of personal expectations, are summarized schematically in figure 3.

Toward an Empirical Model

Consider again the observed government popularity series described in figure 1. The series reported is the monthly average of the five major British opinion polls,[7] a measure that is generally regarded as providing a more accurate reflection of the state of political opinion in Britain than any single poll. Two features of the popularity series are immediately noticeable. First, there is a

---

6. For a discussion of these issues in the British context, see Glasgow University Media Group 1985.

7. These are: Gallup, MORI, NOP, Harris, and Marplan. In some months, Harris and/or Marplan did not ask a question about government popularity. The general question asked by all agencies is: "If there were a general election tomorrow, which party would you support?"

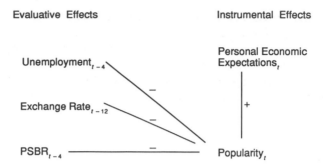

Fig. 3. Hypothesized macroeconomic model of government popularity in Britain, 1979–83

clear acceleration or discontinuity in popularity between April and May, 1982, an increase in popularity of fully eleven percentage points. It is this discontinuity that Crewe (1985) indirectly attributes to the Falklands factor and that Dunleavy and Husbands (1985) indirectly utilize when they find that their Falklands dummy variable produced a sixteen percentage point increase in government popularity during the first Thatcher term. We shall offer a rather different analysis of this discontinuity later. The second—and more important—feature of figure 1, however, is the overall *trend:* popularity suffers a general decline until the end of 1981 and then experiences a recovery through to the 1983 election.[8] As table 2 shows, the trend can be described quite well by a simple curvilinear function of the form $Y_t = a + bt + ct^2$. As the table also shows, moreover, this same decline-recovery pattern is also experienced by two of the variables—personal expectations and the exchange rate—that were identified above as being of theoretical importance in any analysis of Mrs. Thatcher's first-term popularity. The fact that these trend

---

8. One way of interpreting this broad decline-recovery pattern, of course, is to regard it as a manifestation of the "midterm effect" that is frequently observed in democratic polities. Governments are often obliged to take unpopular measures in the early period of office, which adversely affects their opinion poll ratings, but equally often they manage to effect some sort of economic recovery in the run-up to the next election, with beneficial consequences for their own popularity. When the consequences of this sort of "political" economic management are combined with the generally lower levels of political stimulation typically associated with the periods between elections, it is relatively easy to appreciate why the midterm effect is so frequently observed. However, although this account is consistent with the decline-recovery pattern of the first Thatcher term, we do not find it satisfying to describe that pattern simply as a midterm phenomenon. If something is happening, either in the real economy or in public perceptions of it, then the model being employed is not strictly a midterm effect model at all: rather, it is one that relates government popularity to objective and/or subjective economic circumstances. For a review of the relevant literature, see Hudson 1985.

TABLE 2. Trend Patterns in Government Popularity and Its Correlates, June, 1979–June, 1983

Variable	Time Trend Function	Graphic Representation of Function	Month of Maximum/ Minimum
Government popularity	$Y_t = 40.66 - 1.13t + .02t^2$ $R^2 = .54$; all coefficients significant at .05 level		December, 1981
Personal economic expectations	$Y_t = 1.01 - 1.44t + .03t^2$ $R^2 = .57$; all coefficients significant		December, 1981
Exchange rate (£ against \$; lagged 12 months)	$Y_t = 1.74 + .04t - .009t^2$ $R^2 = .77$; all coefficients significant		October, 1980

relationships are so strong (indeed, the expectations and popularity curves reach their respective minimum points at exactly the same time: December, 1981) leads us to conclude that it would be unwise to remove the trends in the data prior to estimation: to do so (by first- or second-differencing) would be to remove an important part of the association between the variables that may well reflect some sort of causal connection between them. As a result, the models that we estimate below all use "unprewhitened" data, an approach that has the considerable substantive merit of providing easily interpretable coefficients.[9]

Table 3 estimates the parameters of the simple macroeconomic model of government popularity described in figure 3. No coefficients are reported for inflation as this variable consistently failed to furnish a significant parameter whenever it was included in any of the models estimated in the present study. The model does not suffer from multicollinearity.[10] Three features of the table are immediately noticeable. First, although the reported OLS model exhibits an AR(1) in its residuals, the maximum likelihood (ML) model provides

---

9. For a discussion of the rival attractions of prewhitened versus unprewhitened data, see Sanders and Ward 1989.

10. The bivariate intercorrelations among the independent variables were as follows:

	Expectations (t)	Unemp $(t - 4)$	Exchange $(t - 12)$
Unemployment $(t - 4)$	.44		
Exchange rate $(t - 12)$	−.69	−.27	
PSBR $(t - 4)$	−.37	−.28	.39

TABLE 3. Estimates of Macroeconomic Model of Government Popularity, October, 1979–June, 1983 (*t*-statistics in parentheses)

	OLS Model	Maximum Likelihood (ML) Model
Personal Expectations	0.24	0.25
	(4.13)	(3.89)
Unemployment ($t - 4$)	−0.64	−0.69
	(4.59)	(3.48)
Exchange Rate ($t - 12$)	−19.89	−19.74
	(9.89)	(8.16)
PSBR ($t - 4$)	−0.0008	−0.0007
	(4.24)	(3.28)
Constant	87.96	88.12
	(22.45)	(17.44)
$\bar{R}^2$	.90	.91
F	99.84	86.16
	(5,39)	(6,37)
DW	1.37	1.88
AR(1)		.31
		(1.95)

parameter estimates very similar to those obtained using OLS. Second, the model as a whole accounts for some 90 percent of the variation in government popularity between October, 1979, and June, 1983. Third, and most important, all the parameters of both the OLS and ML models are highly significant and in the predicted direction: unemployment, as previous research has shown, has a reductive effect on popularity ($b = -.69$); and, as predicted in the previous section, equally important negative effects are also evident for the lagged exchange rate ($b = -19.74$) and PSBR ($b = -.0007$) variables, while personal expectations ($b = .25$) clearly exerted a positive influence on popularity.

What all of these observations suggest is that a combination of instrumental and evaluative macroeconomic factors seem to have been extremely important in determining variations in government popularity during Mrs. Thatcher's first term in office. Moreover, as figure 4 shows, the operation of purely macroeconomic factors predicts a continuing recovery in government popularity after December, 1981, with a clear acceleration in popularity in the spring and early summer of 1982. This conclusion, in turn, seems to contradict the accepted view that it was the political effects of the Falklands campaign that were primarily responsible for the Conservatives' electoral revival during 1982 and 1983.

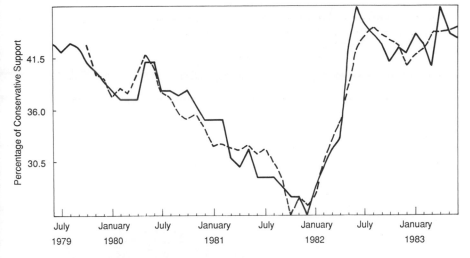

Fig. 4. Observed and predicted popularity scores from table 3. Solid line: observed Conservative support (%): average of major monthly polls (Gallup, MORI, NOP, Marplan, and Harris). Dashed line: predicted Conservative support (%) from table 3 (ML model).

Measuring the "Falklands Effect"

Table 4 reports the consequences of adding a variety of "Falklands factor" effects to the purely "economic" model outlined in table 3. The "Falklands effect" is operationalized in six different ways.

— FALK 13 is a dummy variable that, following Dunleavy and Husbands (1985), takes the value 1 for the 13 months May, 1982, through June, 1983, and zero otherwise;

— FALK 14 is a dummy variable that takes the value 1 for the 14 months April, 1982 (when the war began), through June, 1983, and zero otherwise;

— FALK 3 is a dummy variable that takes the value 1 for the three months May–July, 1982, and zero otherwise;

— FALK 4 is a dummy variable that takes the value 1 for the four months April–July, 1982, and zero otherwise;

— FALK-NORPOTH provides an approximation of the sort of gradual-temporary effect observed by Norpoth that was referred to earlier: it takes the value zero until April, 1982, the value 11 for May and June of 1982, and subsequently decays at a rate of 0.05 per month through the June, 1983, election.

TABLE 4.   Estimates of the Impact of the Different Falklands Effect Variables in Combination with Macroeconomic Controls, October, 1979–June, 1983 (*t*-statistics in parentheses)

	OLS	ML	FALK 13 OLS	FALK 13 ML	FALK 14 OLS	FALK 14 ML
Personal	.24	.25	.16	.17	.22	.24
expectations	(4.13)	(3.89)	(3.09)	(2.73)	(4.01)	(3.86)
Unemployment	−0.64	−0.69	−1.44	−1.42	−0.24	−1.18
($t - 4$)	(4.58)	(3.47)	(6.71)	(5.82)	(4.82)	(4.34)
Exchange rate	−19.89	−19.74	−10.52	−10.87	−13.55	−14.40
($t - 12$)	(−9.89)	(8.11)	(3.91)	(3.61)	(4.51)	(4.52)
PSBR	−.0008	−.0007	−.0006	−.0006	−.0005	−.0006
($t - 4$)	(4.28)	(3.28)	(3.53)	(3.88)	(2.58)	(2.53)
Falklands Effect			8.11	7.79	5.46	4.60
			(4.42)	(3.88)	(2.70)	(2.16)
C	87.96	88.12	76.35	71.04	76.38	78.35
	(22.45)	(17.44)	(13.70)	(11.91)	(13.58)	(12.97)
$\bar{R}^2$	.90	.91	.93	.93	.91	.91
F	99.84	86.16	120.86	100.50	93.92	75.81
DW	1.37	1.88	1.53	1.98	1.80	1.89
AR(1)		.31		.27		.09
		(1.95)		(1.45)		(.58)

— FALK-DECAY, like FALK-NORPOTH, seeks to estimate some sort of gradual-temporary effect. The effect, however, is assumed to have petered out completely by the time of the June, 1983, election: FALK-DECAY takes on the value 13 for May of 1982 and then drops one percentage point per month through to a figure of zero in June, 1983.

Two major conclusions can be drawn from table 4. First, in each of the twelve models estimated all four of the macroeconomic variables specified in our purely "economic" model continue to furnish significant parameter estimates with the predicted signs: the unemployment, exchange rate and PSBR variables consistently yield significant negative coefficients while the personal expectations coefficients are uniformly significant and positive. This suggests that no matter how the "Falklands effect" is operationalized, the macroeconomic factors that we have identified continue to be of considerable statistical importance as predictors of government popularity. The second main implication of the findings reported in table 4 is that the estimated magnitude of the "Falklands effect" depends, to a considerable degree, on the way in which the effect is specified:

— the FALK 13 ML model suggests an effect of almost 8 percent, in line

FALK 3		FALK 4		FALK-NORPOTH		FALK-DECAY	
OLS	ML	OLS	ML	OLS	ML	OLS	ML
.25	.26	.26	.28	.22	.22	.25	.25
(4.82)	(4.55)	(4.73)	(4.57)	(4.40)	(3.75)	(4.80)	(4.31)
−0.69	−0.74	−0.71	−0.76	−1.06	−1.10	−0.83	−0.89
(5.65)	(4.84)	(5.30)	(4.72)	(6.49)	(5.41)	(5.97)	(4.75)
−20.11	−19.97	−20.02	−19.82	−15.11	−15.09	−17.92	−17.89
(11.45)	(10.14)	(10.60)	(9.52)	(7.06)	(6.15)	(9.35)	(8.01)
−.0005	−.0005	−.0005	−.0005	−.0005	−.0004	−.0005	−.0004
(2.73)	(2.40)	(2.55)	(2.31)	(2.49)	(2.06)	(2.32)	(1.89)
4.24	4.16	2.92	2.73	0.55	0.56	0.34	0.37
(3.68)	(3.35)	(2.53)	(2.19)	(3.82)	(3.53)	(3.19)	(3.04)
87.8	88.09	88.01	88.29	78.63	78.84	83.83	84.11
(25.69)	(22.33)	(23.93)	(21.38)	(18.85)	(15.70)	(22.27)	(18.15)
.92	.93	.91	.91	.92	.93	.92	.92
107.63	91.66	91.97	77.62	109.99	95.38	100.22	89.00
1.58	1.96	1.65	1.93	1.44	1.97	1.41	1.95
	.17		.14		.27		.28
	(1.09)		(.87)		(1.72)		(1.78)

with the Clarke, Stewart, and Zuk (1986) finding reported earlier;

— the FALK 14 OLS model suggests an effect of almost 5.5 percent per month over 14 months;

— the FALK 3 ML model suggests that the war increased the government's popularity by just over 4 percent, though only for a period of three months during the early summer of 1982;

— the FALK 4 OLS model suggests that the effect was worth only 3 percent for four months during the summer of 1982;

— the FALK-NORPOTH ML model suggests that the effect was indeed a gradual temporary one, but that the magnitude of the effect ($b = .56$) was almost half the size of that estimated by Norpoth (1987), so that by June, 1983, the war was worth under three percentage points to the Conservative government;

— the FALK-DECAY model also suggests that the effect was a gradual-temporary one but that the effect, during the summer of 1982, was under half that suggested by Norpoth (1987) ($b = .37$) and that by the time of the June, 1983, election the effect had entirely disappeared.

The question that obviously follows from these conflicting findings is whether or not any statistical criterion or criteria can be employed in order to decide between their competing merits. Given that all of the models provide significant parameters with the predicted signs, the t-values are of little assistance in this matter. A similar conclusion follows from an examination of the corrected R^2 values from the various equations: the differences between the models are so slight as to render them virtually indistinguishable. In terms of the F-values, the "best" ML model is FALK 13, with FALK-NORPOTH and FALK 3 close behind. However, before this is taken as conclusive evidence of the superiority of the FALK 13 model, it should be emphasized that, strictly, the F-statistic can only be employed as a means of deciding whether or not a particular model is statistically significant. Indeed, if the F-ratio were to be taken as the decisive criterion for evaluating rival models, the "best" model would undoubtedly be the Dunleavy-Husbands (1985) "unemployment plus Falklands factor" model reported in figure 1 ($F = 160.49$), which, as we saw, fails to explain the marked recovery in popularity that occurred several months before General Galtieri's intervention. Since the F-value for each of the models reported in table 4 is greater than the required critical value, all that can be said with certainty is that all the models are indeed significant; all of which gets us nowhere in terms of deciding which model is somehow "the best."

If it is the case that we cannot choose between models that seek to assess both macroeconomic and "political" effects simultaneously, it is perhaps advisable to approach the question of the character and magnitude of the "Falklands effect" from a different angle. If we think in terms of "Granger-causality"—in which some X_t might be said to "Granger-cause" some Y_t to the extent that Y_t is not explained by its own past history—then it is possible to estimate the effect of the "Falklands factor" by seeing how far some Falklands effect variable can explain the variation in government popularity over and above the variation that cannot be explained by past values of government popularity. Given that the popularity series itself displays a classic AR(1), the general form of the model to be tested is

$$\text{Popularity}_t = a + b_1 \text{Popularity}_{t-1} + \text{FALK} + U_t$$

Substituting each of the six "Falklands effect" variables into this equation for the 1979–83 period yields the results presented in table 5. Table 6 reports the same calculations for a longer time-series that includes the first *two* Thatcher terms, 1979–87. At first sight, tables 5 and 6 seem to provide little enlightenment. In both tables, the different "Falklands effect" variables *all* yield significant coefficients, while the corrected R^2 and F-values are all so similar as to render the models indistinguishable. Yet the models also provide *different*

TABLE 5. OLS Estimates of the Impact of Different "Falklands Effect" Variables, controlling for Popularity $t - 1$, June, 1979–June, 1983 (t-statistics in parentheses)

	Pop-1	FALK 13	FALK 14	FALK 3	FALK 4	FALK-NORPOTH	FALK-DECAY
Pop-1	.92	.81	.82	.89	.91	.81	.84
	(15.83)	(12.09)	(12.82)	(17.06)	(17.11)	(12.88)	(14.57)
Falk		2.52	2.31	4.64	3.65	0.32	0.32
		(2.89)	(2.80)	(3.62)	(3.19)	(3.30)	(3.39)
C	2.96	6.45	5.84	3.71	3.05	6.39	5.38
	(1.35)	(2.72)	(2.55)	(1.89)	(1.52)	(2.85)	(2.55)
$\bar{R}^2$	.84	.86	.86	.87	.87	.87	.87
F	250.55	149.56	147.86	164.75	155.54	157.85	159.56
DW	1.79	1.74	1.95	2.12	2.35	1.77	1.81

estimates of the magnitude of the Falklands effect: in table 5, for example, the effect varies from 2.31 percentage points per month for 14 months (FALK 14) to 4.64 points for 3 months (FALK 3); in table 6, the effect varies from 1.52 points for 14 months (FALK 14) to 4.43 points for 3 months (FALK 3). Clearly all the models cannot be "correct" if we really believe that there was a specifiable "Falklands effect." Yet faced with the separate pieces of evidence presented in tables 4–6, we seem unable to arrive at any kind of firm conclusion.

Table 7 goes some way toward resolving the problem. It reports the extent to which each "Falklands effect" variable produces uniform coefficients across the different models estimated in tables 4–6. What is clear from table 7 is that the FALK 3 variable produces a similar parameter ($b = 4.16$ in the model that contains macroeconomic controls; $b = 4.64$ in the popularity$_{t-1}$ model for 1979–83; and $b = 4.43$ in the popularity$_{t-1}$ model for 1979–87: range $= 0.48$) across all three models. This contrasts sharply with the FALK 13 model (range $= 6.09$) and even with the FALK-NORPOTH model (range $= 2.62$ for the spring 1982 effect).

In short, therefore, it is FALK 3 that produces the most consistent estimate of the "Falklands effect" regardless of the statistical controls that are applied: using the classic principles of convergent validity,[11] this suggests that it is the FALK 3 operationalization—which assumes a short-term, three-month effect for the Falklands factor—that most adequately captures the "true" Falklands effect.[12] This conclusion, in turn, supports the notion that macroeconomic forces were extremely important in the recovery of Conservative support in 1982 and 1983. As we saw in relation to the "purely

---

11. See Campbell and Fiske 1959.

12. If we add popularity at time $t - 1$ to the FALK 3 plus macroeconomic effects model described in table 4, we obtain the following results:

Independent Variable	OLS estimate	t-value
Personal Expectations	.20	3.62
Unemployment ($t - 4$)	−.51	3.43
Exchange rate ($t - 12$)	−14.93	4.86
PSBR ($t - 4$)	−.0004	2.29
FALK 3	4.12	3.70
Popularity ($t - 1$)	.23	2.02
Constant	66.26	5.94

$R^2 = .94$ $F(6,38) = 97.47$ DW $= 1.97$

These results (with all parameters significant and a FALK 3 coefficient of 4.12) again corroborate our conclusion that the FALK 3 operationalization offers the "best" approximation of the "true" Falklands effect.

TABLE 6. OLS Estimates of the Impact of Different "Falklands Effect" Variables, controlling for Popularity, June, 1979–June, 1987 (t-statistics in parentheses)

	Pop-1	FALK 13	FALK 14	FALK 3	FALK 4	FALK-NORPOTH	FALK-DECAY
Pop-1	.92	.87	.88	.90	.92	.87	.88
Falk		1.70	1.52	4.43	3.47	0.22	0.25
		(2.74)	(2.51)	(3.90)	(3.48)	(2.97)	(3.30)
C	2.95	4.56	4.14	3.89	2.99	4.42	4.15
	(1.94)	(2.88)	(2.67)	(2.79)	(2.08)	(2.87)	(2.78)
$\bar{R}^2$	.85	.86	.86	.87	.86	.86	.86
F	529.46	286.86	282.84	312.28	301.97	291.22	298.04
DW	1.76	1.75	1.84	1.94	2.08	1.76	1.77

TABLE 7. Summary of Different Estimates of the "Falklands Effect"

	Macro Economics Controls	Pop-1 1979–83	Pop-1 1979–87	Range
FALK 13	7.79	2.52	1.70	6.09
FALK 14	4.60	2.31	1.52	3.08
FALK 3	4.16	4.64	4.43	0.48
FALK 4	2.73	3.65	3.47	0.92
FALK-NORPOTH	5.04–2.80	3.52–1.60	2.42–1.10	2.62–1.70
FALK-DECAY	4.81–0	4.16–0	3.25–0	1.56

economic" model described in figure 3 and table 3, personal expectations, unemployment, the exchange rate, and PSBR were well able, on their own, to explain the recovery in popularity after December, 1981. An inspection of the coefficients derived from the "purely economic" ML model and those derived from the FALK 3 ML model (see cols. 2 and 8 of table 4) reveals that they are remarkably similar: the significant coefficient for the FALK 3 variable indicates that the much-vaunted "Falklands effect" gave a boost of just over 4 percent per month to Conservative popularity for the period May–July, 1982. By the late summer of 1982, the effect had disappeared; and it was certainly of no consequence by the time of the general election in June, 1983. The Conservatives' victory derived primarily from the more flexible approach adopted in relation to the exchange rate after May, 1981, and from the recovery in personal expectations that began in January, 1982.[13]

Conclusion

Our prime intention in this chapter has been to show that macroeconomic factors were at the root of Mrs. Thatcher's political revival in 1982. Certainly the evidence of the models that we have presented supports the conclusion that economic factors were much more important than political ones. In particular, we have shown that the effects on government popularity of the Falklands War were relatively small.

13. One question we have been unable to address here, because of space constraints, is why expectations should have recovered after December, 1981. Our statistical analysis of this question (not reported here) suggests that, during the 1979–83 period, personal expectations were strongly influenced (negatively) by two variables: interest rates and the level of taxation. (It is important to note that in Britain, given the high level of homeownership—over 60 percent of homes by the late 1980s—interest rate movements have a substantial impact on many household budgets). Interest rates were falling throughout the autumn and winter of 1981–82, which undoubtedly fueled the initial recovery of government popularity in January, 1981. This recovery was then given a substantial boost by the tax cuts made in the 1982 budget, the first cuts to be made after almost three years of austerity. For a more detailed analysis, see Sanders, Ward, and Marsh 1987.

What we have also sought to establish is that if the effects of the macroeconomy are estimated purely in terms of unemployment (and inflation, the effects of which are clearly nonsignificant), serious problems of model misspecification may arise. We have argued that in the early Thatcher years, electors' *evaluations* of the government's economic performance depended not only on movements in unemployment but also on movements in sterling's external value and in the public sector borrowing requirement: movements that were important because of the prominence they were accorded in contemporary political discourse. We have also argued that there was an important *instrumental* aspect to the Thatcher government's electoral resurgence. The fact that, notwithstanding the continued growth of unemployment, electors-as-consumers experienced a marked revival in their aggregate economic expectations from the beginning of 1982 onward made an additional and continuing contribution to the Conservative recovery. We would argue that the outbreak of the Falklands War—and especially the outpouring of nationalist sentiment that accompanied it—merely served to mask these macroeconomic effects. The Conservative revival was well under way before the war began. And there is certainly good reason to suppose that it would have continued even if the war had not interposed itself.

Where does this leave us? Do we have a statistical model for predicting government popularity after 1983? In response to these questions we are obliged to err on the side of caution. Our analysis has been an exercise in (recent) quantitative history rather than an attempt to generalize about the determinants of the popularity of British (or even Thatcher) governments: our models are posited primarily as descriptive explanations of what happened between 1979 and 1983, not as general predictive guides. Our reticence in this regard, however, does not stem from a lack of conviction about the adequacy of the models we have reported. Rather, it results, in part, from our belief that the political reactions of the British electorate are not susceptible to universal generalization and in part from our conviction that both the exchange rate and PSBR took on very different roles after 1983: by 1985, as the £ plummeted to $1.08, serious concern was being widely expressed that sterling was dangerously *undervalued* rather than overvalued, as it had been in 1979–80; PSBR, on the other hand, simply faded away both as ideological totem and as a publicly touted indicator of policy success.

REFERENCES

Alt, James E. 1979. *The Politics of Economic Decline.* Cambridge: Cambridge University Press.
Campbell, Donald T., and Donald W. Fiske. 1959. "Convergent and Discriminant Validation by the Multitrait-Multimethod Matrix." *Psychological Bulletin* 56:81–105.

Clarke, Harold D., Marianne C. Stewart, and Garry Zuk. 1986. "Politics, Economics, and Party Popularity in Britain, 1979–83." *Electoral Studies* 5:123–41.

Crewe, Ivor. 1985. "How to Win a Landslide Without Really Trying: Why the Conservatives Won in 1983." In *Britain at the Polls,* ed. Austin Ranney. New York: Duke University Press.

Dunleavy, Patrick, and Christopher T. Husbands. 1985. *British Democracy at the Crossroads: Voting and Party Competition in the 1980s.* London: George Allen and Unwin.

Frey, Bruno S., and F. Schneider. 1978. "A Politico-Economic Model of the United Kingdom." *Economic Journal* 88:243–53.

Glasgow University Media Group. 1985. *War and Peace News.* Milton Keynes: Open University Press.

Goodhart, C. A. E., and R. J. Bhansali. 1970. "Political Economy." *Political Studies* 18:43–106.

Hibbs, Douglas A. 1982. "Economic Outcomes and Political Support for British Governments among Occupational Classes." *American Political Science Review* 76:259–79.

Hudson, John. 1985. "The Relationship between Government Popularity and Approval for the Government's Record in the United Kingdom." *British Journal of Political Science* 15:165–86.

Mosley, Paul. 1978. "Images of the Floating Voter, or the Political Business Cycle Revisited." *Political Studies* 26:375–94.

Mosley, Paul. 1984. *The Making of Economic Policy: Theory and Evidence from Britain and the United States since 1945.* Brighton: Wheatsheaf Books.

Norpoth, Helmut. 1987. "Guns and Butter and Government Popularity in Britain." *American Political Science Review* 81:949–59.

Paldam, Martin. 1981. "A Preliminary Survey of the Theories and Findings of Vote and Popularity Functions." *European Journal of Political Research* 9:181–99.

Sanders, David, and Hugh Ward. 1989. "Analyzing Government Popularity: Classical Regression versus Box-Jenkins Methods." Paper presented to the ESRC Workshop on the Analysis of Social and Political Change, Nuffield College, Oxford.

Sanders, David, Hugh Ward, and David Marsh. 1987. "Government Popularity and the Falklands War: A Reassessment." *British Journal of Political Science* 17:281–313.

Whitely, Paul. 1984. "Inflation, Unemployment, and Government Popularity." *Electoral Studies* 3:25–46.

Part 3
Economic Perceptions and
Government Accountability

Explaining Explanations of Changing Economic Conditions

Stanley Feldman and Patricia Conley

It is by now fairly well accepted that the fortunes of incumbent politicians depend upon the performance of the economy. A number of studies of the popularity of political leaders and the success of incumbents at election time well document the consequences of recent changes in national economic conditions (for a review of many of these studies see Kiewiet and Rivers 1985a). What remains controversial is the interpretation of this relationship. One line of research has used time-series data to examine the effects of changes in macroeconomic conditions on popularity functions and election outcomes. Although the identification of the specific economic variables that have the most substantial effects on political outcomes often varies from study to study, the vast majority of these studies find robust relationships between economic and political variables. The problem is that the nature of the mechanism producing the observed relationship is unclear. Or, more correctly, various causal mechanisms are confounded in the time-series specification.

A second line of research proceeds by specifying individual-level models that are estimated (most frequently) with cross-sectional survey data. These studies have also found strong connections between changing economic conditions and political evaluations, but the survey data analyses have raised the issue of the mechanism that produces this relationship. Perceptions of change in economic conditions have been measured in at least two different ways in the individual-level studies. People have been asked about changes in their own financial well-being and they have been asked about (perceived) changes in national economic conditions. (Recently, there have also been questions concerning economic conditions among the group that the respondent most

The data used in this chapter were collected by the National Election Studies and made available by the Inter-University Consortium for Political and Social Research. This chapter is based in part upon work supported under a National Science Foundation graduate fellowship. Any opinions expressed are those of the authors and do not reflect the views of the National Science Foundation.

identifies with.) A consistent set of results from these studies is that the relationship between changes in personal economic well-being and political evaluations is small while the effect of changes in national economic conditions is sizable (see Kinder, Adams, and Gronke 1989 for a recent demonstration).

These results from survey studies have been interpreted both as support for a sociotropic hypothesis—people evaluate politicians based on their apparent success in managing the national economy—and as lack of support for an economic self-interest hypothesis—people evaluate politicians based on perceived changes in their own financial well-being. This is, of course, consistent with the time-series results, but so would be stronger evidence of personal self-interest effects.

These conclusions concerning sociotropic and self-interest effects have been dealt with in two very different ways. One group of researchers has attempted to understand why the effects of financial well-being are small. One explanation argues that people are selective in their attribution of blame for changing financial well-being, with incumbent members of the majority party most likely to be held responsible (Hibbing and Alford 1981). A second explanation also deals with attributions of responsibility but in a more general sense. According to Kinder and Kiewiet (1979; 1981), Feldman (1982; 1985), and Kinder and Mebane (1983), Americans tend to see themselves as responsible for their own financial conditions and therefore do not connect changes in their own fortunes with the performance of incumbent politicians. Among those people who do make a connection between their financial well-being and the broader political and economic environment there is a strong relationship between changes in well-being and political evaluations. More generally, these results from studies of economic conditions are often seen as a piece of the general pattern of a lack of self-interest effects in political evaluations (see Feldman 1985 for a more detailed discussion of this).

A second approach to the survey results has been to argue that they are wrong. Using a simple model to distinguish between overall changes in personal financial well-being and that part of the movement of personal conditions that is "politically relevant," Kramer (1983) has asserted that the models used in the survey research studies are misspecified or, alternatively, that the results are contaminated by substantial measurement error induced by the politically irrelevant component of financial well-being. Kramer argues that because of the confounding of the two components of changing personal well-being, cross-sectional survey analyses will not be very useful in understanding economic effects on political evaluations and vote choice.

In an effort to deal with Kramer's criticism of cross-sectional survey results both Markus (1988) and Rivers (n.d.) have utilized pooled cross-sectional data sets. Working with the same series of CPS/NES surveys, Markus and Rivers are able to take advantage of over-time variability in presidential vote and economic conditions as well as cross-sectional variation. The two analyses proceed in very different ways. Using a fairly straightforward specification, Markus uses two-stage least squares to deal with measurement error in the personal well-being indicator. His results yield an estimate of the effect of change in personal conditions on vote choice that is somewhat higher than is obtained in the cross-sectional studies and smaller than the estimated effect of changing national conditions. Rivers attacks the problem differently. Working explicitly from Kramer's distinction between politically relevant and irrelevant sources of variation in personal financial well-being, Rivers uses the pooled data set to specify a model that estimates the percentage of change in financial conditions that is politically relevant and, based on that, estimates the effect of this variability on vote choice. Rivers's findings indicate that the impact of change in personal well-being is now substantial—roughly eight times the estimate derived from the simple indicator of financial conditions and an effect only somewhat smaller than his estimate of the impact of changes in the national economy.[1]

Although there is general agreement that political factors are not seen by most people to be the major determinant of changes in their financial conditions, the way in which this is incorporated into alternative models varies considerably. On the one hand, Kramer (and Rivers) assumes that those people who see personal factors determining much of their recent financial fortunes can still discern some impact that political factors have on them. The result is an attempt to partition those changes in financial conditions into the politically relevant and irrelevant. On the other hand, the attribution argument is that most people do not make *any* connection between their financial conditions and political or economic forces. But those people who do will base their political evaluations at least in part on their financial well-being. In the first case, the politically relevant component of financial conditions is to be found as a fraction of all (or most) people's overall economic well-being. In the second case, that politically relevant variance is located only (or largely) within a small group of people. These two specifications have very different implications for the interpretation of the evidence from the cross-sectional studies.

The aim of this chapter is to consider, once again, people's perceptions of recent changes in their financial conditions and the explanations they offer to account for this. Using a recent National Election Studies survey that is especially rich in instrumentation regarding economic perceptions, we will

---

1. It should be noted that both Rivers and Markus consider only temporal variation in the state of the national economy; cross-sectional variation in perceptions of change in national conditions is ignored in both studies. This almost certainly leads to an underestimate of the effects of national conditions on vote choice.

examine the distribution of these explanations, the connection between these explanations and the perception of political influence on personal well-being, and the determinants of people's explanations. We will thus be concerned with the ways in which personal economic fluctuations are translated into political judgments.

The Nature of Explanations for Changing Economic Conditions

The data for this analysis were drawn from the 1984 NES pre- and postelection study. All of the questions used are from the preelection wave of the survey, based on interviews done in September and October from a probability sample of the adult population. As in past NES studies, respondents were asked whether their own financial situation had gotten better or worse over the past year and whether the national economy had improved or worsened. In addition, people were questioned in a similar way about the economic conditions of a group they felt most close to economically.[2] Following these three questions the respondents were asked why these changes had occurred. Up to three responses to each question were recorded. For the first time, 1984 respondents were also asked directly about the influence the economic policies of the federal government had on their own financial condition, as well as the effect it had on the financial conditions of the national economy and their designated closest group. The comparison of the explanations offered for economic change and the perceptions of government influence should provide a way of determining the extent to which people attribute any part of their economic fluctuations to political causes.

The first task is to impose some order on the numerous explanations that people offered for changes in personal, group, and national economic conditions. This was done by considering first, the nature of the activity that the explanation references and, second, the scope of the impact of that activity. As shown in figure 1, we distinguished between three broad types of activities: those having to do directly with politics, those dealing with the economic environment, and those related to private behavior. The impact of these activities can be broad (society-wide) or narrow (personal impact). The result of combining these two dimensions is a six-category framework for these reported explanations. We then examined the specific explanations respondents gave to produce major subcategories of responses within each of the six types of explanations (as shown in the cells of fig. 1).

The distribution of the responses for the three levels of economic condi-

---

2. See Kinder, Adams, and Gronke 1989 for a more complete analysis of the group economic questions on the 1984 NES.

Nature of Impact	Nature of Activity		
	Political	Economic	Private
Societal	1. Reagan / Reaganomics 2. Government spending 3. Debt / deficit 4. Government policies 5. Taxes 6. Politics 7. Trade / dollar	1. Inflation / costs 2. Unemployment / jobs 3. Business conditions 4. Business cycle 5. Interest rates / borrowing	1. Consumer / worker behavior 2. Social class / minorities 3. Nongovernmental sources of help 4. Social problems
Personal	1. Own government benefits 2. Own taxes 3. Politics relative to group	1. Own business 2. Own employment	1. Family income 2. Expenses, health costs, education 3. Personal outlook / behavior

Fig. 1. Types of explanations for changing economic conditions

tions (personal, group, and national) is shown in table 1. Each entry indicates the percentage of respondents who made at least one comment in that category when asked to explain changes in their own, their identified group's, or the nation's economic well-being. Total percentages for each of the six major categories are also noted. (Since multiple responses were recorded the percentages in each column total to more than 100 percent.) The explanations offered for personal conditions are similar to those found in previous studies (Feldman 1982; Kinder and Mebane 1983). There are few explicit references to political actions and even fewer direct references to the president or his policies. The largest single type of explanation within the political-societal category is references to taxes. Not only did people fail to explain changes in their economic conditions in broad political terms, but there were also few references to the personal impact of government benefits or tax liabilities. On the other hand, slightly over a third of the respondents did make reference to general economic conditions in explaining their personal fortunes. The majority of these explanations related to inflation. Although it is not clear that the open-ended questions used in previous studies have elicited exactly the same information, it does appear as if the proportion of people giving a political or economic explanation for recent changes in their economic well-being is higher in 1984 than in past election years for which we have data. For example, in 1972 a similar coding of open-ended responses produced an estimate of 34.8 percent of respondents giving a political or economic explanation; the corresponding estimate for 1984 is 45.5 percent. If this difference is not the result of inconsistencies in the questions and coding or sampling error, it suggests that the economic problems experienced by the United States in the early 1980s and/or the policies or rhetoric of the Reagan administration may have increased the extent to which people relate changes in their own financial conditions to politics and the economy.

The distributions of explanations for group and national economic conditions are very different from the responses to the personal questions and very similar to each other. As Kinder and Mebane (1983) have noted, people's explanations for changes in the national economy often are little more than

TABLE 1.   Distribution of Explanations for Change in Personal, Group, and National Economic Conditions (percentages)

	Personal		Group		National	
Government-societal		11.8		30.6		39.4
Reagan	2.3		2.6		10.6	
Spending	3.4		20.8		11.1	
Debt/deficit	0.1		0.5		5.7	
Policies	1.1		3.4		9.6	
Taxes	5.5		4.4		7.1	
Politics	0.1		0.2		2.2	
Trade/dollar	0.3		0.2		1.9	
Government-personal		7.0		5.6		1.3
Own benefits	6.2		0.8		0.2	
Own taxes	0.3		2.4		0.4	
Politics: group	0.4		2.5		0.7	
Economic-societal		37.3		64.2		70.8
Inflation	22.0		20.1		22.7	
Jobs	5.1		16.2		35.3	
Business conditions	4.5		15.3		13.1	
Business cycle	10.9		24.3		24.1	
Interest rates	5.4		6.5		17.2	
Economic-personal		32.7		1.0		0.8
Own business	7.1		0.4		0.2	
Own job	26.1		0.6		0.7	
Private-societal		3.7		11.3		10.7
Consumer behavior	2.7		3.7		7.9	
Class/minorities	0.6		5.5		1.6	
Non-government help	0.1		0.5		0.0	
Social problems	0.4		1.7		1.4	
Private-personal		54.3		4.3		2.0
Income	39.1		3.3		1.4	
Expenses	19.9		0.7		0.4	
Behavior/outlook	6.3		0.4		0.3	

restatements of the fact that the economy has gotten better or worse. Thus, in 1984, 70 percent of the sample "explained" changes in the national economy by saying that inflation was better, unemployment was better or worse, or the business climate was improved. Almost 40 percent made some reference to politics, noting various aspects of the president's policies, government spending, taxes, and the deficit. It is perhaps surprising that so many respondents made no reference at all to government activity in explaining why the economy was better or worse. This may simply be a result of people's tendency to explain why things are better or worse by describing how they are better or worse. Or, more substantively, it may indicate that many people do not see the government to be a major cause of economic fluctuations. We will return to this question shortly. It is also worth noting that the distribution of explanations for group economic conditions shows that the tendency to personalize changes in one's own financial situation does not extend to explanations of group financial conditions. Respondents are almost as likely to cite political or macroeconomic explanations for changing conditions of their identified group, as they are for the national economy. This may be a reason why perceptions of group economic conditions are more closely related to political evaluations (directly or indirectly) than are personal conditions (see Kinder, Adams, and Gronke 1989).

It is still not entirely clear what to make of these responses to the requests for explanations. The few political explanations offered for changes in personal financial conditions could mean that most people see *no* connection between their own financial well-being and the government or that other factors are *more important* than politics. As Kiewiet and Rivers (1985b, 219) observe:

> do voters, having experienced a stream of economic outcomes, attempt to discriminate between that part of it which is properly attributable to the actions of the incumbent policymakers and that part of it which is not? Or do they simply take this stream of outcomes at face value and evaluate the incumbents more or less favorably on the basis of it? Strict notions of voter rationality would certainly suggest that they would attempt to differentiate between income change which is "government-induced" and that which is not; after all, why should an individual choose between competing candidates on the basis of things that neither could possibly control? On the other hand, this task may well place large information costs and unreasonable demands on the inferential powers of the typical voter.

It may be that respondents are telling us the most important determinants of their financial conditions at the time; they may still be able to ascertain whether the activities of the incumbent administration helped or hurt them.

Some evidence on this point may be obtained from a second set of three questions that were included in the 1984 NES. The questions were worded as follows: "Would you say that the economic policies of the federal government have made (you/group/nation's economy) better off, worse off, or haven't they made much of a difference either way?" Respondents who answered better or worse off were then asked whether that was much better (worse) or somewhat better (worse). As opposed to the open-ended explanations questions, this set of questions does not require that the effects of federal government policy be most important or even very important determinants of financial conditions. Respondents were only asked if there was any effect for the better or worse. It is therefore entirely possible that many of those who explain their personal financial situations in nonpolitical or noneconomic terms may still respond that the government did have some effect.

The frequency distributions for these three questions are shown in the bottom half of table 2. For comparison, the distributions for the simple retrospective evaluations are given in the top half of the table. Looking first at the simple evaluations, we see a pattern that for the most part conforms to expectations. By a fairly wide margin (43 percent to 28 percent) more people reported that their financial condition improved rather than worsened. By a similar margin (43 percent to 24 percent) people saw the national economy as having improved. The odd result is for assessments of the financial condition of the group people most identify with. Here, by an equally large margin (44 percent to 21 percent), respondents reported that the financial condition of the groups got worse. It is not obvious why this is the case. Perhaps disaggregating the groups would shed some light. In any case, this one result seems somewhat anomalous.

TABLE 2. Perceptions of Personal, Group, and National
Economic Conditions (percentages)

	Personal	Group	National
Change in Economic Conditions over Past Year			
Much better	11.0	3.2	7.7
Somewhat better	32.5	17.6	35.0
Same	28.7	35.0	33.6
Somewhat worse	17.5	26.5	15.4
Much worse	10.3	17.6	8.4
Effect of Government Economic Policies on Economic Conditions			
Much better	3.3	1.9	4.8
Somewhat better	15.0	16.6	31.7
No difference	58.9	42.4	41.2
Somewhat worse	15.0	24.2	14.8
Much worse	7.7	14.8	7.6

The first thing to note about the responses to the government influence questions is the high proportion of people who reported that the government had no effect either way on economic conditions. This tendency is most pronounced for the question on personal conditions. Here, barely 40 percent say that the economic policies of the federal government had any effect on their financial situations. For the group and national conditions almost 60 percent report some effect of the federal government. In the case of the national economy, those people who did report some effect of the federal government said that, on average, its policies helped the economy. The reverse is true for the group and personal questions. This is perhaps not surprising for the group question since the respondents seem to believe that group economic conditions worsened, but it runs counter to the general perception of improvement in personal economic conditions. Not only did a majority of people feel that the government had no effect on their financial situation, but of those who perceived some impact, a majority felt that it was detrimental. Yet, by generally accepted notions of economic voting, the state of the economy in 1984 was strongly to the advantage of Reagan (see, for example, Kiewiet and Rivers 1985a). If people were, in fact, voting on the basis of changes in their own financial conditions attributed to government policy, responses to this question suggest that Reagan should have suffered, not gained.

An important issue for establishing the validity of these questions is whether the responses to the direct question on personal impact of government policies are in accord with the explanations respondents gave for their financial conditions. The simple answer is yes. Looking at those respondents who reported some change in their financial situations, 70 percent of those who gave a political explanation also said the federal government had some effect. Among those who reported a macroeconomic explanation (but not a political one), 55 percent answered that the government had some effect. Among all others, only 33 percent said that the economic policies of the federal government had any effect on their financial situation. Moreover, among the last group, it made virtually no difference whether their explanation was that their level of government benefits or taxes changed, or that their business was doing better or worse, or that their expenses had gone up or down; without some explicitly political or macroeconomic explanation, few people saw any effect of government policies on them personally. It is not just that the government is not a major contributor to personal financial conditions; for many people it has no effect at all.

Government Responsibility and Political Evaluations

Do these attributions of responsibility make any difference in the extent to which people relate changes in their economic situations to evaluations of incumbent politicians? Prior research suggests it makes a great deal of difference (Feldman 1982; Kinder and Mebane 1983; Abramowitz, Lanoue, and Ramesh 1988). It is, however, important to reexamine that issue with these questions in order to provide a better sense of just how widespread the connection between personal economics and political evaluations is. Shown in table 3 are OLS estimates for a simple model predicting approval ratings of Ronald Reagan. The model includes retrospective evaluations of personal and national economic conditions. To complete the specification of the model, party identification, ideology, positions on social, economic, and international issues, race, sex, income, and education are also included. All of the variables are scaled from 0 to 1 except for income (thousands of dollars) and education (years). For example, the national economic conditions variable is scored 0, 0.25, 0.50, 0.75, or 1.0. The model was estimated separately for those people who gave a political explanation for changes in their personal economic conditions, those who gave a macroeconomic explanation, and those who gave some sort of personal explanation. Since party identification, at least, has been shown to be responsive to short-term forces, it is likely that this specification underestimates the impact of the economic variables on Reagan evaluations, although it is not clear that this bias is more or less pronounced for either one of the economic variables.

The estimates from this model reinforce earlier demonstrations that explanations of personal well-being do matter. Among those who gave a political explanation, change in personal economic conditions is a strong predictor of Reagan evaluations and the size of the coefficient compares favorably with the effect of national economic conditions. The effect of personal economic conditions is somewhat smaller but still pronounced for those who gave an economic explanation; it almost completely disappears for those people who provided a personal explanation for changes in their financial well-being. The difference in the size of the coefficient for personal conditions between the first two groups and the personal explanation group is statistically significant at well beyond $p = .01$.[3]

A similar result is obtained using the direct question about the impact of government economic policies on financial conditions. Separating those people who said the government had no effect from those who attributed some effect to the government and reestimating the same model for these two groups yields an estimate of the impact of personal conditions of .06 for the former and .21 for the latter group (the difference in coefficients is again significant at beyond $p = .01$). It therefore seems to matter little which question is used to assess government responsibility. In either case, the con-

---

3. We have also found that the relationship between responses to the personal conditions question and the national conditions question is much stronger among those who give political or economic explanations than for those who give personal explanations. However, the causal direction of this relationship is unclear.

TABLE 3. Effects of Economic Assessments on Reagan Approval by Explanation for Change in Financial Well-Being

	Political		Economic		Personal	
	b	SE	*b*	SE	*b*	SE
Personal conditions	.26	.07	.20	.04	.05	.03
National conditions	.30	.08	.29	.05	.38	.04
Party id (Republican)	.34	.07	.45	.04	.38	.03
Ideology (conservative)	.06	.07	.02	.04	.08	.03
Social issues	.08	.10	.18	.05	.19	.04
Domestic issues	.38	.11	.18	.07	.11	.05
International issues	.34	.10	.31	.06	.38	.05
Race (nonwhite)	−.04	.05	−.13	.04	−.12	.03
Sex (female)	.05	.04	.04	.02	.01	.02
Income	−.004	.011	−.005	.005	.009	.005
Education	.012	.007	.002	.004	−.006	.003
R^2	.63		.58		.49	
SE	.26		.26		.28	
N	224		654		1,103	

Note: Entries are unstandardized OLS regression coefficients. All variables are coded on a 0–1 interval except for education (years) and income ($1,000s).

nection between personal economic conditions and Reagan evaluations is substantial when people perceive an effect of the government and almost nonexistent when they do not. As shown before, at least 60 percent of the U.S. public seems to deny any impact of government policies on their financial situations.

Explanations for National Economic Conditions

What about the consequences of the explanations respondents give for changes in the national economy? Do these affect the connection between assessments of the nation's economy and political evaluations in the same manner just displayed for personal well-being? First, it is worth noting that the relationship between explanations for national conditions and the closed-ended question on the effect of the federal government is not as large as the comparable relationship for personal conditions. Among those who gave explicitly political explanations for changing economic conditions (40 percent of the sample), 73 percent reported that the government had some effect on the nation's economy. Among those who did not give a political explanation, the figure is 56 percent. This difference is sizable and in the right direction, but it is not as sharp as the relationship between the personal economic explanations and the perceived impact of the government on financial conditions.

To determine if the perception of government influence on the economy moderates the effect of national economic conditions on Reagan evaluations, the same model was estimated separately for those who gave a political explanation for changes in the national economy and those who did not. The estimated coefficients for the two groups were virtually identical. Specifically, the effect of perceptions of the national economy on Reagan evaluations was no larger for those who gave a political account than for those who did not. As before, the closed-ended question on the impact of government policies on the national economy can be used to divide the sample into those who reported some effect of the government and those who did not. Reestimating the model for these two groups of respondents produces a difference in the effect of national conditions on Reagan evaluations. For those who reported an influence of the government the coefficient was .39; for those who did not it was .27. This difference is clearly in the expected direction and is significant at the .01 level.

These results for the impact of perceptions of the nation's economy on Reagan evaluations are at odds with the results for personal economic conditions. In the latter case, the estimated effect of financial conditions on evaluations of Reagan depended greatly on people's assessments of the determinants of changes in their financial situations. For those people who saw only personal factors affecting their well-being, no connection appeared between financial conditions and political evaluations. For perceptions of national economic conditions, the role of attributions is not nearly so pronounced. Even among people who admit to seeing no influence of government policy on economic conditions there is a strong relationship between assessments of the national economy and evaluations of Reagan. These results are consistent with a similar analysis by Kinder and Mebane (1983) that showed some effect of explanations of the national economy on the political consequences of perceptions of the state of the economy but one substantially weaker than the impact of explanations of personal conditions. These discrepant results may indicate that most of the public has a poor understanding of the dynamics of macroeconomic change (and asking them about it provides little useful information) or that people will reward or punish incumbent politicians for fluctuations in the national economy even when these politicians are not held directly responsible for the economy.

Accounting for Explanations of Personal Financial Conditions

Having found that a majority of the public not only fails to explain their financial condition in political or macroeconomic terms but also claims to see no influence of the government on their economic situation, it is still possible that those who do perceive some broader influence do so in response to the consequences of public policies. Some people may be more directly affected by the actions of the government and the distribution of explanations may reflect that. If so, the tighter connection between economic conditions and political evaluations found for those people who gave political or economic explanations would, in fact, reflect their own economic circumstances rather than their perceptions of national economic conditions.

What factors should predict the explanations people give for their financial well-being? Research in economics (Katona 1975) and attribution theory (Fiske and Taylor 1982) suggests that those people who feel better off economically should be more likely to take credit themselves, while those who feel worse off should make more external attributions. Such is the case here. Among those who said their financial condition was the same or better, 62 percent offered a personal explanation, 30 percent gave an economic explanation, and 8 percent specified a political cause. In contrast, among those who reported their financial condition to be worse, 41 percent gave a personal explanation, 40 percent offered an economic explanation, and 19 percent said it had to do with politics. By a wide margin, those who are worse off were more likely to see external forces as responsible. This result provides an explanation for the earlier finding that, in 1984, more people reported that the actions of the federal government hurt their financial well-being rather than helped. It is simply that more people who feel worse off blame the government than those who are better off give it credit. As a result, even in a year like 1984, the government comes off poorly in assessments of its impact on personal well-being.

It is still possible that variations in these explanations are related to the actual effect politics had on individual finances. Although the 1984 NES is not ideal for identifying groups of people that are differentially affected by government economic policy, it is possible to look for some differences in explanations among people in various locations in the social structure, ones that would reflect the operation of individual self-interest. On the other hand, it may be that these explanations primarily reflect differences in political attitudes or variations in information about politics and the economy. To assess this, table 4 shows a series of bivariate relationships between economic, social, and political variables and explanations for personal economic conditions. Given the large difference in explanations between those who feel worse off financially and all others, the relationships are shown separately for these two groups of respondents.

Shown first in the table are the relationships of explanations with job status and occupation. If political and economic explanations for changing financial conditions are a response to the felt impact of politics and the economy, we should best observe that for various aspects of job experience. By and large, explanations are unrelated to job status and occupation. For

TABLE 4. Percentage Breakdown of Explanations for Change in Financial Well-Being

	Worse-Off Financially				Better/Same Financially			
	Political	Economic	Personal	N	Political	Economic	Personal	N
Job status								
Unemployed	14.5	30.4	55.1	69	7.3	19.5	73.2	41
Laid off	20.0	40.0	40.0	20	7.7	23.1	69.2	13
Working	17.4	43.8	38.7	333	8.1	31.1	60.8	1,133
Other	21.9	37.5	40.6	192	8.7	27.5	63.8	403
Occupation								
White collar	14.6	41.1	44.4	151	9.5	34.3	56.2	621
Farmers	17.2	41.4	41.4	29	15.6	24.7	59.7	77
Construction	14.6	58.3	27.1	48	5.9	35.3	58.8	102
Service	21.3	38.7	40.0	150	6.8	24.1	69.2	237
Protective	25.0	25.0	50.0	8	0.0	22.7	77.3	44
Blue collar-craft	21.5	46.2	32.3	65	8.8	32.4	58.8	148
Blue collar-manual	19.8	36.4	43.8	121	7.2	26.5	66.3	291
Not working	22.9	17.1	60.0	35	10.6	16.7	72.7	66
Labor union								
Nonmember	19.4	38.2	42.4	490	8.9	29.7	61.4	1,253
Member	16.0	48.0	36.0	125	6.4	29.7	63.8	343
Sex								
Male	21.2	43.3	35.5	231	10.5	33.8	55.7	742
Female	17.2	38.3	44.5	384	6.6	26.1	67.3	854
Race								
White	17.7	40.4	42.0	498	8.7	30.9	60.4	1,426
Nonwhite	23.1	39.3	37.6	117	5.9	19.4	74.7	170
Age								
17–29	23.1	30.0	46.9	130	6.8	20.5	72.6	409
30–39	14.9	41.8	43.3	141	8.2	32.8	59.0	402
40–49	16.3	45.7	38.0	92	8.4	39.6	52.0	227

50–64	18.0	39.1	42.9	133	10.4	33.6	56.0	268
65+	18.2	46.4	35.5	110	8.9	27.9	63.2	280
Income								
<$7,000	17.8	37.9	44.4	169	7.5	21.3	71.3	240
$7,000–12,000	22.3	37.5	40.2	112	7.0	21.9	71.1	201
$12,000–20,000	23.4	40.2	36.4	107	8.3	23.7	68.0	266
$20,000–30,000	19.8	38.7	41.4	111	8.0	33.9	58.0	336
$30,000–50,000	11.9	48.8	39.3	84	8.7	37.0	54.2	378
>$50,000	9.4	43.8	46.9	32	11.4	35.4	53.1	175
Education								
Less than h.s.	18.0	38.8	43.2	206	7.9	25.1	67.0	342
High school	19.4	42.4	38.2	217	7.3	28.3	64.4	551
Some college	17.9	39.3	42.7	117	7.9	34.0	58.1	382
College degree	15.8	39.5	44.7	38	8.3	32.0	59.8	169
Graduate work	22.9	37.1	40.0	35	14.4	32.2	53.4	146
Media attention								
Lowest fifth	15.0	35.3	49.7	153	6.4	24.1	69.6	299
	19.3	43.7	37.0	119	6.2	28.3	65.0	321
	19.0	45.5	35.5	121	8.7	28.8	62.5	323
	14.7	39.2	46.1	102	8.6	32.2	59.2	302
Highest fifth	25.8	38.3	35.8	120	11.7	34.4	53.9	349
Party identification								
Strong Democrat	21.9	45.0	33.1	151	7.7	25.3	67.0	221
Weak Democrat	17.2	40.4	42.4	151	6.9	23.9	69.2	289
Lean ng Democrat	22.2	43.3	34.4	90	4.8	27.9	67.3	147
Independent	19.3	33.7	47.0	83	7.7	27.3	65.1	209
Leaning Republican	17.6	41.2	41.2	51	8.1	34.5	57.4	223
Weak Republican	14.5	40.0	45.5	55	8.6	32.7	58.7	269
Strong Republican	8.8	23.5	67.6	34	13.9	36.1	50.0	238

(continued)

TABLE 4—*Continued*

	Worse-Off Financially				Better/Same Financially			
	Political	Economic	Personal	N	Political	Economic	Personal	N
Ideology								
Strong liberal	30.8	44.2	25.0	52	7.1	26.8	66.1	112
Liberal	16.3	45.0	38.8	80	5.4	24.0	70.7	167
Weak liberal	20.5	39.7	39.7	78	6.4	27.5	66.1	171
Moderate	19.0	35.9	45.1	142	5.7	22.4	71.9	317
Weak conservative	18.2	38.2	43.6	110	10.1	36.4	53.4	335
Conservative	15.6	43.3	41.1	90	10.1	32.5	57.4	227
Strong conservative	14.3	39.7	46.0	63	12.0	34.1	53.9	217
Individualism								
Lowest fifth	21.9	44.4	33.7	187	9.8	25.1	65.1	275
	18.1	41.8	40.1	177	6.2	26.9	66.9	338
	17.4	41.2	41.3	42	8.7	26.0	65.3	150
	16.9	33.1	50.0	118	8.5	31.3	60.2	402
Highest fifth	14.3	35.2	50.5	91	9.0	31.6	59.4	431

example, the unemployed are somewhat more likely than others to give a personal explanation for either improving or worsening financial conditions. This is consistent with Schlozman and Verba's (1979) findings that the unemployed do not see the government to be a cause of their difficulties. There is also little variation in explanations by occupation. The one major exception is the group of construction-related occupations. When they feel themselves to be worse off they are significantly more likely to attribute this to the economy. This does make sense given the fluctuations in the construction industry due to the state of the economy. However, when conditions improve for the construction workers, they are as likely as others to attribute it to personal factors. On the other hand, farmers, who we thought would be more likely to give external explanations for changes in their financial conditions, do not. There is a slight tendency for them to cite the government as a determinant of their well-being (especially when they are better off) but, overall, farmers do not seem to have been highly politicized by the debates over the plight of the farmers and the government's role in dealing with this problem.

We also find that neither labor union membership nor race is highly related to these explanations. Blacks are somewhat more likely to claim credit for themselves when their financial conditions improve—perhaps a reasonable response to the expressed policies of the Reagan administration. Membership in labor unions in this country seems not to politicize workers. One interesting difference that does emerge is between men and women. Regardless of change in financial conditions, women were more likely to give personal explanations than men. This result held up when we controlled for differences in job status between men and women. This result is consistent with social psychological findings that women are more likely than men to make internal attributions for the outcomes of male-oriented tasks. Age, income, and education appear to be somewhat related to the explanations, although not very strongly or consistently. Older people are more likely to give an external explanation when their financial condition deteriorates; it is not clear whether this is due to the impact of social security and Medicare on older people or just years of experience. Both education and income are inversely related to the likelihood of giving a personal explanation, but only when conditions improve. Again, this could be the result of the greater impact of politics and economic conditions on the financial situations of those with higher income and occupational status, or it may just reflect increased attention to external influences.

The possibility that the differences in proportion of political and economic explanations by income and education are due to higher levels of information or attention draws support from the relationship between media attention and explanations. More clearly, for those whose financial conditions improved, increased attention to the media is significantly related to giving more political and economic explanations. It thus appears as if the likelihood of giving a political or economic explanation for changing financial conditions is more a function of attention to the media than actual work and economic experiences. People are more likely to learn that the government has had an impact on their well-being from the media than from firsthand experience.

The explanations people offer are not just a function of learning or job experience; they are also strongly related to party identification. The relationship is interesting, not only for what it says about the explanations, but also as an illustration of the power of partisanship. Among those whose financial condition worsened, Democrats are much more likely than Republicans to blame it on the government. For those who are better off, the difference between Democrats and Republicans is just the reverse. These results make perfect sense from a partisan rationalization perspective: Democrats are quite willing to blame the (Republican) government directly or indirectly (through economic conditions) when their conditions deteriorate but are reluctant to give Reagan and the Republicans credit when things improve. Republicans, on the other hand, are unwilling to blame their party's leaders when conditions worsen but are somewhat more likely to assign them credit. These explanations are thus, in large part, political. It would be difficult to explain this relationship between party identification and explanations for change in financial well-being on the basis of actual differences in the impact of politics and the economy on partisan groups. Rather, partisanship provides one basis for assigning responsibility for financial conditions. This does not mean that these explanations are just a reflection of partisanship, but again we find evidence that variations in these explanations have more to do with political attitudes and exposure to information than with any actual impact of government policies.

To round out the discussion of table 4 we note that the effects of ideological identification and individualism resemble the pattern for party identification. The impact of ideology is very similar to partisanship in a less pronounced form. Individualism has a substantial effect, in the expected direction, for those who report being worse off: those most individualistic are most likely to give a personal explanation. Just the opposite is observed for those better off, but the relationship here is much weaker. It seems that both ideology and this measure of individualism (to a lesser extent) are contaminated by the powerful effect of party identification.

In order to assess the joint impact of these bivariate relationships a probit model was estimated. The dependent variable was a simple distinction between political or economic versus personal explanations. The independent variables were the set of variables examined previously in table 4. In addition, an interaction term between party identification and change in financial condition was constructed to specify the nature of the effect of partisanship on the likelihood of giving a personal explanation. The results of the analysis are shown in table 5 (the dependent variable is coded 0 for political and economic explanations and 1 for personal). The multivariate results closely mirror the bivariate relationships reported in table 4. Simply being worse off has a substantial effect on the likelihood of giving an external explanation; the controls do not diminish this effect. Nor do the multivariate estimates diminish the impact of partisanship; the political reactions of Democrats and Republicans remain highly significant. Otherwise, the conclusions drawn from the bivariate analyses remain intact. Job status and occupation have virtually no effect on the likelihood of giving a political or economic explanation. The effect of sex remains significant as does the effect of media attention. In addition, age and income have small but significant coefficients. Overall, the model does only passably well in accounting for the distinction in the two types of explanations; 63 percent of the cases are correctly predicted while 55 percent would be correctly predicted by a null model.

Conclusions

As Markus (1988) has shown, it can make a difference politically whether people base their evaluations of presidents on perceived changes in their own

TABLE 5.   Probit Estimates for Explanations of Change in Financial Well-Being

	b	SE	Beta/SE
Worse-off	−.91	.10	−8.85
Party id (Republican)	−.33	.10	−3.31
Party id × worse-off	.79	.20	3.39
Ideology (conservative)	−.16	.10	−1.58
Individualism	.09	.16	0.55
Media attention	−.33	.15	−2.26
Race (nonwhite)	.03	.09	0.28
Sex (female)	.25	.06	4.16
Income	−.05	.02	−2.93
Age	−.005	.002	−2.55
Unemployed	.11	.14	0.74
Working	−.08	.09	−0.86
Union member	.09	.07	1.19
White collar	−.01	.09	−0.16
Farmer	−.02	.15	−0.13
Construction	−.18	.13	−1.44
Service	−.04	.09	−0.38
Blue-collar craft	.00	.11	0.02
Not working	.24	.17	1.42
N	2,203		
Percent predicted correctly	63		
Rank order correlation	.24		

financial conditions or whether they respond to objective changes in the national economy. Both Rivers (n.d.) and Markus (1988) show that by pooling cross-sectional survey data, estimates of the total effect of macroeconomic fluctuations on presidential vote choice can be obtained that coincide nicely with estimates from time-series studies. But Rivers estimates a coefficient for the effect of changes in personal-level financial conditions that is much larger than simple cross-sectional studies or Markus's pooled cross-sectional study. Rivers's model also shows that roughly half of the variance in the personal finances question is due to "politically irrelevant" factors. Alternatively, almost 50 percent of the variance in this question is estimated to be due to changes in personal financial conditions brought about by government actions. Whether or not this fraction of financial situations is actually a consequence of politics, it is clear that not many people see their own conditions to be a function of the government. Considering the analysis in this and earlier studies, it appears that between 60 percent and 70 percent of the U.S. public perceives little or no connection between recent changes in their financial conditions and politics or the economy.

These results have major implications for constructing models of the relationship between perceived economic conditions and political evaluations. Although there seems to be fairly widespread agreement that only a portion of the variance in personal well-being can be linked to the government or macroeconomic activity, the specification of that key variance is disputed. Kramer's model assumes that a proportion—constant across people—of the variance in reported personal well-being is due to government economic policy. This is the specification in Rivers's model as well. The analysis in this chapter strongly suggests that this is not the correct way to identify the politically relevant portion of personal well-being. Whether or not people do in fact make such complex calculations, it is clear that many people do not attribute any significant part of recent changes in their personal well-being to the government. Thus, if we are to identify adequately the politically relevant component of personal well-being, it will require a model that recognizes that the proportion of personal well-being that is linked to societal factors differs enormously across people.

REFERENCES

Abramowitz, Alan I., David J. Lanoue, and Subha Ramesh. 1988. "Economic Conditions, Causal Attributions, and Political Evaluations in the 1984 Presidential Election." *Journal of Politics* 50:848–63.
Feldman, Stanley. 1982. "Economic Self-Interest and Political Behavior." *American Journal of Political Science* 26:446–66.

Feldman, Stanley, 1985. "Economic Self-Interest and the Vote: Evidence and Meaning." In *Economic Conditions and Electoral Outcomes,* ed. Heinz Eulau and Michael Lewis-Beck. New York: Agathon Press.

Fiske, Susan T., and Shelley E. Taylor. 1984. *Social Cognition.* Reading, MA: Addison-Wesley.

Hibbing, John R., and John R. Alford. 1981. "The Electoral Impact of Economic Conditions: Who Is Held Responsible?" *American Journal of Political Science* 25:423–39.

Katona, George. 1975. *Psychological Economics.* New York: Elsevier.

Kiewiet, D. Roderick, and Douglas Rivers. 1985a. "The Economic Basis of Reagan's Appeal." In *The New Direction in American Politics,* ed. John E. Chubb and Paul E. Peterson. Washington, DC: Brookings Institution.

Kiewiet, D. Roderick, and Douglas Rivers. 1985b. "A Retrospective on Retrospective Voting." In *Economic Conditions and Electoral Outcomes,* ed. Heinz Eulau and Michael Lewis-Beck. New York: Agathon Press.

Kinder, Donald R., Gordon S. Adams, and Paul W. Gronke. 1989. "Economics and Politics in the 1984 American Presidential Election." *American Journal of Political Science* 33:491–515.

Kinder, Donald R., and D. Roderick Kiewiet. 1979. "Economic Grievances and Political Behavior." *Amercan Journal of Political Science* 23:495–527.

Kinder, Donald R., and D. Roderick Kiewiet. 1981. "Sociotropic Politics: The American Case." *British Journal of Political Science* 11:129–62.

Kinder, Donald R., and Walter R. Mebane. 1983. "Politics and Economics in Everyday Life." In *The Political Process and Economic Change,* ed. Kristen Monroe. New York: Agathon Press.

Kramer, Gerald. 1983. "The Ecological Fallacy Revisited: Aggregate- versus Individual-Level Findings on Economics and Elections and Sociotropic Voting." *American Political Science Review* 77:92–111.

Markus, Gregory B. 1988. "The Impact of Personal and National Economic Conditions on the Presidential Vote: A Pooled Cross-Sectional Analysis." *American Journal of Political Science* 32:137–54.

Rivers, Douglas. N.d. "Macroeconomics and Macropolitics: A Solution to the Kramer Problem." *American Political Science Review.* In press.

Schlozman, Kay L., and Sidney Verba. 1979. *Injury to Insult.* Cambridge, MA: Harvard University Press.

Explaining Aggregate Evaluations
of Economic Performance

Henry W. Chappell, Jr., and William R. Keech

Many studies have developed models explaining aggregate approval ratings for presidents or governments on the basis of economic performance variables. Recent contributions have provided new insights, but answers to apparently simple questions, e.g., how increases in the unemployment rate affect approval ratings, remain elusive.

In this chapter we provide additional evidence on these matters for the case of the United States. Using a modeling framework previously set forth in Chappell and Keech 1985, we estimate political support functions using recent Gallup Poll approval ratings. Perhaps of greater interest, we also study an alternative data series for approval ratings. For about ten years the Louis Harris poll has regularly asked a question regarding respondent evaluations of the president's handling of the economy. This contrasts with the traditional Gallup question about overall job performance which has most often been used in political support function studies. The Harris question has obvious advantages for analysts interested in evaluations of economic performance, since it asks respondents to focus attention exclusively on economic issues. Although the available time-series is short, it is long enough to make an interesting statistical analysis.

Several questions related to the use of the Harris economic approval variable will be investigated. First, to what extent are economic and overall approval ratings related? Do honeymoons, trends, and political events affect economic evaluations as they do the overall performance ratings? What models of voter behavior are best able to explain the series of economic evaluations? Are there substantive differences in conclusions produced by models respectively explaining economic and overall performance of the president?

Preliminary Analysis

Our empirical work will model the paths of two approval ratings. The first rating is defined by survey responses to the Gallup poll question: "Do you approve or disapprove of the way that (the president) is handling his job as president?" We define the variable *GPOS* to be the fraction of respondents reporting approval as the answer to that question. Our second rating is based on the similar Harris poll question that focuses attention on the economy: "Do you approve or disapprove of the way that (the president) is handling the economy?" The variable *HPOS* is the fraction responding positively to this question. Our sample period includes the first quarter, 1977, to the second quarter, 1986, for *GPOS*, and the first quarter, 1977, to the third quarter, 1986, for *HPOS*. Each variable is measured as an average of polls within the relevant quarter.[1]

Figure 1 provides time plots for both series. Several results are apparent from the figure. First, the two series tend to move together. The correlation between the two series is + 0.95 in the Carter years and + 0.89 in the Reagan years. Although it is rare for one rating to move up when the other moves down, there are a few exceptions. For example, in the first quarter, 1980, economic approval ratings went down when the overall approval rating briefly increased (the latter possibly caused by early reactions to the seizure of the U.S. embassy in Iran and the Russian invasion of Afghanistan). Thus, the possibility remains that paths of the two series are determined somewhat differently.

A second finding is that economic approval ratings are usually lower than overall approval ratings. This occurs even though there are fewer undecideds for the economy-specific question. In other words, respondents are more likely to disapprove of economic performance than performance in general.

Third, we note that the difference between economic and overall approval ratings is more pronounced for Carter than for Reagan. On average, Carter's overall approval rating was 0.217 points above his economic approval rating, while the difference was only 0.044 for Reagan. These differences are striking; however, we do not pursue an explanation for this phenomenon in this chapter.[2]

Fourth, for the Reagan administration, there is a strong suggestion of a relation between approval ratings and the business cycle. His approval ratings ebbed as the economy headed into recession in 1982, increased as the recovery proceeded in 1983 and 1984, and leveled off as the economy stabilized in 1985 and 1986. The correlation between the unemployment rate and the economic approval rating during the Reagan years was − 0.95, strongly suggesting a relation between the economy and approval ratings. However, the analogous correlation for the Carter years was + 0.33, so simple explanations for the path of approval ratings are not apparent.

---

1. For *HPOS*, there were two quarters when no polls were taken. For that series, we have replaced those missing values with extrapolated values.

2. One possibility is that Reagan's microeconomic policies were viewed more favorably.

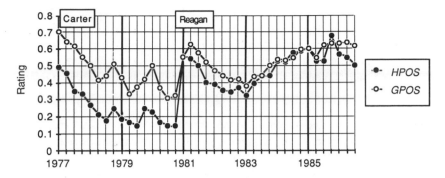

Fig. 1. Economic (*HPOS*) and overall (*GPOS*) approval ratings

Last, we note the possible presence of honeymoon and trend effects in both series, like those described by previous researchers. Both Carter and Reagan approval ratings fell over the early months of their administrations. Reagan's popularity rose in 1986 to levels comparable to those prevailing when he first took office, however.

The Specification of Political Support Functions

We have previously distinguished what we term "naive" and "sophisticated" measures of economic performance. Naive voting occurs when voters evaluate performance by looking at current and past outcomes, for example inflation and unemployment rates, and reward or punish incumbents according to values of these variables. Presumably, higher values of either of these variables would be punished. For naive voters, we measure performance for period t by N_t, which is defined as:

$$N_t = \gamma_1 U_t + \gamma_2 \dot{P},$$ (1)

where U_t and $\dot{P}_t$ are unemployment and inflation rates and γ_1 and γ_2 are positive constants. Higher values of N_t indicate lower levels of performance. Use of this measure, a generalization of the familiar "misery index," implicitly assumes that current incumbents are responsible for current outcomes, and it ignores any possible long- and short-run constraints which might relate U_t and $\dot{P}_t$. Voters using such a standard could be manipulated by cynical vote-maximizing politicians, as described by some political business cycle models (Nordhaus 1975).

Chappell and Keech (1985, 13) have described a more sophisticated standard of evaluation:

> In contrast . . . a sophisticated voter would have some sense of feasibility constraints in evaluating outcomes and would be concerned with future as well as current implications of present choices. He would reward incumbents for selecting desirable policies even when times are bad and punish them only for those undesirable outcomes for which they could reasonably be held responsible.

Thus a voter might reasonably reward *higher* unemployment if it was perceived as necessary to fight an inherited inflation. Many macroeconomic theories, in fact, do imply that sustained inflation can be reduced only at the expense of a temporary excess of unemployment over its natural rate. If this is the case, voters would be likely to support policies leading to unemployment in excess of the natural rate when inflation is high. Specifically, we suppose that desirable policies can be defined by the following feedback rule:

$$Z_t^* = d\dot{P}_{t-1} \tag{2}$$

where Z_t^* refers to the optimal value of Z_t, a measure of slackness in the economy, and d is a positive constant. In the following work, Z_t is computed as:

$$Z_t = U_t/UN_t - 1 \tag{3}$$

where UN_t is the natural or "nonaccelerating inflation" rate of unemployment. The feedback rule calls for more contractionary policies when the inflation rate is higher. Performance, S_t, is measured as the absolute value of the difference between actual and optimal policies:

$$S_t = |Z_t - Z_t^*| \tag{4}$$

$$= |U_t/UN_t - 1 - d\dot{P}_{t-1}| \tag{5}$$

Higher values of S_t indicate lower levels of performance according to the sophisticated voter standard.

   Having described sophisticated and naive standards of performance, we next consider the specification of political support functions in which these measures of performance are embedded. The political support functions that we use are variants of those we have described in Chappell and Keech (1985). In general, they take the following forms:

$$POS_t = \alpha_0 T_t^{*.5} + \alpha_1 T_t^{*.5}\bar{S}_t + X_t\beta_t + e_t \tag{6}$$

for the "sophisticated" voter model, or

$$POS_t = \delta_0 T_t^{*.5} + \delta_1 T_t^{*.5}\, \bar{N}_t + X_t\beta_t + e_t \tag{7}$$

for the "naive" voter model. In equations 6 and 7, $\bar{S}_t$ and $\bar{N}_t$ respectively refer to weighted averages of sophisticated and naive performance measures computed over the history of an administration, T_t^* is the number of quarters the current administration has been in office, and X_t is a vector of noneconomic variables (including dummy variables providing president-specific intercepts) that might affect approval ratings.

The weighted averages $\bar{S}_t$ and $\bar{N}_t$ are computed as follows:

$$\bar{S}_t = \frac{\displaystyle\sum_{k=0}^{31} |Z_{t-k} - d\dot{P}_{t-k-1}|\, D_{t,t-k}g^k}{\displaystyle\sum_{k=0}^{31} D_{t,t-k}g^k} \tag{8}$$

$$\bar{N}_t = \frac{\displaystyle\sum_{k=0}^{31} (\gamma_1\dot{P}_{t-k} + \gamma_2 U_{t-k})\, D_{t,t-k}g^k}{\displaystyle\sum_{k=0}^{31} D_{t,t-k}g^k} \tag{9}$$

where $D_{t,t-k} = 1$ if the administration in office in quarter t was also in office in quarter $t - k$, and is equal to 0 otherwise. Parameter g indicates the relative weighting of past periods' performance. If $g = 1$, all periods are weighted equally; as g approaches 0 the importance of current (as opposed to past) performance is greater.

For estimation purposes, it is convenient to rewrite equation 7 in the following form:

$$POS_t = \delta_0 T_t^{*.5} + \omega_1 T_t^{*.5}\bar{U}_t + \omega_2 T_t^{*.5}\bar{P}_t + X_t\beta_t + e_t \tag{7b}$$

where $\bar{U}_t$ and $\bar{P}_t$ again refer to the appropriate weighted averages and $\omega_1 = \gamma_1\delta_1$ and $\omega_2 = \gamma_2\delta_2$. The parameters γ_1, γ_2, δ_1, and δ_2 are not identified; thus ω_1 and ω_2 are estimated in our empirical analysis.

Our model has several distinguishing attributes. We have already noted the distinction between naive and sophisticated voting behavior, so the specification of performance by N_t or S_t is a major interest. A second key feature involves the weighting of economic performance by $T_t^{*.5}$ (i.e. $\sqrt{T_t^*}$). This weight increases with time in office, but at a decreasing rate. This weighting scheme is consistent with a Bayesian decision-making calculus, by which voters would attach more weight to average performance as the number of performance observations used in computing that average is increased. Note that $T^{*.5}$ also appears independently in the model so that trend effects will not be spuriously attributed to the economic performance measures. Other variables, including honeymoon indicators, the presidential dummies, and political phenomena are included in the X_t vector in equations 6 and 7. Our honeymoon effects are captured by a series of six dummy variables (Pk, $k = 1, \ldots, 6$) respectively indicating each of the first six quarters in office for a new administration. These dummies allow a flexible pattern for the honeymoon effect. Specific political events variables are discussed later.

Empirical Analysis

The equations to be estimated are given by equations 6 and 7, where the expressions provided in equations 8 and 9 are substituted for $\bar{N}_t$ and $\bar{S}_t$. In principle, all parameters of these equations, including d (which reflects degree of inflation aversion in the sophisticated voter model) and g (the memory, or weighting, parameter), could be estimated using nonlinear least squares. As a matter of practice, collinearity makes achieving convergence difficult—and when convergence is achieved parameter values may be implausible. We have therefore imposed plausible values for d and g and estimated remaining parameters by least squares (correcting for first-order serial correlation). For the case of g, the "memory" parameter, we alternately let $g = 1.0$ (indicating equal weighting of past periods) or $g = 0.8$ (indicating moderate discounting of past periods). For the inflation aversion parameter, d, we consider cases of strong inflation aversion ($d = .050$), moderate inflation aversion ($d = .025$), or weak inflation aversion ($d = .010$). To get a sense of what is implied by "strong inflation aversion," note that if $d = .05$, and the inflation rate is 10 percent, the desired policy rule would call for unemployment 50 percent above its natural rate. If the natural rate of unemployment were 6 percent, the rule implies that voters would consider 9 percent unemployment a tolerable short-run cost of fighting inflation. For each model, we report results only for the values of d and g that achieved the lowest sum of squared residuals (for the corrected error process) of the regression.

Quarterly data were employed for all variables. The key economic variables, unemployment and inflation rates, were obtained from the CITIBASE data tape. Both variables are expressed as percentages, the latter as an annualized percentage rate of change in the GNP deflator. The natural rate of unemployment was computed as the predicted value of a regression explaining unemployment as a cubic function of time over the first quarter, 1947, to the fourth quarter, 1986, sample period.[3]

---

3. The natural rate of unemployment for the fourth quarter, 1986, was constrained to take a value of 6.5. Unconstrained equations would have assigned rates that appear a bit too high (around 7.5), primarily because of the severity of the recession of the early 1980s.

Overall Performance and Economic Performance

Our first task is to compare how our models explain overall evaluations (*GPOS*) and economic evaluations (*HPOS*) over the period from 1977 to 1986. Table 1 provides estimates of various sophisticated and naive voter models for each of these variables.[4] The table provides several important findings. First, results for *GPOS* and *HPOS* are quite similar for the sophisticated voter model. The sophisticated performance measure has the hypothesized negative coefficient, which is significantly different from zero, and setting $d = .05$ (indicating strong inflation aversion) provides the best fit for the equations. Large honeymoon effects are indicated by coefficients for *P* 1, . . . , *P*6. The similarity of the *HPOS* and *GPOS* results appears to imply that responses regarding overall performance closely parallel those for economic responses. The naive model, however, yields somewhat different results for overall and economic evaluations. Unemployment has the hypothesized negative sign in the *GPOS* equation, but has a positive coefficient in the *HPOS* equation. Naive and sophisticated models are again comparable in terms of "goodness of fit"; however, the naive model does provide a lower sum of squared residuals for both *GPOS* and *HPOS* equations.

All equations are consistent in indicating strong inflation aversion, but there are a few puzzling results. For the naive voter models the perverse positive sign on the unemployment variable in some equations is bothersome. The sophisticated voter model can potentially explain why increases in unemployment would sometimes be rewarded, but the results from that model also present some questions. In particular, in regressions where d is not constrained to a range of plausible values (these runs are not reported here), it takes on unreasonably large values, implying extreme inflation aversion. This was also true of results reported in our earlier paper, but is all the more surprising given the fall in popularity that accompanied the Reagan recession. Two possible explanations can be suggested. The first involves collinearity problems. In the regressions reported here, the honeymoon variables *P*1, . . . , *P*6 have much larger coefficients than they did in our earlier paper, which employed a longer sample period. The drop in popularity in 1982 is largely, and perhaps inappropriately, attributed to huge honeymoon effects instead of poor economic performance. Further regressions (not reported) show that when the honeymoon terms are omitted from the model, strong inflation aversion is still indicated, so this explanation is not completely satisfactory. An alternative explanation is also possible. If voters believe that inflation is controllable, but that the unemployment rate is not (a belief consistent with some economic theories), then results indicating apparent extreme inflation aversion may be sensible. The d parameter appearing

---

4. Variable definitions are summarized in the appendix.

TABLE 1. Political Support Functions: Economic and Overall Evaluations (t-statistics in parentheses)

Variable	Sophisticated Voter Model		Naive Voter Model		Sophisticated Voter Model		Naive Voter Model	
	GPOS	HPOS	GPOS	HPOS	GPOS	HPOS	GPOS	HPOS
g (Memory)	1.000	1.000	0.800	1.000	1.000	1.000	0.800	1.000
d ($\dot{P}$ aversion)	0.050	0.050	0.200	0.300	0.050	0.050	0.000	−0.300
ρ (Autocorrelation)	0.300	0.400	0.154	0.050	0.000	−0.100	0.167	0.184
$T*.5$	0.110 (5.174)	0.110 (4.675)	0.154 (4.777)	0.050 (0.522)	0.138 (9.392)	0.163 (10.228)	0.167 (6.124)	0.184 (2.618)
$T*.5\,\bar{S}$	−0.224 (−4.710)	−0.196 (−3.465)			−0.248 (−8.517)	−0.254 (−8.168)		
$T*.5\,\bar{P}$			−0.014 (−6.464)	−0.012 (−1.961)			−0.014 (−7.940)	−0.019 (−4.355)
$T*.5\,\bar{U}$			−0.009 (−1.957)	0.010 (0.911)			−0.007 (−1.771)	0.001 (0.094)
Carter	0.338 (3.937)	0.090 (0.908)	0.459 (5.600)	0.113 (1.087)	0.237 (3.901)	0.108 (−0.490)	0.348 (4.599)	0.032 (0.436)
Reagan	0.308 (3.726)	0.235 (2.487)	0.453 (5.110)	0.234 (1.934)	0.222 (3.862)	0.108 (1.740)	0.353 (4.339)	0.192 (2.142)
P1	0.286 (4.076)	0.330 (4.110)	0.204 (3.061)	0.334 (4.021)	0.351 (7.170)	0.411 (7.692)	0.286 (4.847)	0.389 (6.766)

Note: The value 0.110 / 0.110 and 0.138 / 0.163 appear on the $T.5$ line for the Sophisticated Voter Models; the ρ (Autocorrelation) values for the Naive Voter Models are 0.154 (4.777), 0.050 (0.522), 0.167 (6.124), and 0.184 (2.618).*

	(1)	(2)	(3)	(4)	(5)	(6)	(7)	(8)
P2	0.275	0.285	0.212	0.290	0.339	0.361	0.282	0.340
	(4.522)	(4.114)	(3.692)	(4.089)	(7.831)	(7.520)	(5.466)	(6.337)
P3	0.216	0.193	0.167	0.203	0.274	0.258	0.230	0.245
	(3.931)	(3.103)	(3.249)	(3.199)	(6.966)	(5.878)	(4.953)	(5.074)
P4	0.137	0.112	0.112	0.133	0.190	0.166	0.168	0.171
	(2.711)	(1.980)	(2.428)	(2.359)	(5.182)	(4.039)	(4.052)	(3.908)
P5	0.070	0.061	0.053	0.080	0.118	0.103	0.102	0.112
	(1.523)	(1.211)	(1.256)	(1.580)	(3.424)	(2.669)	(2.702)	(2.784)
P6	−0.003	0.007	0.001	0.029	0.038	0.029	0.045	0.054
	(−0.081)	(0.163)	(0.032)	(0.691)	(1.185)	(0.771)	(1.321)	(1.442)
David					0.111	0.059	0.082	0.051
					(3.628)	(1.739)	(2.444)	(1.480)
Cartiran					0.126	0.093	0.804	0.070
					(4.325)	(2.838)	(2.902)	(2.384)
Geneva					−0.052	−0.061	−0.050	−0.072
					(−1.374)	(−1.393)	(−1.341)	(−1.699)
Libya					−0.030	−0.153	−0.052	−0.159
					(−0.764)	(−4.354)	(−1.287)	(−4.710)
Marines					0.027	0.024	0.035	0.007
					(1.026)	(0.801)	(1.245)	(0.243)
$\bar{R}^2$	0.992	0.986	0.993	0.987	0.995	0.990	0.995	0.991

in the model reflects not only voters' preferences, but also their beliefs about the structure of the economy.

The Relation between Overall and Economic Evaluations

In this section we focus more intensively on some possible differences in the behavior of the *GPOS* and *HPOS* series. A priori, we would expect that noneconomic political events would have greater effects on *GPOS* (overall evaluation) than on *HPOS* (economic evaluation). We would also expect that economic performance outcomes would be more important in explaining *HPOS* and *GPOS*. If so, we would expect the following:

1. Support functions with *GPOS* as the dependent variable should have greater unexplained variation than those explaining *HPOS*, other things equal. This should result because of the greater impact of random political events (which are not controlled for within the models) for the *GPOS* variable.
2. If dummy variables indicating particular political events are added to the models, their coefficients are likely to be larger in the *GPOS* equations than in the *HPOS* equations.
3. Coefficients of economic performance measures should be larger in absolute value in equations explaining *HPOS* than *GPOS*.
4. As an alternative way of testing for larger impacts of economic performance on *HPOS* than on *GPOS*, consider the following regression specifications (eq. 10 and eq. 11).

$$HPOS_t = \beta_0 + \beta_1 GPOS_t + \beta_2 T_t^{*.5} + \beta_3 T_t^{*.5} \bar{S}_t + e_t \qquad (10)$$

$$HPOS_t = \beta_0 + \beta_1 GPOS_t + \beta_2 T_t^{*.5} + \beta_3 T_t^{*.5} \bar{P}_t \qquad (11)$$

$$+ \beta_4 T_t^{*.5} \bar{U}_t + e_t$$

If the *HPOS* and *GPOS* variables are determined by identical processes, except that economic performance has a larger impact on *HPOS* than on *GPOS*, then β_3 and/or β_4 should be less than zero in the regressions above. We have again included $T^{*.5}$ independently in the regressions to avoid confounding economic impacts and trends.

We will now consider each of these four propositions in turn.

1. We see from our results in table 1 that there is little difference in explanatory power of the *GPOS* and *HPOS* models, in contrast to the proposition suggested above. However, there are explanations

for this result that would not rule out the possibility that *HPOS* and *GPOS* are differently determined by economic and political variables. First, voters may find it more difficult to assess economic performance than overall performance, so that economic evaluations may have more random error. Second, if *GPOS* is based on more polls per quarter and more respondents per poll, its sampling error will be smaller.

2. To test the importance of political events, we added the following dummy variables to the X_t vector in the political support functions:

David	A dummy variable equal to one for the third and fourth quarters, 1978, otherwise equal to zero. This variable coincides with the Camp David peace accords.
Cartiran	A dummy variable equal to one for the fourth quarter, 1979, and the first quarter, 1980, otherwise equal to zero. This variable coincides with the seizure of the U.S. embassy in Tehran, and also with the Russian invasion of Afghanistan.
Geneva	A dummy variable equal to one for the second quarter, 1985, otherwise equal to zero. This variable coincides with the Geneva summit meeting.
Marines	A dummy variable equal to one for the fourth quarter, 1983, and the first quarter, 1984, otherwise equal to zero. This variable coincides with the bombing of the Marines' barracks by terrorists in Beirut, and also with the invasion of Grenada by the United States.
Libya	A dummy variable equal to one for the second and third quarters, 1986, otherwise equal to zero. This variable coincides with the U.S. bombing of Libya.

Choosing important political events is necessarily subjective, and the effects of events will vary depending on the precise nature of those events. We have previously been hesitant to include political or "rally" variables in support functions; we instead prefer to let such effects remain in equation error terms. However, we are now specifically interested in the differential impacts of political events on *HPOS* and *GPOS,* so we have added the variables noted above to models explaining those variables. Table 1 also provides results of regressions including the political events variables. The results show a lack of support for the relevant proposition—that political events should affect *GPOS* more than *HPOS*. There is evidence that both the Camp David agreement and the seizure of the U.S. embassy increased Carter's overall rating, *GPOS* (at least initially), but they apparently had large effects on the economic rating, *HPOS,* also. For Reagan, the *Libya* variable appears significantly (and negatively) in the *HPOS* equation, but not in the *GPOS* equation, contrary to expectations. A glance at figure 1 suggests that the significance of this variable in the *HPOS* equation is probably spurious, since Reagan's economic rating started to drop one quarter before the bombing. Nevertheless, these results must be considered disappointing, since they indicate that voters do not specifically focus on economic outcomes when answering the economics-specific question. It is interesting to note that inclusion of the political events variables does dramatically increase the significance of the economic performance variable in the sophisticated voter models, however.

3. Inspection of the results in table 1 reveals that coefficients of economic performance variables do not differ greatly in explaining *GPOS* and *HPOS*. In some cases, performance coefficients are slightly larger in equations explaining *GPOS*, in contrast with the proposition.[5]
4. Estimates of equations 10 and 11 are provided below (*t*-statistics in parentheses):

$$HPOS_t = .286 + .545 \ GPOS_t - 0.013 \ T_t^{*.5} - 0.178 \ T_t^{*.5}\bar{S}_t \quad (10)$$
$$(3.61) \qquad\qquad (0.43) \qquad\quad (2.49)$$

$$g = 0.8, \ d = 0.05, \ \rho = 0.9, \ R^2 = .909$$

$$HPOS_t = 0.130 + 0.637 \ GPOS_t - 0.269 \ T_t^{*.5} - .0009 \ T_t^{*.5}\bar{P}_t \quad (11)$$
$$(3.58) \qquad\qquad (2.04) \qquad\quad (0.094)$$

$$+ \ 0.033 \ T_t^{*.5}\bar{U}_t$$
$$(2.84)$$

$$g = 1.0, \ \rho = 0.7, \ R^2 = .904$$

In equation 10, the coefficient of the sophisticated performance measure is negative and significant, supporting the notion that performance does contribute to the explanation of the *HPOS* above and beyond its influence captured by *GPOS*. In the naive voter model, the coefficient on unemployment is significantly different from zero as well, but not in the direction predicted by the theory. These modest results provide the only evidence we have found to suggest that variations in macroeconomic variables affect overall and economic evaluations differently.

---

5. In the estimated models, $\bar{S}_t$ and $\bar{N}_t$ may not be precisely identical in equations explaining *HPOS* and *GPOS* because *d* and *g* are permitted to vary. However, we find that even when identical performance measures are employed, their coefficients do not vary much for the *GPOS* and *HPOS* equations.

Conclusions

Results reported in this chapter reaffirm those of our earlier work, Chappell and Keech 1985. They show that aggregate evaluations of the president are consistent with a "sophisticated" voter model, but they do not rule out less sophisticated voting behavior. Indeed, the "naive" voter model works somewhat better in more recent years than it did for earlier samples, at least in explaining overall performance evaluations. All of our models indicate that voters are inflation averse. The extreme degree of that inflation aversion provides an unresolved puzzle.

On the whole, there is little convincing evidence that respondents behave much differently in making marginal adjustments of their "economic" and "overall" performance evaluations in response to economic outcomes. One might argue that this is consistent with an assertion that economic performance dominates evaluations of overall performance. This seems unlikely, particularly given the apparent impacts of purely "political" events on economic performance judgments. Instead, it is likely that voters make judgments about the overall performance of an administration, based on economic and other considerations, and then let these overall impressions color their responses to the question specifically focusing on economic events. This is somewhat disappointing, in that the Harris data set appears not to provide new and better information than the Gallup polls previously available. However, it is reassuring that inferences about economic evaluations based on the overall Gallup approval ratings are not likely to be reversed as more data on economy-specific evaluations become available.

APPENDIX: SUMMARY OF VARIABLE DEFINITIONS

GPOS	The fraction of respondents responding yes to the Gallup Poll question: "Do you approve or disapprove of the way that (the president) is handling his job as president?"
HPOS	The fraction of respondents responding yes to the Harris Poll question. "Do you approve or disapprove of the way that (the president) is handling the economy?"
N	Economic performance for naive voters (as defined by eq. 1).
$\dot{P}$	The rate of inflation, defined as an annualized percentage rate of change in the GNP deflator.
Pk ($k = 1, \ldots, 6$)	A series of dummy variables indicating the kth quarter of the current presidential administration's tenure in office.

S	Economic performance for sophisticated voters (as defined by eq. 5).
T*	The number of quarters the current administration has been in office.
U	The civilian unemployment rate.
UN	The natural rate of unemployment (estimated as the predicted value from a regression equation explaining unemployment as a cubic function of time).
David *Cartiran* *Geneva* *Marines* *Libya*	A series of dummy variables indicating political events (defined in detail in the text).
Carter *Reagan*	Dummy variables indicating the Carter and Reagan presidencies respectively.

REFERENCES

Chappell, Henry W., and William R. Keech. 1985. "A New View of Political Accountability for Economic Performance." *American Political Science Review* 79:10–27.
Nordhaus, William D. 1975. "The Political Business Cycle." *Review of Economic Studies* 42:169–90.

Public Perceptions of Parties'
Economic Competence

Manfred Kuechler

Economic voting is a multifaceted topic. Many of the controversies past and present can be easily resolved by carefully separating a number of different subtopics. All deal with the impact of the state of the economy on voting behavior or—more generally—on the popularity of political actors. However, while all these subtopics are closely related, findings from empirical analyses may appear inconsistent at first sight. Closer inspection typically reveals that the underlying research question was different in the first place. Further elaboration notwithstanding, three major research questions related to economic voting can be identified:

1. Is there a correlation between electoral success (popularity) of a polit ical actor and global measures of the state of the economy? More daringly: Does the state of the economy at large have a causal effect on elections?
2. Is there an association between the individual voter's economic well-being and/or the perceived state of the general economic situation on the one hand and his or her voting decision on the other?
3. Is there an association between the individual voter's perception of a political actor's ability to handle economic problems and his or her voting decision?

Obviously, the answers to these three questions are fully independent. We may see a correlation on the macrolevel, but this may not emanate from an individual-level relationship. The success of the Nazis in the late Weimar Republic is a case in point. On some aggregate level, the Nazis' electoral success correlates with the level of unemployment. Yet, more refined analyses indicate that the unemployed did not have a higher than average propensity to vote for the Nazis (e.g., Lohmöller et al. 1985; Kuechler 1988). The first of the three questions is typically addressed by economists. It is an interesting topic, but findings from this strand of research shed little light on individual voting behavior.

The second question is sometimes referred to as "pocketbook" voting. Answered in the affirmative, it implies that voters hold political actors directly responsible for their economic well-being. However, there is little empirical evidence to support this claim. Controlling other factors, the personal economic situation does not have a relevant effect on the voting decision. Stronger support is found for the impact of the individual's assessment of the general economic situation (see, e.g., Eulau and Lewis-Beck 1985 for an overview).

Finally, in order to focus on the process by which the individual makes his or her political choices, the status of the economy must be linked to the political actors. The third question, then, looks at the individual's perception of the political actors' competence to deal with economic issues and the possible influence of this perception on political choices. Or, to put it in slightly different words, do perceptions of the parties' competence to handle economic issues affect voters' decisions? In this chapter, I will address this third research question.

Previous Analyses

In earlier analyses of the U.S. presidential elections of 1976 and 1980 (Kuechler and Wides 1980; Wides and Kuechler 1981, and Kuechler and Wides 1982) an indicator of perceived economic competence was identified as the most important factor directly influencing the voting decision. This indicator was constructed combining separate seven-point-scale ratings of both presidential candidates on inflation and unemployment into a trichotomy of perceived relative economic competence. Not surprisingly, the evaluation of past government policy and party identification were both found to contribute significantly to shaping the perception of economic competence. These analyses also confirmed the hypothesis that global economic judgments are far more important than personal economic concerns. This had been suggested by, e.g., Kinder and Kiewiet (1979) based on their analysis of the 1974 and 1976 congressional vote.

This (simple) model of economic voting was subsequently tested with data from the 1983 German Election (Kuechler 1985). For both conceptual and practical reasons, a strict replication was not feasible, but the central hypothesis of a major impact of perceived economic competence was well supported by the data. For reasons detailed below, the economic competence indicator was tested against a baseline model of sociodemographic factors marking the traditional cleavages in the German electorate—rather than against party identification—as well as against a similar indicator reflecting perceived competence with respect to noneconomic issues and, furthermore, against the (retrospective) evaluation of the government's economic policies.

In this chapter I will present empirical findings from the 1987 German election—for the most part following the approach in the 1983 analysis—in an attempt to gain additional empirical support for the claimed prevalence of economic issues.[1] The 1987 election provides a particularly severe test of this assertion for two reasons.

First, economic conditions had greatly improved since 1983 with improvements becoming most visible in the last six months before the election. Most notable to the general public, in 1986 the index of consumer prices (inflation rate) experienced the first yearlong decline since 1953; the index was down by 0.2 percent compared to 1985. Real wages for industrial workers increased by 3.4 percent (the largest rise since 1977); the foreign trade surplus reached a new record high of DM 110.2 billion (surpassing the old mark set in 1985 by more than DM 30.0 billion). In addition, the rise of the unemployment rate was curbed during the preceding four years, though no significant improvement was achieved. An annual decrease was achieved for the first time in 1986 with a rate of 9.0 percent, down from 9.4 percent for 1985 (which still amounts to 2.23 million officially unemployed). Given the seasonal variation, this first real decline became apparent in the summer of 1986, well in time for the upcoming elections. With steady economic improvement one might expect a decline of salience of economic issues and, consequently, diminishing manifestation of economic concerns.

Second, and much more important, a growing concern with environmental problems in the wake of the Chernobyl nuclear accident had permanently affected the political agenda. Radiation and contamination of food and soil had changed the public's awareness more than any amount of "Green" rhetoric would have ever achieved. The nuclear threat was no longer seen as a nightmarish vision fostered by environmental radicals, but as a real problem affecting all citizens. A chemical spill in Switzerland and the ensuing contamination of Germany's major waterway, the Rhine River, provided a second drastic reminder of environmental threats. Public opinion data show a steep increase of manifest public concern with problems of environmental protection and the use of nuclear energy following Chernobyl; from about 30 percent in February, 1986, to over 60 percent in June, 1986. It turned out to be a short-lived peak, but post-Chernobyl data consistently show a level between 40 percent and 50 percent, indicating an enduring effect.[2] Public awareness (not

---

1. As in the 1983 analysis, data for the present analysis were provided by the Forschungsgruppe Wahlen, Mannheim, West Germany. Special thanks to Manfred Berger, Wolfgang Gibowski, and Dieter Roth for providing the data as well as additional material; and to Ekkehart Mochmann and Rolf Uher (Central Archive for Empirical Social Research at the University of Cologne) for their efficiency in transferring the data sets.

2. All data are taken from the monthly POLITBAROMETER surveys of the Forschungsgruppe Wahlen. Respondents are (open-endedly) asked to name the three problems seen as personally most important.

hysteria) and—most important in its reinforcing function—media attention have increased considerably. Minor chemical leaks and spills that most likely occurred equally frequently in the past now get prime attention, resulting in public warnings, if not temporary evacuations: a constant reminder of the problems at hand. Beyond the environment, other issues central to the concerns of new social movements—most notably peace and disarmament—have been established on the political agenda, constituting a challenge to the existing political order (see, e.g., Dalton and Kuechler 1990) and its preoccupation with economic wealth.

Given this situation, a continued prevalence of economic voting in the German election of 1987 was not a foregone conclusion. Before displaying the data and discussing their implications, I will address some conceptual and methodological problems posed by the notion of economic voting, with particular emphasis put on the West German context and its party-centered political system.

Issue Voting in a Party-Centered Political System

Voting based on perceived differential competence of the political actors in regard to any set of issues—including economic voting—is a central element of the traditional Michigan Model of voting behavior. In its simple form, this model postulates a "normal" inclination toward a particular party (party identification) affecting the vote choice both directly and indirectly (and in part modified) through issue and candidate evaluations. This model, however, was developed in view of the particular political system of the United States. Any attempt to extend the model to another political context, then, should be prefaced by a careful evaluation of the limits of its applicability. In particular, three aspects need to be discussed: (1) the role of parties and the specific nature of "party identification" in a given political system; (2) construction, validity, and reliability of indicators measuring party identification; and (3) the transition from personal actors (candidates) to institutional actors (parties) as primary objects of voter perceptions.

In the United States the two major parties lack a sharply focused programmatic image. There are marked differences of opinion and political preference within each party on almost every important issue. Parties are not expected to speak with one voice and intraparty debate and competition is considered as an integral part of the democratic process—notwithstanding the necessity to "close ranks" at times. In the absence of a clearly defined party line, the relationship between parties and their constituencies is "open" as well. Voters may identify with a party; they may consider themselves Democrats or Republicans. Yet, even when a party "identification" is more than purely conventional (e.g., going beyond partisan registration requirements in many states), for the American voter it does not necessarily entail a deep-rooted commitment to stay with this party at the polls. Elected representatives in legislative bodies on federal, state, and local levels routinely deviate from party lines or—in the absence of those—from the party majority. This provides and constantly reinforces a role model of limited loyalty toward one's party. Or to put it more positively: the American voter is by and large willing to evaluate the leading candidates in their own right. Of course, this volatility is much more prevalent in presidential than in congressional elections, where incumbency typically is the most important determinant. Still, given this particular nature of party identification, it is plausible to posit that issue evaluations constitute one of the causes that affect the voting decision rather than assuming that these evaluations are predominantly rationalizations of the individual's vote choice.

In contrast, European party systems in general—West Germany being no exception—have been described as reflections of fundamental social cleavages representing particular class interests. Overemphasizing the difference, the relationship of party and individual in the United States can be described as of pragmatic utility—easily set aside in any particular instance—whereas this relation is built upon class interests and corresponding ideological beliefs (*Weltanschauung*) in Germany and a lasting affective commitment—not easily abandoned at all. On the elite level, members of parliaments are required to stay with the party line unless the party leadership —on very rare occasions—suspends this obligation. Members of parliament defying the party leadership and/or switching parties are typically held in low esteem by the public and are rarely able to continue their political career. Obviously, this is an "ideal-type" characterization. Further qualifications are needed to validly describe the relationship between party and individual in its empirical detail, but it captures the essence of an important conceptual difference.

However, it has been argued that the once stable ties between the major parties and clearly defined segments of the electorate have been weakened and that a new era of volatility has dawned (see, e.g., Dalton 1984). True, due to social change (e.g., the numerical decline of the working class, drastically changing communication patterns in the "media age," etc.) the social boundaries have become less decisive. The (major) parties have tried to shed their image of representing special class interests. Programmatically, they claim to represent voters coming from all strata of the electorate, to be "Volksparteien" (catch-all parties). However, both major parties have maintained a clear cleavage-related profile in both their actual policies and in the eye of the public. The sociodemographic characteristics (social class, union membership, religious affiliation, church attendance) reflecting the dual cleavage structure in West Germany are still strong factors in determining voting behavior. Compared to the 1950s we observe a decline in the importance of these factors;

compared to the 1970s we find no clear downward trend (see, e.g., Pappi 1986; Schmitt 1988). While the structural pattern (the associations between these factors and voting behavior) seems to be stable, there may be a continued (but rather slow) change in the marginal distributions. With traditional working-class orientations and strong church ties likely to decline slowly, the traditional cleavages will lose their previous significance. However, they might well prevail for some time to come reflecting not necessarily immediate class (cleavage) interests, but affective ties developed by the voter in earlier phases of his or her life (socialization effect).

In sum, the West German voter is much more likely to entertain strong affective ties with a particular party than his or her U.S. counterpart. Further-more, this attachment is not easily ignored, resting solidly on fundamental beliefs (*Weltanschauung*) and/or an internalized allegiance. The structure of these ties is somewhat similar to those of religious affiliations. An individual may not be active in his or her church, he or she may disagree with some of the doctrines (e.g., Catholics with the church's position on birth control), but the basic beliefs still exert a strong impact on the individual's actions. In Germany, political convictions are not changed frequently; conversions do occur, but they are rare.

What follows from this for the prospect of issue voting? In general, attitudes are usually seen as entailing three components: cognitive evalua-tions, emotional attachments, and dispositions to act. However, the emotional attachment is particularly important. It serves as a filter in cognitive informa-tion processing, i.e., information unfavorable to the party of choice will be not processed at all or it will be immediately modified by discrediting its source or by offsetting it with information unfavorable to alternative parties. Evaluations of competence with regard to certain issues—as obtained in survey research—may well be a reflection of social information processing seriously biased by preexisting affective bonds, rather than the independent piece of evidence as we treat it in the routine statistical analysis of survey data.[3] The (statistical) association between issue competence and vote choice, then, may not be due to a causal impact of issue evaluations. Rather, and deliberately overstating the point, responses to issue questions in a survey may be rationalizations of a vote choice grounded in diffuse affections.

This is not to say that individuals are necessarily able to explicate these ideological beliefs or even able to use the terms *left* and *right* consistent with the analytical concepts of political scientists. Also, this view does not imply that voters are ignorant or "irrational." Calculating costs and benefits, it may well be the most rational decision to rely on established attitudinal ties rather

---

3. For a similar view on the American voter see Peffley, Feldman, and Sigelman 1987; for an opposing view on the German voter see Klingemann 1986. Also, the directional approach to issue voting suggested by Rabinowitz and Macdonald (1989)—while still biased toward cogni-tion—offers an interesting alternative to more rigid models of spatial voting.

than paying close attention to platforms, programs, and campaign rhetoric. If cognitive dissonances are not avoided altogether or resolved immediately, they most likely will lead to grudging compliance (voting for the party as a lesser evil) or to less drastic deviations from normal voting behavior. The German party system still reflects the traditional cleavage system with the smaller parties (FDP, Greens) serving basically the same segment of the electorate as their major counterparts. The boundaries of these segments are drawn somewhat differently over time, contingent upon the coalition preference of the FDP. However, with an adjustment in the middle of the spectrum, there is a clear choice between blocks at any particular time. Thus, abstaining or voting for another party in the same block are much less drastic deviations.

The segment of "volatile voters" resting their voting decision on a fresh, unprejudiced assessment of parties and candidates and their competence to handle the salient issues each time around is still fairly small.[4] A quantitative assessment of the size of this segment is difficult. Survey questions dealing with past voting decisions ("recall questions") and, more so, dealing with hypothetical situations ("if elections were held now . . ."; *Sonntagsfragen*) are faced with serious reliability problems and tend to overestimate the amount of change in actual voting—a first proxy to the more fundamental notion of attitudinal attachment discussed here.

Given this conceptual difference of "party identification" between the United States and Germany, the basic Michigan Model does not provide an adequate specification of the German situation. At least, the model would need to allow for a reciprocal relationship between issue evaluations and vote choice. This would account for the possibility that issue evaluations are rationalizations of a vote choice based on diffuse affective ties. And, if—at least for a sizable portion of the electorate—ties of this kind practically all but fully determine vote choice, there may not be enough statistical variation left to reliably estimate the relationship to other factors such as issue evaluations. Unfortunately, turning to the second aspect outlined above, we find additional problems with the measurement (operationalization) of the party identification concept in the German political context.

The indicators currently used are seriously flawed. To a large extent they do not measure a separate concept of "party identification" but current party preference or voting intention. This assertion can easily be tested with panel data. Whatever more precise definition of party identification is used, it needs to include the notion of stability over a longer period of time.[5] Indicators supposedly measuring party identification therefore need to display a high

---

4. A model of this kind was suggested by Himmelweit, Humphreys, and Jaeger (1985) based on British data. An attempt to replicate this "consumer model of voting" in the context of the German election of 1983 (Kuechler 1986) was not successful.

5. See, e.g., Asher 1983 for a cogent discussion of various attempts to reformulate the original concept.

degree of stability over short periods of time. The analysis of the 1983 German election panel has clearly demonstrated a lack of stability (Kuechler 1985 and 1986). The 1987 panel data reconfirm these findings. Due to space limitations, I will not present these results in full detail. Suffice it to say that over a period of about four months (between the first and second wave) only two-thirds of all responses to the party identification question were stable. Even controlling for strength of party identification and looking at the sub-sample of "strong" identifiers only, less than 80 percent named the same party twice. Hence, the very high empirical association between party identification indicators and vote choice is—in part—an artifact of method. Consequently, the use of any of these indicators as a control when assessing the relationship between issue-related factors (e.g., economic competence) and vote choice is highly problematic.

Therefore, I will use social background variables—reflecting the traditional social cleavage structure of the German electorate—as a proxy to measure the impact of the individual voter's predisposition toward the competing political actors (parties) and determine the role of perceived actor competence relative to these controls. While I will employ a statistical model, in which competence evaluations and background variables are considered as independent variables, the question of causal direction is open to further debate—and improvements in measurement.

Finally, turning to the third aspect, we need to consider the choices the voter is faced with. In American presidential elections there is basically a choice between two candidates, a simple alternative totally focused on two personal political actors with parties reduced to minor supporting roles. The internal diversity of the American parties puts little restraint on the image-building efforts of the candidates.

The situation in West Germany (and other European countries) is quite different. For one, there is no separate, highly personalized election for the chief executive post. The personal traits of German chancellor candidates are largely inconsequential. A controversial candidate may fail to satisfy all segments of his or her party's clientele, leading to abstentions and an increase in tactical voting, i.e., switching to the other party in the block. A case in point is Franz-Josef Strauss as the top candidate of the CDU and CSU in the 1980 elections. However, candidate personality never had a decisive impact on the outcome of German elections: German elections are elections of parties, not elections of candidates. The substitution of institutional for personal political actors, however, does not pose a major problem for the study of economic voting, since German parties (in contrast to American parties) have a clearly defined programmatic profile. In addition, the choice is a simple alternative at any given point. Coalition preferences are announced well in advance of the election—sometimes contingent upon certain conditions—and have been

formed with little delay thereafter, saving West Germany the agony of prolonged efforts of coalition building quite typical for other EC countries like
Italy or the Netherlands.[6]

In the German context, then, parties are clearly discernible political
actors. What makes it more difficult to pursue the idea of "issue voting"—
whether economic or noneconomic—are the unresolved methodological
problems of validly measuring party identification in the German political
context.

Data- and Index Construction

The indicators of issue competence are based on a set of thirteen issues.[7] An
English translation of the items used is given in table 1 along with the margin-
als for the second wave and Cramer's coefficient for the association of single
items with vote choice. The same question format was used in 1983. However, only seven items on the issue list are identical; disarmament and Europe's political unification were added; relations with Eastern Europe was split
into two, as was the 1983 inflation item. The five economic issues in table 1
are indicated. Four of those were rated as important (first two categories on the
salience scale) by at least 90 percent of the respondents as compared to only
two of eight noneconomic issues (environmental protection and disarmament).

Following the analysis of the 1983 election (Kuechler 1985), responses
for economic and for noneconomic issues were combined into two competence indices.

Index Type 1: CDU Competence (all important issues)[8]

high   CDU preferred for all important problems *and* at least two

---

6. This holds for the federal level; in recent years, state elections in Hesse and Hamburg
have produced less clear-cut results.

7. Data used for the analyses presented in this chapter are taken from the 1987 German
Election Panel of the Forschungsgruppe Wahlen, Mannheim. The first wave was conducted in
September, 1986, resulting in $N = 1,954$ cases. Data for the second wave were collected in
January, 1987, up to two days prior to the elections, resulting in a total of $N = 1,344$ cases (a
panel attrition of 21 percent). Panel mortality follows the usual pattern; an above-average rate is
found in the younger, presumably more mobile (harder to reach at home) age cohort. Also, the
sample is clearly biased in its voting preference toward the SPD and against the FDP. All
marginal distributions presented here will be biased and should not be taken at face value.
However, the multivariate analyses are less affected by this bias and, consequently, no attempt
has been made to offset this bias by introducing weights. All statistical estimations presented in
this paper are based on unweighted, second-wave data.

8. Throughout this chapter CDU refers to CDU and CSU (the Bavarian counterpart of the
CDU) together. Other options, like the difference between SPD and CDU preferences, result in

(out of five) economic or at least three (out of eight) noneconomic issues rated as important

medium   CDU preferred for at least one important issue

low   no CDU preference for any important issue

In addition, indicators of a second type were constructed based on the issues rated as "very important." Here, only environment and disarmament (items F and N in table 1) were included in the noneconomic set, because these issues represent the agenda of new social movements most directly.

Index Type 2: Competence (very important issues)

CDU   CDU preference for all very important issues

SPD   SPD preference for all very important issues

ambivalent   others with at least one very important issue

indifferent   no issue rated as very important

Sociodemographic Factors, Competence Indicators, and Vote Choice

Not surprisingly—and in line with the theoretical argument developed above—competence evaluations correlate strongly with the vote choice. This holds for individual issues (V ranging between .355 and .454; see last column in table 1) as well as the composite indices. However, the absolute level of these associations is less interesting than the differences between economic and noneconomic issues and the differences over time (see table 2). Notwithstanding minor changes in index construction, a clear pattern emerges. In 1983, the association between competence in noneconomic issues and vote choice was clearly lower than the one between economic issues and vote ($V = .382$ vs. $V = .484$). For 1987 the associations are about equal. Unfortunately, a comparison over time cannot be made for the type 2 indices, since the disarmament issue was not included in the 1983 list.[9] Therefore, I will focus on the type 1 indices for the multivariate analyses below.

First, however, a more detailed look at the conceptually more focused type 2 indices: A cross-tabulation of the economic with the noneconomic

---

extremely skewed distributions or lack clear-cut meaning when trichotomized. In contrast to 1983, the number of issues rated as important by a respondent was taken into account. In addition, results for a 1987 index without modification are shown in table 2.

9. The numerical difference in the value for V is somewhat larger for the type 2 indices than for the type 1 indices. In the absence of a sampling distribution for V, it is hard to tell whether this difference should be considered significant (in substantive terms). One should also note that the V-value for the type 2 indices is generally lower; possibly only due to larger table size (4×4 compared to 4×3).

TABLE 1. Competence Issues

Issue	CDU	SPD	Both	None	Not important	Cramer's V[b]
A. Improving the economy[a]	47.7%	22.1%	16.3%	4.0%	10.0%	.442
B. Fighting unemployment[a]	40.2	32.5	16.2	8.9	2.3	.454
C. Maintaining law and order in the Federal Republic	39.6	19.9	19.0	4.4	17.1	.438
D. Improving relations to the Soviet Union	22.3	38.0	13.2	2.8	23.7	.362
E. Maintaining good relations to the US	39.3	17.9	15.3	2.7	24.9	.362
F. Providing effective environmental protection	27.8	41.5	20.9	5.5	4.3	.424
G. Securing social security payments[a]	40.1	27.7	19.0	6.2	6.9	.444
H. Reducing fiscal debts[a]	42.1	15.5	13.0	6.7	22.7	.386
I. Improving relations to East Germany	22.3	37.4	13.8	3.1	23.3	.374
K. Giving people more say in government decisions	17.4	30.4	10.8	7.4	34.0	.355
L. Keeping prices stable[a]	45.4	21.5	20.1	4.6	8.4	.409
M. Promoting political unification of the European Community	25.6	20.9	18.4	4.9	30.3	.355
N. Advocating disarmament in East and West	26.3	39.8	19.6	5.8	8.5	.413

Source: German Election Study (FGW), second wave, January, 1987, unweighted N = 1,544.

Note: "Here we have a list of tasks and goals people talk about in the Federal Republic. For each one, please tell us whether you think this task is very important, important, not so important, or completely unimportant."

(For all tasks rated as "very important" or as "important":)

"Who is best suited to solve this problem to your satisfaction? Do you think that the present government led by CDU and FDP is more apt, or would it be a government led by the SPD?"

[a]Economic issues

[b]Cramer's coefficient for association with vote choice (CDU, SPD, FDP, Greens), N = 1,429 valid cases in the second wave

index reveals hierarchical patterns in competence attribution. Only 6.4 percent of the respondents who see the CDU as uniformly more competent in noneconomic issues come to a different conclusion with respect to economic issues. Similarly, just 7.6 percent of those favoring the SPD in economic matters are ambivalent or prefer the CDU with respect to noneconomic matters. In other words: for the CDU, perceived competence is transferred from the noneconomic to the economic realm; for the SPD it is transferred from the economic to the noneconomic field. Or, noneconomic issues for the CDU and economic issues for the SPD constitute a political litmus test. If a party has a voter on its side here, it has him or her all the way.

TABLE 2. Competence-Indices and Vote Intention

| Vote Intention | Index 1: CDU Competence | | | | | |
| | Economic Issues | | | Noneconomic Issues | | |
	low	medium	high	low	medium	high
CDU	7.9	43.1	90.2	10.0	59.8	91.9
SPD	76.1	42.8	1.3	72.9	28.3	1.6
FDP	2.1	6.4	7.5	2.2	7.9	6.5
Greens	14.0	7.7	1.0	14.9	4.0	0.0
N = 1,429	573	376	480	638	470	321
Cramer's V		.534			.508	

| Vote Intention | Index 2: Competence (very important problems only) | | | | | | | |
| | Economic Issues | | | | Environment/Disarmament | | | |
	CDU	Ambivalent	SPD	Indifferent	CDU	Ambivalent	SPD	Indifferent
CDU	89.0	29.0	2.2	32.4	91.2	47.0	7.6	57.2
SPD	2.6	59.5	79.9	40.5	1.7	39.0	73.9	34.4
FDP	7.3	4.2	0.6	10.8	7.1	6.1	2.5	6.0
Greens	1.2	7.3	17.3	16.2	0.0	8.0	16.0	2.5
N = 1,429	509	496	313	111	296	362	486	285
Cramer's V		.434				.381		

Looking at the control variables, there is no significant change—compared to 1983—in the level of association between age, religious affiliation, frequency of church attendance, and union membership, on the one hand, and vote choice, on the other. Each of the competence indicators was run against a set of three sociodemographic variables in a multivariate analysis following an approach suggested by Grizzle, Starmer, and Koch (GSK approach).[10]

The results of these analyses are shown in tables 3 and 4. From a statistical point of view, the two models are not identical.[11] However, in terms of substance, the structure of the two models is very similar. As expected, the

10. I will assume that the reader is generally familiar with this technique. However, effects can be understood similarly to an analysis of variance. An introduction to this approach, emphasizing applications in political science, can be found in Kritzer 1978a and 1978b, whose NONMET program (PC version) was used for the computations. The CATMOD procedure in SAS provides another software option.

This weighted least squares procedure is equivalent to the first approximation in ML-oriented general linear models and corresponding software such as GLIM or LIMDEP. These approaches allow the simultaneous inclusion of categorical and interval-level independent variables. However, for conceptual reasons, age should be treated as a (categorical) cohort indicator rather than as a measure (interval-level) of biological existence. One disadvantage of the GSK approach lies in the fact that the number of factors (independent variables) simultaneously included in a model is restricted by sample size. Ideally, all subpopulations formed by the combinations of factor categories should contain at least twenty cases. Consequently, all so-

TABLE 3. Economic Competence Perception and Vote Intention, Results of GSK Analysis

	Percentage		
Effect	CDU	SPD	Greens
Mean	43.4	40.5	8.6
Age up to 35	−2.9	−5.7	6.7
Union member	−5.1	5.9	—
Catholic	4.6	−1.0	—
CDU-competence low	—	—	—
Non-catholic union	−30.0	—	—
Others	−39.9	—	—
Age up to 35	—	28.2	14.1
Age over 35	—	38.6	1.7
CDU-competence medium	—	—	—
Non-Catholic union	−27.3	11.3	—
Other	—	—	—
Wald-statistic	21.15	21.03	19.37
df	17	17	20
p	.219	.225	.498

Note: Results are reported for a "best model," i.e., a model that has sufficient goodness-of-fit (preferably $p > .20$) and in which all effects are significant (at least at the .05 level).

    For dichotomous variables, the effect for the category not shown is the negative of the table entry. For the third category of a trichotomous variable (here, CDU-competence high) this effect is the negative sum of the effects for the two categories directly estimated (and shown in the upper portion of the table).

main effects of the sociodemographic variables are modest at best, but there are significant (statistical) interactions of these variables with the competence indices. With respect to the vote share of the SPD and of the Greens, the effect of the competence indices varies with age group; with respect to the Greens, this effect is considerably stronger for respondents up to 35 years of age. For example, among respondents up to 35 years old who perceive the CDU competence as high, the share of the Greens is practically zero compared to almost 30 percent (24 percent with respect to noneconomic matters), if the CDU competence is rated low.[12] For respondents over 35 years of age this

ciodemographic variables were dichotomized and church attendance (highly correlated with age) was omitted.

    11. Also, combining the three partial models of table 3 (each having a dichotomized dependent variable) into a single model with a four-response dependent variable does not render sufficient goodness-of-fit. Obviously, to model the implicit fourth category (here, FDP) additional terms are necessary.

    12. To aid in reading tables 3 and 4, the predicted value for respondents up to 35 years old and high perceived CDU competence is obtained as 8.6 (mean) + 6.7 (age effect) − 14.1 (high competence) = 1.2 (table 3) and 7.0 + 5.0 − 11.6 = 0.4 (table 4). If CDU competence is perceived as low, the sign of this effect is reversed, rendering 29.4 (table 3) and 23.6 (table 4).

**TABLE 4. Noneconomic Competence Perception and
Vote Intention, Results of GSK Analysis**

Effect	Percentage		
	CDU	SPD	Greens
Mean	52.9	35.5	7.0
Age up to 35	—	−5.8	5.0
Union member	−4.6	5.6	—
Catholic	2.3	−1.7	—
CDU-competence low	−44.0	—	—
Age up to 35	—	32.5	14.4
Age over 35	—	43.6	3.3
CDU-competence medium	—	—	—
Union	—	—	—
Nonunion	10.0	−10.2	—
Age up to 35	—	—	−2.8
Age over 35	—	—	−1.4

Note: Wald-statistic = 51.99
  df = 54
  p = .552

effect is much more modest. Other things being equal, a high evaluation of CDU competence in economic issues lowers the percentage of the Greens by only 3.4 percentage points compared to a low CDU evaluation.

With respect to the CDU share, the effect of perceived competence is markedly different in the segment of non-Catholic union members (the traditional clientele of the SPD). Here, even when the economic competence of the CDU is perceived as medium, the probability of voting CDU is below 10 percent.[13] Obviously, the sociodemographic background producing a structural affinity toward the SPD works as a deterrent, keeping the individual from voting CDU as long as the CDU is not uniformly viewed (the "high" category) as more competent on economic issues. A similar, but less striking, deterring effect of union membership on the impact of perceived competence can be found for noneconomic issues.

Overall, the impact of competence perception as displayed in tables 3 and 4 is fairly similar—notwithstanding some numerical differences (slightly higher effects for the noneconomic index). In a final analysis, both indices are considered simultaneously. As with the type 2 indices, a cross-tabulation of

---

13. Again, to aid in reading table 3, 43.4 (mean) − 5.1 (union) − 4.6 (non-Catholic) − 27.3 (medium competence) = 6.4 ± 2.9 depending on age group, hence 9.3 (old) and 3.5 (young). Also, the proportion for a particular category of the dependent variable (here, vote share CDU) in a specific subpopulation (defined by the factors or independent variables) can be verbally expressed as a probability that a respondent of this type would fall into this category of the dependent variable.

TABLE 5. CDU Competence Perception (Index 1) and Vote Intention, Results of GSK Analysis

	Percentage		
Effect	CDU	SPD	Greens
Mean	49.3	39.0	5.8
Econ. competence low	−41.3	37.8	—
Econ. competence medium	—	—	—
Nonecon. comp. low	−31.5	26.2	7.8[a]
Nonecon. comp. medium	—	—	−2.2

Note: Wald-statistic = 17.68
$df = 15$
$p = .280$
Incomplete design with 8 subpopulations
[a]Effect of noneconomic competence perception for CDU and SPD only if economic competence is perceived as medium (conditional effect); for Greens independent of perception of economic competence (main effect).

the economic with the noneconomic indicator produces several cells with extremely low counts, advising some caution in interpreting the results of the GSK analysis summarized in table 5.[14] However, the overall pattern is quite distinct. The effect of the two indices is not additive.[15] With respect to the vote share of the CDU and of the SPD, the evaluation of noneconomic competence is effective only when CDU competence in economic matters is rated as medium. With respect to the vote share of the Greens, perception of noneconomic competence has a uniform impact (in technical terms, it is a main effect), while economic competence is negligible.[16] In contrast, the parallel analysis for 1983 shows a conditional effect of noneconomic competence for all party shares; the condition being medium *or* high CDU competence in economic matters.

In sum, the perceived party competence in economic matters is more strongly associated with vote choice than the perceived competence in noneconomic matters in 1983 as well as in 1987. Given the qualitative changes in

---

14. Only six of the nine cells generated by the cross-tabulation of the two trichotomous indices show sufficient frequencies for the GSK analysis; one cell does not contain any case at all. However, the frequency requirements in the GSK approach are rules of thumb. Their violation does not necessarily lead to incorrect results, though the danger of biased results increases. However, these low cell counts prevent any attempt to add sociodemographic variables to the model.

15. Interaction between two (or more) factors can equivalently be modeled by conditional or nested effects. It is the researcher's choice for which factor is kept a main effect and which one is represented by conditional effects. At times—as in this case—the parsimony rule (minimizing the overall number of terms in a model) provides an objective criterion for this choice.

16. As is documented in table 3, this is not true when a differentiation according to sociodemographic characteristics is introduced.

the model using both indices simultaneously, it is hard to say whether the relative dominance of economic issues over noneconomic has increased from 1983 to 1987. However, the multivariate analysis presented in table 5 makes it safe to claim that the importance of economic issues has not declined.

Conclusion

In the preceding methodological discussion I have argued that the current way of measuring the impact of issue evaluations in the context of the West German (and probably likewise in the context of any party-centered) political system has serious shortcomings. The Michigan Model, as well as rational (in a normative sense) models of voting behavior, assume that the vote choice is based upon careful assessment of each party's merits and potentials (see, e.g., Klingemann 1986). In this conceptual framework, a longer-lasting affiliation with one party is seen as a predetermining factor at best. Yet competence assessments are seen as an independent cause for the voting decision. In contrast, I contend that models of this type hold for a certain segment of the electorate at best. For another segment (probably the majority of voters), a rather deep-rooted attitudinal attachment is likely to more fully determine both the perception of issue competence and the vote choice. An association between competence evaluations and vote choice, then, would not be due to a unidirectional causal link from evaluation to vote choice, but rather due to a rationalization of the vote choice. Still, the relative degree of the association between vote choice and different types of issues is an indication of the individual voter's issue priorities. In the long run, parties need to be attentive to these priorities. Thus, a focus on issues in studying voting behavior is important, even if issues have no short-term causal impact.

The underlying attitudinal attachment can be conceptualized as "party identification"—though there are important differences in the nature of this identification between the United States (where the construct of party identification was originally developed) and West Germany. However, questions currently used to measure party identification (closely following the U.S. model) are deficient. New avenues are needed to validly discern "identifiers" from "nonidentifiers"—or "movers" from "stayers."

With these caveats in mind, the data from the 1987 German election indicate that perceived economic competence is still very strongly associated with vote choice in spite of major changes in the political and economic context. Compared to 1983, perceived competence with respect to noneconomic issues has drastically gained in importance, reflecting a growing concern with environmental problems in the wake of Chernobyl. The nuclear accident at Chernobyl provided actual firsthand experience of nuclear hazards. It was an important catalyst for reshaping the political agenda, but the growing public concern with environmental issues is not exclusively tied to this singular event. In direct comparison, economic issues still seem to be more important than noneconomic problems, but by a possibly smaller margin. It is obvious that no party can afford to ignore the issues of environmental protection, nuclear energy, and disarmament. However, these issues supplement rather than replace economic problems on the political agenda. Economic concerns are omnipresent, even with inflation close to zero and a halt in the rise of unemployment. There is little evidence, then, for "New Age Politics" and the assertion that the electorate is realigning along a new set of issues, concerns, and interests (e.g., Dalton 1984 and 1986).

REFERENCES

Asher, Herbert B. 1983. "Voting Behavior Research in the 1980s: An Examination of Some Old and New Problem Areas." In *Political Science: The State of the Discipline,* ed. Ada Finifter. Washington, DC: APSA.

Dalton, Russell, J. 1984. "The West German Party System between Two Ages." In *Electoral Change in Advanced Industrial Democracies,* ed. Russell J. Dalton, Scott Flanagan, and Paul Allen Beck. Princeton, NJ: Princeton University Press.

Dalton, Russell J. 1986. "Wertwandel oder Wertwende: Die neue Politik und Parteien-polarisierung." In *Wahlen und politischer Prozess,* ed. Hans-Dieter Klingemann and Max Kaase. Opladen: Westdeutscher Verlag.

Dalton, Russell J., and Manfred Kuechler, eds. 1990. *Challenging the Political Order: New Social and Political Movements in Western Democracies.* New York: Oxford University Press.

Eulau, Heinz, and Michael Lewis-Beck, eds. 1985. *Economic Conditions and Electoral Outcomes: The United States and Western Europe.* New York: Agathon.

Himmelweit, Hilde T., Patrick Humphreys, and Marianne Jaeger. [1981] 1985. *How Voters Decide.* Milton Keynes: Open University Press.

Kinder, Donald R., and Roderick Kiewiet. 1979. "Economic Discontent and Political Behavior: The Role of Personal Grievances and Collective Economic Judgments in Congressional Voting." *American Journal of Political Science* 23:495–527.

Klingemann, Hans-Dieter, 1986. "Der vorsichtig abwägende Wähler: Einstellungen zu den politischen Parteien und Wahlabsicht." In *Wahlen und politischer Prozess,* ed. Hans-Dieter Klingemann and Max Kaase. Opladen: Westdeutscher Verlag.

Kritzer, Herbert M. 1978a. "Analyzing Contingency Tables by Weighted Least Squares: An Alternative to the Goodman Approach." *Political Methodology* 5:277–326.

Kritzer, Herbert M. 1978b. "An Introduction to Multivariate Contingency Table Analysis." *American Journal of Political Science* 21:187–226.

Kuechler, Manfred. 1985. "Ökonomische Kompetenzuteile und individuelles politisches Verhalten: Empirische Ergebnisse am Beispiel der Bundestagswahl 1983." In *Wirtschaftlicher Wandel, religiöser Wandel und Wertwandel: Folgen für das politische Verhalten in der Bundesrepublik Deutschland*, ed. Dieter Oberndörfer, Hans Rattinger, and Karl Schmitt. Berlin: Duncker und Humblot.

Kuechler, Manfred. 1986. "Maximizing Utility at the Polls? A Replication of Himmelweit's 'Consumer Model of Voting' with German Election Data from 1983." *European Journal of Political Research* 14:81–95.

Kuechler, Manfred. 1988. "Die Wahlerfolge der NSDAP bis 1932 im Lichte der modernen Wahlforschung." Paper presented at the 24th Deutschen Soziologentag.

Kuechler, Manfred, and Jeffrey Wides. 1980. "Perzeption der Wirtschaftslage und Wahlentscheidung." *Politische Vierteljahresschrift* 21:4–19.

Kuechler, Manfred, and Jeffrey Wides. 1982. "Economic Perceptions and the 1976 and 1980 Presidential Votes." *ZUMA-Arbeitsbericht*, no. 3: 165–204.

Lohmöller, Jan-Bernd, Jürgen W. Falter, Andreas Link, and Johann de Rijke. 1985. "Unemployment and the Rise of National Socialism: Contradicting Results from Different Regional Aggregations." In *Measuring the Unmeasurable*, ed. Peter Nijkamp. The Hague: Elsevier.

Pappi, Franz-Urban. 1986. "Das Wahlverhalten sozialer Gruppen bei Bundestagswahlen im Zeitvergleich." In *Wahlen und politischer Prozess*, ed. Hans-Dieter Klingemann and Max Kaase. Opladen: Westdeutscher Verlag.

Peffley, Mark, Stanley Feldman, and Lee Sigelman. 1987. "Economic Conditions and Party Competence: Processes of Belief Revision." *Journal of Politics* 49:100–121.

Rabinowitz, George, and Stuart Elaine Macdonald. 1989. "A Directional Theory of Issue Voting." *American Political Science Review* 83:93–121.

Schmitt, Karl. 1988. *Konfession und politisches Verhalten in der Bundesrepublik*. Berlin: Duncker und Humblot.

Wides, Jeffrey, and Manfred Kuechler. 1981. "Economic Perceptions and the 1976 Presidential Vote: A WLS Analysis." *Micropolitics* 1:369–93.

Ambiguous Intervention:
The Role of Government Action
in Public Evaluation of the Economy

James E. Alt

The empirical basis of popularity functions is well-established.[1] However, even a cursory look at Frey and Schneider's (1984) comprehensive review shows that far more changes and differences exist than have been explained. This is not damaging to the field, however. In fact, it is precisely the need to bring such diversity within the scope of general models that gives the field its pleasant sense of challenge. A major desideratum is to find models that are relatively stable or in which the instability is theoretically explicable over time within countries as well as across countries.

Increasingly, scholars argue that the way to do this is to deal explicitly with voters' economic information, concentrating on focus, direction, and sophistication. "Focus" means who is involved. When people think about the economy, do they see it as composed of individuals (with themselves as central), members of groups, or as an aspect of countries as a whole? Certainly, data series reflecting each focus have been accumulated, and one can imagine scholars (with some success) explaining cross-national and cross-temporal differences by differences or changes in the focus of attention. "Direction" means forward- or backward-looking, or retrospective or prospective evaluation. Its study reflects efforts to determine the extent to which people are myopic (shortsighted forward) or amnesic (quick to forget). Then there is "sophistication." Do people who evaluate economic outcomes understand how the economy works, and is their model correct? Do they use information efficiently? How great (and cost-effective) is the demand for such

The author gratefully acknowledges the assistance of the National Science Foundation under grant 80-06488 (data collection) and grants 85-12037 and 86-40444 (analysis).

1. The existence of predictable policy differences between parties vitiates Stigler's (1973) theoretical critique of popularity function models. Norpoth and Yantek (1983) cast doubt on the exogeneity of economic conditions, but their test, of fairly low power, risks failing to find significant cross-time-series effects which do, in fact, exist.

information? Or is information something that people only accumulate when supplied by others (media, politicians)?

This chapter deals with sophistication. My point is to bring government itself into the information-transmission process, to show that insofar as the public responds to mediated cues and/or signals in accumulating information about the economy, the economic policy actions of government affect what the public thinks about, if not necessarily of what it thinks of it.

Importantly, this signaling role also presents mixed incentives for government intervention, a problem hitherto overlooked by students of the feedback between popular evaluation and government economic policy. In a nutshell, the problem is that to intervene is to make the economy better *later,* while the public is made more aware *now* of how bad things have become. Thus, the immediate impact of an intervention on public opinion depends on the balance between any positive effect on expectations (to the extent there is confidence in the effectiveness of the policy) and a negative effect on retrospective evaluations from increased awareness of economic problems. The long-run effect depends on how fast the short-run effect fades and whether improvement is sustained. Section 1 develops some of the complexities of this intervention calculus. Section 2 describes data and method, and section 3 uses British survey data to provide some preliminary estimates of the relative roles of past and future in determining the impact of a policy intervention on public opinion.

1. Government Intervention as a Source of Information

Studies from at least nine countries (Frey and Schneider 1984) establish the impact on political popularity of economic conditions. Most frequently, the conditions include the rate (or changes in it) of growth of real (maybe disposable) income, price inflation, or unemployment, while occasionally studies ascribe effects to the exchange rate, trade balance, or even the tax burden. Additionally, scholars have looked for, measured, and estimated the effect on popularity of noneconomic factors, including the personal popularity of leading politicians, external effects like war, and balance of the government's domestic record. Information about all these conditions accumulates gradually over time in a backward-discounted fashion.[2]

---

2. Personal factors have been incorporated by shifts corresponding to different incumbents (many models) or through explicit modeling of the relationship between the personal popularity of the prime minister and overall vote intention (Hudson 1984). The role of war in popularity has been recognized for a long time (see, e.g., Mueller 1970), though Norpoth (in this volume) has given the debate renewed precision. The connection between incumbents' records and votes received was analyzed by Alt (1979) and has recently received theoretical attention from Hudson (1985), criticized by Stray and Beaumont (1987). Cumulation with backward discounting is usually modeled by including a lagged dependent variable in estimation.

Most of these studies employ a model of individual citizens monitoring and responding to economic conditions in a continuous fashion. A few exceptions concentrate instead on information flow and voter learning, modeling the impact of mass media and dramatic events on public opinion, the reciprocal influences of public opinion and public policy, and the content and efficiency of popular monitoring and learning about the economy. The general framework of this chapter draws on these, first to present a model of the flow of information from economy to vote choice, and then to discuss the ambiguous role of government intervention.

Information Flow from the Economy to the Vote

The transition from real economy to electoral choice[3] contains several cognitive and evaluative steps. The individual's ultimate choice, vote (or its intentional counterpart, popularity), presupposes some judgment about the overall record of the incumbent government. If this approval of record efficiently summarizes all past performance which is deemed relevant to vote choice, any other information affecting voting is either not performance-based (for instance, personal attributes) or not retrospective (for example, expectations, but only insofar as they do not themselves reflect perceptions of past performance). Hudson (1984) deals with the first, and earlier work by Kuklinski and West (1981) and Lewis-Beck's (1988) comparative work establish that future expectations can be just as important as retrospective evaluations.

The government's economic record plays a role in the individual's evaluation of the government's more general record. Alt (1979) estimates the closeness of fit between these stages, and Hudson's (1985) sophisticated analysis confirms the overall result. The contribution of the economy to the government's overall record depends on the extent to which the economy is perceived to be the most important issue facing the country, something intensively investigated by MacKuen (1981), who also shows how the state of the economy influences the perceived importance of economic problems.

Before any of this, the real economy has to be turned into a "subjective" economy, a complex perceptual problem. Once inside the minds of the electorate, the cumulation of information about the economy into a view of how well the incumbents have handled the economy is largely a matter of understanding how individuals attribute responsibility for economic change. Attribution of responsibility can result from persuasion by others, but presupposes (in any case) some model of the economy that explains how things

---

3. See my earlier discussion (Alt 1979, 127). Lewis-Beck's (1988) model is a subset of this one, moving directly from the perceived economy, to government's handling of the economy, to vote.

work, and thus why something either results from or could have been altered by government intervention.[4]

But no one can attribute responsibility for what has not been noticed, so knowledge is also important. The subjective economy has both forward- and backward-looking elements, and contains both general (the health of the economy) and specific (either personal effects or individual conditions like inflation) concerns, all of which must be modeled.[5] Moreover, while direct monitoring has a role, mediation is very important. Both the media and the actions of government can have significant agenda-setting or attention-grabbing effects on public opinion.

Of these, the role of the media has had more scholarly attention. A host of experimental studies attest to media effects. MacKuen (1981 and 1983) demonstrated an agenda-setting role in popular opinions of issue importance and popularity for the mass media. Dalton and Duval (1986) show that attention and content respond to mediation with respect to British public opinion on EC membership. Mosley (1984 and 1985) claims that the instability of the economy-opinion relationship (which was our starting point) occurs because the public pays irregular attention to the economy. In his view, moreover, it is press coverage that signals crisis, draws the attention of an unwary public to economic conditions, and even supplies the information used by the public in evaluating the economy (independent of the underlying, real economic condition). Just how much his data actually reveal is unclear, but the general conclusion is right in step with an incontrovertible theme of the recent literature, that media coverage is an important independent source of information. We will build on this subsequently.

Popular Response to Government Intervention

Think of the average citizen watching the economy flow past and wondering what to make of it. Are things better? Worse? Is it government that is responsible? Is anyone? Naturally, there are some things like income, employment status, and prices that are routinely and inevitably observed. Probably those

---

4. Kramer (1983) points out the critical role of responsibility in measurement and Rivers (n.d.) shows one way to measure it. Peffley, Feldman, and Sigelman (1987) and Conover and Feldman (1986) show the importance of different psychological states in activating a response. Chappell and Keech (1985) raise the possibility that models are subtler and more sophisticated than is often thought, and Beck (1987) shows that information processing in such a model has some characteristics of efficient effort.

5. Beck (1987) argues that people should be most concerned with what most affects them, and finds evidence for popular monitoring of the food price index rather than the general CPI, a point originally made by Mosley (1984). Moreover, efficient use of information would lead one to predict that in time-series analysis of attitudes to inflation, actual inflation (and anything believed to cause changes in it) should have effects while "irrelevant" economic conditions should not.

that strike closest to home are observed most closely. Some things like the external balance, which may nevertheless be very important in policy, are relatively invisible.

Not quite invisible, of course: the air is full of "news" about the economy. One vital conclusion to emerge from media studies is the importance of the dramatic quality of an event in eliciting a political response in the public. Mosley's contrast between the voter patiently monitoring those economic trends that affect him and the voter generally indifferent and only occasionally shocked by some startling occurrence could not be clearer. In fact, much of the news carries attributions of responsibility as well. Nevertheless, these are not unambiguous sources of information: claims of blame are matched by counterclaims of innocence. Many media sources are known to be biased and their claims likely to be discounted by the public. So it is not clear that *only* the media produce the kinds of event which capture the public's attention.

Another such event is the announcement of a major policy change. For instance, annual British budgets come out to much fanfare. Several hours of television coverage and pages in the papers are hard to overlook. Of course, there are more announcements than there are policy changes.[6] Nevertheless, for the voter intermittently exposed to bursts of information about the economy, the sort of big, dramatic, well-covered announcement of a policy change can be a major source of information, not just about the direction of policy and the responsibility of government but also about the underlying conditions that brought about the change of course.

What sort of popular response to a policy change should we expect? Take the case of an incomes policy. There are at least four possible patterns of response. First, if the incomes policy is itself the outcome of a predictable political response to the same conditions the public monitors (inflation), then it will have no effect on public opinion beyond making rational individuals more certain of their forecasts. This is the rational expectations hypothesis. However, maybe the policy is valued in its own right. Then, if people believe it will work, they will both see and expect improvement. By contrast, if people think it will only work temporarily, at best, they may feel the country is now better off (retrospective change) but not expect more improvement in the future (no change in expectations). Finally, if policy change functions as a signal, reminding or alerting people that inflation is worse than they thought, the dominant retrospective effect would be negative, with the prospective effect depending on their confidence in its effectiveness. For modeling purposes, while responses can be measured at both individual and aggregate

---

6. Some events are media events and some are real events covered by the media. Some announcements claim credit but reflect no underlying policy change of importance; their effects are announcement effects. Others signal real policy changes. The voter's problem is to decide which is the case.

levels, their pattern could be any of these. We will see below in fact that there is evidence for all of them in public opinion.

The Intervention Calculus

Students of public policy often model government economic interventions as simple functional responses to past economic outcomes (See Alt and Chrystal 1983, chap. 6). But if

> i) voting has retrospective and prospective elements,
> ii) politicians consider the effect of the economy on voting in deciding whether or not to intervene, and
> iii) intervention acts as a signal in the way just described,

then we can model the complex choice of whether or not to intervene. To see how, let us start by assuming that the political system has two centralized competing parties, which voters support based on both retrospective and prospective economic judgments. Retrospective judgments reflect accumulated perceptions of past performance and depend critically on the rate at which people forget the past. Prospective judgments are expectations of future economic performance, and depend also on individuals' rates of discount. Policy is a function of past economic conditions and politicians' vote hopes. Finally, voting is a function of economy, retrospectively and prospectively judged, with voters' attention stimulated by dramatic announcements of policy changes, as described above. Now if dramatic interventions rekindle hope in the public but also remind people of what has been going on, then governments contemplating intervention face a highly ambiguous choice.

Let us develop a simple example (sketched in fig. 1) that ignores several complications like discounting. Say the economy has been overheating, so that inflation is rising through time on the path labelled ii'. Since an election is coming, it is reasonable to worry about the damage that inflation will do, and so at time t^* the government clearly has some incentive to intervene to reduce inflation. It has, as ever, one instrument, say the bank lending rate, and can use this to raise interest rates. This will restrict demand, leading to reduced inflation along the line i^*i''. If it does not, of course, it continues to have the opportunity to intervene at least until after the next election when either it or (if the incumbents are defeated) the opposition has the opportunity to intervene in the same way. At that point, inflation would head along path $i^e i'''$. However, (at least some members of) the electorate have (reasonably) been paying little attention, and their perceptions lag true inflation, so that on average the electorate believes it to be proceeding along path $i^p i^{p'}$. Should the government intervene?

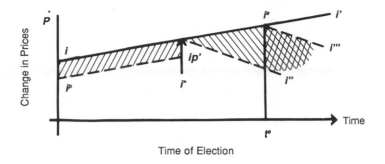

Fig. 1. Intervention timing, costs, and benefits

Obviously, the answer is no longer unambiguous. It depends on the relative sizes, within the subjective economy, of at least five different sorts of effects. These include:

1. The cumulative *gain* in popularity that the government derives from publicly observed reduced inflation before the election. This benefit is proportional to the size of the triangle between i^*i^e and i^*i'', from t^* to t^e, which in turn depends on the effectiveness of the scale of the reduction in inflation and the amount of time left before the election. The gain increases the incumbents' probability of reelection, though ex ante it has to be discounted for uncertainty both about the economic model used, the possibility of exogenous effects on inflation, and the extent to which the improvement in inflation will be observed by the public.

2. The cumulative *gain* to the incumbents from their improved position in the next administration (the inverse of the opportunity costs of inaction), reflecting the cumulative benefits of beginning at t^e on the path i^*i'' rather than at i^e. This is proportional to the parallelogram between $i^e i'''$ and i^*i'', bounded on the left by t^e and to the right by the rate of discounting the future. These gains, naturally, have to be discounted ex ante by the probability of reelection given early intervention and the same sorts of uncertainty as in 1.

3. The cumulative *loss* in popularity from the increase in interest rates, normally ignored or assumed to be small in the empirical study of popularity functions, in which voters are normally assumed to focus on ends rather than means.

4. The cumulative *loss* from signaling the severity of past deterioration of the economy through heightened awareness of inflation. This is in proportion to the parallelogram between ii^* and $i^p i^{p'}$, bounded to the

right at t^*. To the left it is bounded by backward discounting, or the rate of forgetting, given the signal of intervention.

5. Finally, the cumulative *gain*, if any, from improved expectations of future expectations, which has the same effects as 1 but is less certain, given lack of knowledge about the process of expectation formation, and possibly smaller, for several reasons. First, if 4 is large, the effect of discovering one's self to be worse off may, other things being equal, reduce expectations of improvement. Second, while certainty grows as observed inflation falls, the benefits of the observation may increasingly move from 5 to 1: there is no guarantee of both sorts of benefit accruing simultaneously. All in all, this is a risky term on which to depend very heavily.[7]

This has some further consequences. First, the closer one is to an election, the less benefit will accrue from 1 and 5, and, equally, the less will be the inaction opportunity cost in 2; all in all, the closer to an election, the less likely is intervention. This is paradoxical, since the closer to the election, other things being equal, the greater the pressure to heed reelection prospects is likely to be.

Second, with a dynamic model of the economy, one could probably calculate an optimal time for intervention. From the logic of the last paragraph, it would be early in the term: not too early, as that increases the uncertainty of effect, but not too late, since that increases the signaling cost, 4. As a guess, as 4 increases relative to 1, 2, and 5, an early midcourse correction seems to be what this sort of model calls for, rather than a later dash for economic correction.

More results could doubtless be derived. For present purposes, one observation is sufficient. Given the assumptions I have made, without a specification of the intervention calculus, the relationship between the economy, policy interventions, and voting will appear highly unstable. This depends mostly on whether intervention acts as a signal, that is, informs people about the past while changing their expectations of the future. The rest of the chapter investigates that question empirically.

2. Data and Method

We hope to estimate government-mediated links between the real and subjective economy, independent of the effects of individual monitoring and the mass media. To do this separately for the four parts of the subject economy—

---

7. I deliberately omit a further complication. If expectations set the future standard against which performance is judged, all future retrospective judgments have to be calculated net of the changed expectations. Any positive effect on expectations must diminish the positive impact of future observed performance.

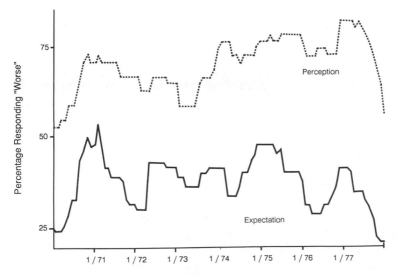

Fig. 2. Perceptions and expectations of general situation worsening, Britain, 1970–77

specific and general, past and future—for the case of Britain from 1961 to 1981 requires combining data from three separate sets of surveys conducted monthly by two different political/market research companies.[8] I will take a first cut here at only two series: retrospective and prospective views of general economic conditions. Policy-relevant extensions of the results discussed in Section 1 will be taken up in another publication.

Dependent Variables

The dependent variables are taken from a subset of the British Market Research Bureau financial expectations survey, from February, 1970, to December, 1977, or 95 observations in all. Figure 2 displays the results of these two series of monthly British market research surveys in which respondents were asked whether they thought the "country was in a better or worse state than it had been a year ago," and whether it would again "be in a better or worse state a year hence." The figure displays the proportions believing that

8. Gallup conducts two of the surveys. One, from 1961–79, contains predictions of inflation and unemployment; the other, from 1972–79, contains retrospective and prospective questions on family finances, inflation, and the general economic health of the country, and a prediction of unemployment. The British Market Research Bureau's "financial expectations" survey, monthly from 1971–81, contains past and future general conditions, past personal finances, and a prediction of unemployment. All data were provided by the ESRC Data Archive at the University of Essex, whose assistance is gratefully acknowledged. All these surveys are done monthly (with occasional gaps) and average about 1000 respondents each.

things had become or would become "worse," as opposed to "better" or "the same." The two series behave rather differently, apart from the fact that throughout the period expectations are uniformly less negative than perceptions. The perception of the past series moves toward increased negativism in a steady fashion for about six years, and then shows a very sharp upswing at the end. The expectation series, on the other hand, appears to be stationary in the sense of oscillating around a constant value (about 35 percent to 40 percent thinking things will get worse), but oscillate is just what it does, and a great deal more—though over fairly short periods—than does the perception series.

Independent Variables

Economic Conditions. To preserve our ability to investigate dynamic relationships, I restricted my attention to measures of economic conditions that were available monthly and of some obvious central concern, at least to a subset of the population. I will use six variables: unemployment, the rate in percent, which varies in this period from 2 percent to nearly 6 percent; inflation, the annual rate of increase in the retail price index, which varies from 5 percent to 25 percent; short-time work, as a percentage of the labor force, which normally varies between 0.5 percent and 2.5 percent but on the occasion of major industrial disputes exceeds 20.0 percent;[9] bank or minimum lending rate, in percent, an indicator of credit market conditions, which varies from 6 percent to 15 percent; exchange rate, dollars per unit sterling, from $1.61 to $2.61; and finally, real incomes, the ratio of average earnings to the retail price index, as an annual percentage growth rate which varies from about −5 percent to +10 percent. The incorporation of these variables will be taken to reflect individual monitoring.[10] One would generally expect people to dislike inflation, unemployment, short-time work, and high interest rates, and to like higher real incomes, and feel the economy was accordingly better when real incomes were higher. People could like a higher exchange rate for status reasons, which would be my prior guess, or dislike it for its adverse effects on exports or the balance of trade. We expect that people will feel that prevalence of things they like puts themselves and the country, other things being equal, in a better state.

Government Policy Events. The most important precondition for any event study is to declare ex ante what will count as a significant event and

---

9. It is thus a spiky alternative to using strikes data, which I also collected. In addition to the data used, I accumulated series on housing and food prices and dollar reserves, as alternate measures of prices and monetary conditions.

10. I have also coded a media series, reflecting whether the balance of economic news was positive or negative in a given month, and what the subject predominantly was, but will not report those findings here.

TABLE 1. Chronology of Events

Date	Type	Event
October, 1970	B	Budget (neutral)
February, 1971	S	Rolls Royce bailout
April, 1971	B	Budget (major reflation)
July, 1971	B	Budget (marginal reflation)
October, 1971	S	National Union of Mineworkers overtime ban
January, 1972	S	National Union of Mineworkers strike
March, 1972	S	Budget (tax cuts, credit squeeze)
July, 1972	I	Floating of sterling/snake established
November, 1972	P	Incomes policy "Stage 1"
March, 1973	P	Stage 2 (obscures budget)
October, 1973	P	Stage 3
December, 1973	S	Miners' Strike (budget cuts, OPEC)
March, 1974	B	Budget (neutral)
July, 1974	B	Budget (subsidies, mild reflation)
November, 1974	B	Budget (mild restraint)
April, 1975	B	Budget (contractionary)
July, 1975	P	Social Contract policy
March, 1976	B	Budget (cash limits, neutral)
June, 1976	P	TUC accepts 4 percent
December, 1976	I	IMF demands expenditure cuts
March, 1977	I	IMF arranges loan
(October, 1977)	B	Budget (omitted in data)

Note: Table lists events divided into four types: B = budgets, S = strikes or industrial disputes, P = incomes policy, and I = international crises. Dates are taken from *The Times Index*, various volumes.

why; any other strategy leads to ad hoc residual fitting. We chose four categories of policy events: budgets, imposition of incomes policies, international crisis negotiations, and major industrial disputes (strikes or closures) in which government played an active part. These are listed in table 1. For estimation purposes, an event is coded by a 1 in the first month that survey interview dates indicate was subsequent to the event.[11] Data were taken from the "Calendar of Economic Events" published intermittently in *Economic Trends*.

---

11. The largest empirical problem with such event studies is that there is no way to demonstrate (other than through consistency of results) that the impact of the designated event in some month really stemmed from that event, and not from something else happening that month, let alone from random variation.

Estimation

If all sources of change in the subjective economy were economic, but if there were no inflation, no unemployment, and so on, so that no government response was triggered, then all respondents would recognize that the state of the country's economy had remained the same, and would choose that response alternative. In that case, the proportions choosing "worse" would be zero, errors of perception and judgment apart.[12] If there were some economic bads, the proportion would not be zero, but in the absence of change would be constant, representing an equilibrium value. Ignoring errors, only some event or change should move people to perceive change relative to this equilibrium, and it is reasonable to characterize the departure from equilibrium in terms of the reattractiveness of the "same" position (which is unknown but probably constant over time) and the dramatic quality or perceptibility of the various events and conditions. Letting the deviation from equilibrium perceptions at time t in response to the jth input event be written as P_{jt}, then the movement in P_{jt} from one time to the next may be written ΔP_{jt}, which is equal to

$$\Delta P_{jt} = b_j I_j - c_j P_{jt-1}, \tag{1}$$

where b scales the immediate impact of the input and c represents the reequilibration rate, so that the amount of reequilibration is proportional to the previous deviation.

Since ΔP_{jt} can be rewritten as $P_{jt} - P_{jt-1}$, equation 1 may be transformed into

$$P_{jt} = b_j I_j + (1 - c_j) P_{jt-1} \tag{2}$$

which, as MacKuen (1981 and 1983) shows, can be estimated by nonlinear least squares, assuming only the additivity of the effects of the individual inputs. This nonlinear procedure has two advantages. First, it allows a separate reequilibration rate to be estimated for each input.[13] It also estimates the outputs solely in terms of the inputs, without gaining benefit from any acci-

---

12. I use the response alternative "worse" rather than "better" because the proportions choosing this alternative were consistently larger, hopefully minimizing the biasing effects of random response and measurement error on the regression results.

13. The sensitivity of the method to choice of initial conditions is lessened by including a unit spike in the first period, to represent cumulative effects of disequilibrium prior to the start of the data period, under the assumption that these past effects fade in the same ways as other inpu. . The model allows opinion to adjust only partially to the latest development without imposing the same adjustment speed on the opinion response of all variables, the effect of the more usual inclusion of a lagged dependent variable.

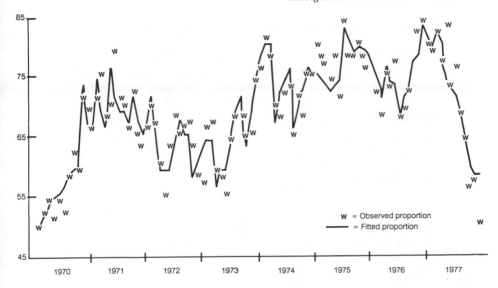

Fig. 3. Actual and fitted proportions perceiving economic deterioration, Britain, 1970–77

dental autocorrelation in the disturbances, as can afflict lagged dependent-variable models. An algorithm for such estimation is published in the appendix to Alt 1985.

3. Modeling Economic Perceptions and Expectations

Retrospective Evaluations

The results from estimating such a model of the retrospective general question are shown in table 2. The fit is very good: the residual error sum of squares is only about 12 percent of the original. The most the six economic conditions do on their own is to explain less than half the variance, so the events are clearly making an independent contribution, and more than randomly selecting one data point in five would achieve. Figure 3 shows that the model's tracking is very good.[14]

The impacts of the independent variables are presented in the table as cumulative impacts, which equal b/c in terms of equation 2. The cumulative

---

14. Two of the largest residuals are data problems. There should be an international crisis spike in January, 1976, as there were important IMF negotiations that month. There was an expansionary budget in October, 1977, but this came too close to the end of the series to be included.

TABLE 2. Estimates for Perceptions of Deterioration

Variable	Expected Sign	Cumulative Impact	Time Constant
Exogenous			
Constant		(53.4)	
Past		−27.6	12.1
Economic			
Inflation +1%	+	0.46	1.06
Unemployment +1%	+	2.63	1.11
Short-time work +1%	+	0.03	1.06
Bank rate +1%	+	3.55	2.50
Exchange rate +10%	−	2.29	10.00
Real incomes +1%	−	−1.02	5.00
Budgets			
October, 1970	+	27.3	2.1
April, 1971	+	38.0	3.2
August, 1971	+	2.7	1.8
March, 1972	−	−7.7	2.7
March, 1974	−	−33.9	2.4
July, 1974	−	−26.7	2.4
October, 1974	+	+3.9	1.4
March, 1975	+	−48.0	20.0
March, 1976	+	+18.3	2.9
Incomes Policies			
Stage 1 (10/72)	−	−37.6	5.9
Stage 2	−	−17.1	2.2
Stage 3	−	−24.3	2.7
Soc. Cont. (6/75)	−	+10.7	1.6
TUC 4% (1976)	−	−10.2	2.3
International			
Float/snake (6/72)	+	+24.2	3.0
IMF cuts (12/76)	+	+23.7	5.3
IMF loan (3/77)	+	+71.1	5.6
Strikes, bankruptcies			
Rolls Royce (2/71)	+	+19.1	2.0
Miners OB (1971)	+	+12.9	1.9
Miners strike (1972)	+	+3.6	1.5
Miners strike (12/73)	+	+1.4	1.3

$R^2 = .88$ $N = 95$

Source: Survey data are from the British Market Research Bureau, Financial Expectations surveys, 1970–77. Labor market data are from the Department of Employment *Gazette*, various issues. Other economic data are from the Central Statistical Office, *Economic Trends*, various issues.

impact is the total (i.e., measured in percent-months) over the whole of reequilibration, which is largely complete after two temporal units known as time constants, which are equal to $1/c$. A sustained unit input induces a shift in equilibrium of b/c, again after a similar delay (see MacKuen 1981 for details). Finally, $[b(k + 1)/c]$ is a linear approximation for the cumulative impact of a unit change sustained initially for k months.

Among the six economic variables, all but short-time work have scalar impact b coefficients that can be estimated significantly, for a given estimate of the dynamic parameter.[15] Short-time work has insignificant effects under any hypothesis. The exchange rate coefficient is consistent with the view that people reject the status of a high exchange rate and recognize that high sterling-to-dollar rates are bad for the country, though I find this somewhat hard to credit. The other coefficients show that increases in inflation, unemployment, and interest rates, and declines in real income growth, are associated with popular perception of economic deterioration.

For example, a 1.00 percentage point increase in interest rates, according to these estimates, makes a 1.42 percentage point difference in the extent of perceived deterioration immediately, and ultimately makes a difference of 3.55 percentage points spread over only a few months, since reequilibration is fairly quick ($c = .4$). Of course, were the increase in interest rates to be permanent, the equilibrium level of perceived deterioration would rise by 3.55 percentage points. A 1.00 percentage point increase in interest rates that lasted six months would have a cumulative impact of about 25, similar in size to that of some of the more dramatic economic policy announcements.

Turning to policy events, international crises clearly are significantly associated with a heightened public sense of economic deterioration. The typical immediate impact is about 5 to 10 percentage points, and the effects are among the longest lasting of the events. Some are clearly still present six to twelve months after the initial crisis. In one case, the cuts after December, 1976, public opinion could simply be reflecting dislike of the changes in public expenditure. In others, signaling appears to be more important as the public appears to become more aware of the underlying situation's gravity.

By contrast, incomes policies generally appear to have made people feel that the country was better off. Only the announcement of the Social Contract, in June, 1975, did not have this effect. The retrospective effects of incomes policy commencements typically lasted less than six months. In this way they resembled industrial disputes, which consistently increased the proportions feeling the country was worse off, though significantly so in only two cases.

Budgets also display fairly consistent short-run dynamics, with only one reequilibration coefficient very different from about 0.5, so that the perceptual effects of budgets appear to dissipate within three to four months. The signs of the effects are inconsistent. The two budgets corresponding to major changes of fiscal direction (see Mosley 1985), those of April, 1971, and March, 1975,

---

15. Estimating all the parameters simultaneously strains the algorithm, so for all practical purposes an iterative convergence routine of estimating first the bs and then the cs is used. I will comment here on the significance of the bs contingent on the last estimated set of cs.

appear to act as signals, with the reflationary 1971 budget serving to heighten the perception of the recession it was designed to cure and the later budget apparently underscoring the boom it was designed to damp.[16] Beyond these, other reflationary budgets are generally seen as good for the country (the perception of decline goes down), and so on. We cannot explain the large increase in negative perceptions after October, 1970.

Still, the perception of events marking policy innovations appears to influence evaluation of the state of the economy significantly. Monitoring of the underlying conditions also counts, but probably less so, at least unless changes in these conditions are very large or long-sustained.[17] With these results, we can try to explain how perceptions of economic change influence popular expectations of the economy.

Adaptive Expectations

The literature on economic expectations is dominated by the conflict between two models, rational versus adaptive expectations.[18] The rational expectation efficiently summarizes all information available at the time it is formed. Testing, say, inflation expectations for rationality would involve determining whether people efficiently used known causes of inflation in making their forecasts. What the "right" model of a general belief about the country's future economic state would be is unclear, but at least we would expect economic variables to appear as significant predictors.

By contrast, an adaptive model of expectation formation is one in which the agent periodically revises his or her expectations in the light of the discrepancy between his or her last forecast and the actual outcome since it was made. The simplest such scheme is a first-order adaptive or error-learning process in which expectations adjust only as a proportion λ of the last recorded error, thus:

$$E_t - E_{t-1} = \lambda(P_t - E_{t-1}),$$

where E_t denotes an expectation and P_t a perception or observation made at time t. These adaptive schemes can be extended by letting the observations

---

16. The dynamic parameter for the spring 1975 budget is out of line with all others, so there may be some misspecification of effects here.

17. It remains to be determined separately whether the media have an independent role in both the transmission of information about events and economic conditions.

18. It is also dominated by one particular data set, the set of data on expected prices submitted by a panel of businessmen and economic and financial consultants in response to a regular survey conducted by journalist Joseph Livingstone. Economic analyses of this set have focused almost entirely on the question of rationality, in a variety of senses.

accumulate over longer periods or by allowing adjustment to be made in response to more than the most recent error. In general, the adaptive process is:

$$E_t - E_{t-1} = \sum_i \lambda_i (P_{t-1} - E_{t-i-1})$$

where $0 < \lambda_i < 1$ and the λ_i decrease as i increases. The bigger λ_0 is, the more expectations are updated in accordance with present perceptions; $\lambda_0 = 1$ and $\lambda_i = 0$ for $i > 1$ is the special case in which expectations are formed extrapolatively from present perceptions.[19] Mincer (1969) points out that the first-order adaptive model is a form of "exponential" forecasting, in the sense that weights on successive terms decline exponentially, as above.

A class of forecasts in which the weights decline at less than an exponential rate is called "convex" forecasting. Convex forecasting is a generalization of "return-to-normality" forecasting, where each individual guesses the likely long-term rate of inflation and makes shorter-term forecasts based on the discrepancy between the current observed rate of inflation and the long-term expected rate. Such forecasts generally reveal a negative correlation between present values of the series being forecast (e.g., presently high) and the predicted direction of future flow (e.g., down). Mincer (1969, 97–98) proves that if many individuals forecast exponentially, their aggregated (summed or averaged) forecast will appear to be convex if not all individual adaptation parameters are equal (see also Bierwag and Grove 1966). So an aggregate finding of return-to-normality forecasting (Kane and Malkiel 1976) is consistent with a model of individual variation in adaptive forecasting.

Time Series Models of Expectations

Table 3 presents the results of an attempt to estimate general economic expectations from variables similar to those discussed previously. The model is a variant of adaptive expectations, in which expectations adjust to the difference between current perceptions and previous expectations, but it is estimated in the same nonlinear fashion as before, so the reequilibration coefficients provide the evidence about the speed of partial adjustment or, alternatively, length of memory. Perceptions are represented by the fitted values from the

---

19. Some confuse expectation as prediction with its other sense of customary or habitually accepted values, where the "expected" values are obtained by summing a geometric series of past values taken to represent the levels people have become used to and thus "expect." The confusion arises precisely because an infinite sum of past values with geometrically declining exponential weights and the first-order adaptive scheme above are the *same* thing.

TABLE 3. Estimates for Expectations of Deterioration

Variable	Cumulative Impact	Time Constant
Exogenous		
Constant	48.5	
Past	15.9	1.6
Economic		
Inflation +1%	0.15	0.0
Unemployment +1%	2.22	0.0
Short-time work +1%	−3.00	20.0
Bank rate +1%	1.80	1.9
Exchange rate +10¢	2.40	12.0
Real incomes +1%	−1.50	7.5
Budgets		
October, 1970	62.0	5.3
April, 1971	0.0	0.0
August, 1971	−0.3	0.0
March, 1972	−1.6	0.0
March, 1974	−9.3	7.5
July, 1974	30.8	5.9
October, 1974	95.0	6.7
March, 1975	45.0	3.8
March, 1976	5.0	0.0
Incomes Policies		
Stage 1	2.6	0.0
Stage 2	−1.7	2.0
Stage 3	2.2	0.0
Soc. contr.	−7.3	4.1
TUC 4%	64.0	20.0
International		
Float/snake	113.0	20.0
IMF Cuts	1.4	0.0
IMF Loan	22.5	4.8
Strikes, bankruptcies		
Rolls Royce	26.0	3.3
Miners OB	−2.2	0.0
Miners strike (1972)	−5.3	0.0
Miners strike (1973)	5.5	1.1
Economic Perceptions	0.41	0.0
	$R^2 = .80$ $N = 95$	

Source: Data sources are as in table 2.

equation reported in table 2, so it is the anticipated component: anything else represents the surprise, or the part of expectations not already reflected in perceptions.

These results are not encouraging, and suggest that the model is not right, at least in its present form. In the first place, the fit is greatly inferior to that observed in the case of perceptions. Not only do expectations oscillate more, but they are less explicable by these variables. Only the contemporaneous fitted values of perceptions appear to matter: there is absolutely no evidence of dynamic reequilibration. Alternately, there is no evidence of adaptation to, only extrapolation from, anticipated deterioration. An encouraging part of this analysis is that the coefficient of fitted perceptions is .41, similar in magnitude to an expected value I derive below.

Independent of this effect of perceptions, only a few of the economic conditions and events have further demonstrable effects, and they show a mixed pattern. Some, like the effect of real income growth, add a little direct reinforcement to the indirect effect of the same condition through perceptions. For instance, in the case of real incomes, a 1.0 percentage point increase in growth translates into a direct cumulative effect of about -1.5 percentage points, to which can be added another -0.4 ($= .41 \times 1.02$) for the indirect effect through perceptions, making the overall effect on expectations about twice as large as on perceptions. The same is true of the exchange rate; all other conditions have apparently smaller effects on expectations than perceptions, but as yet we have neither a theoretical explanation for these differences nor convincing empirical evidence that they exist. The effects of events are typically smaller and less well determined in this case than in table 2, but again we are far short of evidence for the proposition that events move perceptions rather than expectations. Most important, the cluster of three large negative effects attaching to the budgets from July, 1974, to March, 1975, needs further investigation: this is a period including a general election, and the observed negativism could have something to do with that.

Microstructure of Perceptions and Expectations: The Survey Response

Recall the observation above that perceptions wandered while expectations oscillated (fig. 3). Apparently, expectations are generated by a stronger self-equilibrating dynamic process than perceptions. Perceptions are driven by observations of events. These observations accumulate into a sense of whether things are going better or not, which has little inherent tendency to return to a particular level. Aggregate expectations, on the other hand, return to "normal" levels after being driven off these levels by shocks that may or may not be reflected in the accumulated perceptions.

Such a dynamic relationship between perceptions and expectations could arise even in the absence of any information about economic change or individual decisions whatsoever. Consider a hypothetical cross-tabulation of replies to two survey questions: (1) whether things have recently gotten better or worse; and (2) whether people expect things to become better or worse.

Assume that the interviews take place under a cloudless sky—that is, that there are no momentous events occurring. Since we don't know what information people use in responding, methodological conservatism dictates spreading about 10 percent of cases equiprobably around the table to allow for measurement and response error. Assume further that under a cloudless sky each category of perceptions is equally likely, and that people expect what they perceive to continue or *cumulate*. People who think things have gotten better should expect them to continue to get better, for instance. Some will think the opposite, but these will be few. Arbitrarily, we allow 10 percent to expect such unexplained reversals of fortune.

However, people can communicate the expectation of cumulative effects in two ways: by saying "better-better" or, having given a perception of "better," saying "same" to indicate that things would be much the same— that is, "better"—in the future. For this reason one would expect a disproportionate regression to the mean from both extremes in expectations, and we might want to break responses down in a 60-40 proportion to represent this. What to expect of people whose perception is "same" is more difficult; "same" should predominate as an expectation with equal, though smaller, probabilities of saying either "better" or "worse." We can use 25-50-25 as possible proportions. These numbers don't matter too much as long as they are not totally unreasonable. These assumptions produce this result for 100 hypothetical respondents:

Expect		*Perceive*	
	Worse	Same	Better
Better	4	9	17
Same	12	16	12
Worse	17	9	4

Now, if "better-same-worse" is coded $\{1, 0, -1\}$ and the expectation is regressed onto the perceptions for these 100 hypothetical cases, the resulting equation is Expectations = .393 Perceptions. The coefficient is about .4 and arises out of the assumed distribution (or any numerically similar set of assumptions) described above.[20] It is similar in magnitude to the time-series aggregate result reported above.

Assume that when something happens, that is, when there is some shock introduced into this system and the assumed "cloudless sky" disappears, people will stop having this sort of cumulative expectation and more com-

---

20. In a completely independent study, Lewis-Beck (1988,88) regressed "expectations of future economic policies" on "assessment of past economic policies" and obtained a coefficient estimate of .36.

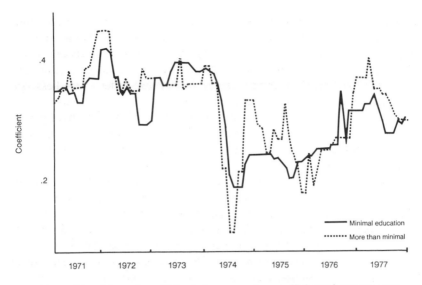

Fig. 4. Monthly series of bivariate regression coefficients between general expectations and perceptions, Britain, 1970–77

monly expect reversals of fortune. Then it will be more likely that people thinking things have become better will now expect them (owing to the shock) to become worse, and vice versa. The result is a relative shift toward the depopulated corners of the table above. Hence the coefficient from a regression of expectations on perceptions after a shock will be smaller, and perceptions will be less of a guide to expectations. As time passes, the effects of the shock diminish and expectations again begin to sort themselves out around perceptions in the cumulative manner described above, though individuals may now have changed places in the table.[21] Unless more shocks intervene, after a while the sky will again be truly cloudless and the coefficients should return to a level of about .4, on the assumptions made above. Thus, .4 is a sort of steady state or equilibrium value for the coefficient of the cross-section regression of expectations on perceptions, below which the coefficient drops after shocks and toward which it returns as calm is restored.

Figure 4 displays a time-series of the monthly bivariate regression coefficients of general economic expectations on perceptions. Separate series are shown for those with more than minimal education and those with minimal

---

21. Compare the discussion of "surprises" in Konig, Nerlove, and Oudiz 1981, as well as their approach to modeling adaptive expectations in the context of categorical survey data. Their ideas are inapplicable to the present study, since they are analyzing repeated panels, and the subjects are spokesmen for firms rather than the mass public.

education. The figure has been heavily smoothed by taking moving averages of groups of five adjacent entries in order to mask very short-term disturbances. The regression coefficient in the period studied only exceeds .4 once or twice. Most of the series is near equilibrium, but many shocks are evident.

The biggest shock is obvious. It is the Oil Crisis of October, 1973, and both series turn down sharply after the October, 1973, interviews.[22] The series rise through the first few months displayed, which immediately follow the election of June, 1970, as the uncertainties surrounding a new incumbency disappear. In fact, the election month coefficient—the interviews were before the election—is extremely low (.15 or so) in each series, but this shock is transitory, and confidence is largely restored so quickly that the real election shock is smoothed out of the series.[23] Other noteworthy shocks include mid-1971 (the announcement of the decision to enter the Common Market) and January, 1977, when the Labour government accepted terms for an IMF loan and committed itself to massive expenditure cuts. These shocks produce uncertainty, though they need not be the worst news of the period, which might have simultaneously depressed perceptions and expectations, but left the relationship between them unaffected.

The disaggregation shown in figure 4 is also noteworthy. Different population subgroups probably process and evaluate information differently, leading to different patterns of adaptation and misleading results when different groups are aggregated. Unfortunately, the surveys from which these questions were taken do not contain a good direct measure of information usage. However, when one group processes more information than another, the time path of its expectations-perceptions relationship should be characterized by more variability, as more shocks will be observed which shift the relationship off its equilibrium path. Figure 4 clearly indicates that both the frequency and amplitude of swings are greater in the series representing those with more than minimal formal education. This would also happen if the information that moves expectations relative to perceptions is generated in the communications media and therefore disproportionately received, evaluated, and reacted to by the more educated portion of the population. Thus, the generally slower movement of the series representing those with minimal education is con-

---

22. Recall that this did not appear to be a major factor in perceptions of well-being, but appears to affect the relationship between expectations and perceptions.

23. Two features of this election-time uncertainty are important. First, it is pronounced, albeit transitory. This is consistent with its treatment in Alesina and Sachs 1988. Second, it is so transitory that most national election surveys will not pick it up, since their fieldwork is largely undertaken more than a month after the election, by which time expectations and perceptions have realigned. Hence, tests of the role of prospective judgments on (even recently) past voting are of doubtful value.

sistent either with insulation from many shocks or with a multistage model of communication in which information is dispersed interpersonally and, hence, more slowly in this part of the population.

4. Conclusion

Governments adjust policy instruments in response to cumulative changes in economic conditions. But if public opinion responds to the policy changes, then the *real* economy will appear in the *subjective* economy in an intertemporally lumpy, nonlinear fashion. This is true even if we do not assume ex ante that people know whether a dramatic announcement signifies real change or not. But it is an empirical matter whether dramatic shifts in what we have called the subjective economy correspond more closely with steady monitoring of the real economy or with the aftereffects of sudden announced changes. If it is the latter, for instance, cumulative inflation will be perceived—but only all at once, after the government has acted to cure it.

In that case, it will be no surprise to find long, peculiar, nonlinear lags of the economic conditions in the subjective economy (Mebane 1987), not because people monitor two years back but because they are intermittently reminded of what has transpired when governments act to do something about it. When interventions themselves bring the real economy into the subjective economy, changes in policy regimes and partisan incumbencies become more important, for these signify changes in the structure of the relationship between interventions and the underlying economy. Moreover, there will be instability simply because interventions are sporadic and different time periods would be dominated by different sorts of intervention. So in this case instability in popularity functions is hardly puzzling: it is natural.

In spite of the unclear results on the formation of expectations, it seems worth pursuing this line of analysis. Events in the form of government announcements of policy changes clearly seem to have an impact on perceptions of national well-being, independent of monitoring of the underlying conditions that may have motivated the policy interventions in the first place. In this way, the rational expectations view, while not contradicted, has to be modified to allow for events themselves to communicate a great deal of information. Beyond that, there was some evidence for perceived effectiveness of policy and some for the idea of signaling or cuing, by which the intervention simply brings out the public response to the underlying conditions. Clearly there is a lot more to be done: we need tests of equality restrictions on the dynamic parameters, models of learning rather than static perception, and a role for the media, as well as a vastly improved understanding of future expectations. An exploratory chapter like this can well end by concluding that a better understanding of the relative magnitudes of retrospective and prospective elements in voting still seems like a rich direction for future politico-economic research to pursue.

REFERENCES

Alesina, Alberto, and Jeffrey Sachs. 1988. "Political Parties and the Business Cycle in the United States, 1948–1984." *Journal of Money, Credit, and Banking* 20:63–82.
Alt, James, 1979. *The Politics of Economic Decline*. Cambridge: Cambridge University Press.
Alt, James. 1985. "Political Parties, World Demand, and Unemployment." *American Political Science Review* 79:1016–40.
Alt, James, and K. Alec Chrystal. 1983. *Political Economics*. Berkeley: University of California Press.
Beck, Neal. 1987. "A Model of Public Opinion with a Theoretical Foundation." Paper presented to the joint sessions of the European Consortium for Political Research, Amsterdam.
Bierwag, Gerald O., and M. Grove. 1966. "Aggregate Koyck Functions." *Econometrica* 34:828–32.
Chappell, Henry, and William Keech. 1985. "A New View of Political Accountability for Economic Performance." *American Political Science Review* 79:10–27.
Conover, Pamela, and Stanley Feldman. 1986. "Emotional Reactions to the Economy: I'm Mad as Hell and I'm not Going to Take It Any More." *American Journal of Political Science* 30:50–78.
Dalton, Russell, and Robert Duval. 1986. "The Political Environment and Foreign Policy Opinions: British Attitudes toward European Integration, 1972–79." *British Journal of Political Science* 16:113–34.
Frey, Bruno, and Friedrich Schneider. 1984. "Public Attitudes toward Inflation and Unemployment and Their Influence on Government Behavior." In *Inflation and the Political Business Cycle*, ed. T. Willett. San Francisco: Pacific Institute.
Hudson, John. 1984. "Prime Ministerial Popularity in the UK: 1960–81." *Political Studies* 32:86–97.
Hudson, John. 1985. "The Relationship between Government Popularity and Approval for the Government's Record in the United Kingdom." *British Journal of Political Science* 15:165–86.
Kane, Edward, and Burton Malkiel. 1976. "Autoregressive and Nonautoregressive Elements in Cross-Section Forecasts of Inflation." *Econometrica* 44:1–16.
Konig, Heinz, Marc Nerlove, and Gilles Oudiz. 1981. "On the Formation of Price Expectations: An Analysis of Business Test Data by Log-Linear Probability Models." *European Economic Review* 16:103–38.
Kramer, Gerald. 1983. "The Ecological Fallacy Revisited: Aggregate- versus Individual-Level Findings on Economics and Elections, and Sociotropic Voting." *American Political Science Review* 77:92–111.

Kuklinski, James, and Darrell West. 1981. "Economic Expectations and Voting Behavior in the United States House and Senate Elections." *American Political Science Review* 75:436–47.

Lewis-Beck, Michael. 1988. *Economics and Elections*. Ann Arbor, MI: University of Michigan Press.

MacKuen, Michael. 1981. *More Than News*. Beverly Hills: Sage.

MacKuen, Michael. 1983. "Political Drama, Economic Conditions, and the Dynamics of Presidential Popularity." *American Journal of Political Science* 27:165–92.

Mebane, Walter. 1987. "Varieties of Economic Evaluation over Time." Paper presented to the annual convention of the Midwest Political Science Association, Chicago.

Mincer, Joseph. 1969. *Economic Forecasts and Expectations*. New York: NBER.

Mosley, Paul. 1984. "'Popularity Functions' and the Role of the Media: A Pilot Study of the Popular Press." *British Journal of Political Science* 14:117–29.

Mosley, Paul. 1985. *The Making of Economic Policy*. Brighton: Wheatsheaf.

Mueller, John. 1970. "Presidential Popularity from Truman to Johnson." *American Political Science Review* 64:18–34.

Norpoth, Helmut, and Thom Yantek. 1983. "Macroeconomic Conditions and Fluctuations of Presidential Popularity: The Question of Lagged Effects." *American Journal of Political Science* 27:785–807.

Peffley, Mark, Stanley Feldman, and Lee Sigelman. 1987. "Economic Conditions and Party Competence: Processes of Belief Revision." *Journal of Politics* 49:100–121.

Rivers, Douglas. N.d. "A Solution to the Kramer Problem." *American Political Science Review*. Forthcoming.

Stigler, George. 1973. "General Economic Conditions and National Elections." *American Economic Review Papers and Proceedings* 63:155–60.

Stray, Stephanie, and C. Beaumont. 1987. "Government Popularity and Attitude toward the Government's Record Revisited." *British Journal of Political Science* 17:122–28.

Part 4
Models of Politico-Economic
Behavior

Forms of Expressing Economic Discontent

Bruno S. Frey

Economic Discontent and Politics

A population dissatisfied with the state of the economy, and putting the blame on the government, has a variety of possibilities for expressing its discontent. One may distinguish seven main forms:

1. Retreat from the *economy* and *polity*. The individuals concerned decide to become passive, or to use an apt German expression, to resort to *innere Emigration*. No clear indication is given to the government of what is causing the dissatisfaction, but the government experiences a general decline in support.
2. Exit to the *shadow economy*. In this form of expressing discontent with the government's performance, individuals switch from the official economy, in which the state functions by taxing, expending, and regulating, to the hidden economy defined by the absence of government intervention (see e.g., Frey and Weck 1984).
3. Expressing discontent as measured in *surveys* or opinion polls. There are two different types of such surveys: (*a*) questions on the level of *satisfaction* with the way the economy is handled by the government or with the politico-economic system as a whole (e.g., Inglehart 1986); and (*b*) questions referring to the *popularity* of the government or of specific parties. There is, by now, a very extensive literature on the connection between popularity and the state of the economy (see, e.g., Paldam 1981; Schneider and Frey 1988).
4. *Conventional political participation*. There are, again, two forms that may usefully be distinguished: (*a*) issue-related participation in direct referenda (see Schneider, Pommerehne, and Frey 1981); and (*b*) party-oriented participation in (general) elections (see, e.g., Monroe 1979; Rattinger 1980).
5. *Articulation through interest groups*. It has been one of the earliest

notions in the economic theory of politics (Public Choice) that interest group activity responds to the economic well-being of its members. In a modern society with a large government sector, interest groups step up their political activities when their members' relative income share decreases.

6. *Nonconventional participation.* There are many specific forms of such peaceful protest, ranging from demonstrations to politically motivated strikes.

7. *Use of force.* When economic conditions worsen, individuals may use violence to effect a change of the politicians in power or to bring about a change in the political system.

The many forms of expressing discontent have been duly observed by researchers but the interdependence between the various forms has been neglected, or has been treated in a superficial way. This has made it impossible to answer the following important questions: What form of expression is used to what intensity under what circumstances? To what extent is one form of expressing economic discontent substituted for another form? What forms of expression are typically used by the members of different social strata? What forms of expression are mainly employed in democracies, and what forms in authoritarian regimes?

The econometric studies of how economic discontent affects the polity have concentrated on one form of expression. This is clearly evidenced in the most advanced scientific endeavor in this area, popularity and election functions. No study seems to have taken into account the fact that government popularity and election support does not directly depend only on economic discontent but also on the extent to which discontent is expressed in other forms. The choice of the form of expression may be analyzed as the result of a rational calculus of individuals. There is an interdependence between various forms of expression depending on the costs and benefits connected with each form. Each form of expression depends, in general, on the other forms of expression, as well as on the underlying economic conditions. Disregarding this interdependence may result in a misspecification of the estimation equation. Testable propositions on the type and intensity of interactions between the forms of expression may be derived.

The Choice of Expression

Rational decision makers choose that form of expressing economic discontent from which they expect to derive the highest expected (marginal) benefits and/or which is accompanied by the least expected (marginal) cost. The utility of using a particular form of expression (or political activity) consists of gaining either a private good or a public good.

Private goods may be an increase in monetary income or in psychic income such as prestige and publicity, both with respect to the population as a whole or to a reference group. In many forms of expression, such as replying to surveys or participating in elections and demonstrations, no monetary income can be gained. This potential exists, however, when force is used, such as when terrorists or guerillas raid banks or take hostages for ransom. Psychic income may be gained through several forms of expression, such as in voting (the benefit consists of a good civic conscience) or in demonstrations that yield high private benefits in terms of social acceptance among the other demonstrators (see, e.g., Muller and Opp 1986), or in terms of publicity. Public goods, on the other hand, consist of improvements of general economic conditions. Here again, the various forms of expression have a different capacity to lead to such improvement.

There are three cost components connected with the various forms of expression: (*a*) The *monetary* cost. In several forms of expression it is zero, such as in surveys and voting, but it is often positive in nonconventional forms of political activity such as participating in demonstrations. (*b*) The *time* cost. Some forms of expressing discontent use very little time, such as answering surveys or participating in elections, while others involve heavy time costs, such as participating in strikes or engaging in a professional terrorist activity. (*c*) *The expected punishment.* This is a function of the expected size of punishment and the expected probability of being caught in a form of expression subject to punishment. The cost of punishment takes the form of time cost in the case of imprisonment, and of money cost in the case of fines. For simplicity, and without loss of generality, they are subsumed here under monetary cost.

More formally: individuals are supposed to use those forms of expression and to that extent that maximize their individual utility subject to the various constraints they are faced with. Individual utility (U) is higher, the more private market goods X_j ($j = 1, 2, \ldots, m$) are consumed, the higher is the free time or leisure F, the more private goods gained by participating in political activities (G_k, $k = 1, 2, \ldots, l$), and the more of the public good E (the state of the economy) is achieved by expressing discontent:

$$U = U(X_1, X_2, \ldots, X_m; F; G_1, G_2, \ldots, G_l, E); \tag{1}$$

with all partial derivatives

$$U' > 0, U'' < 0.$$

This maximand is subject to two kinds of constraints:

a. *Production functions.* The private goods, G_k, may be "produced" by the various forms of expression (or intensity of political activities A_i, $i = 1$, 2, . . . , n):

$$G_k = G_k(A_1, A_2, \ldots, A_n); \tag{2}$$

where $k = 1, 2, \ldots, l$ and with $G_{ki} \equiv \partial G_k / \partial A_i \geq 0$;

$$G_{kii} = \partial G_{ki} / \partial A_i \leq 0.$$

The state of the economy, E, may also be influenced by the forms of expressing discontent

$$E = E(A_1, A_2, \ldots, A_n; Z); \tag{3}$$

with $E_i \equiv \partial E / \partial A_i \geq 0$; and

$$E_{ii} \equiv \partial E_i / \partial A_i \leq 0.$$

Z stands for the exogenous influences on the state of the economy unrelated to the pressure exerted by individuals through their political activities A_i.

Finally, income Y is produced by the input of labor time, L, payed at wage rate w:

$$Y = wL. \tag{4}$$

b. *Resource constraints.* The individuals are limited in their activity by the income available to them and used for the purchase of market goods X_j at price p_j, and the expenditure on the various forms of expression A_i at price p_i:

$$Y = \sum_{j = i}^{m} p_j X_j + \sum_{i = 1}^{n} p_i A_i. \tag{5}$$

Time also limits activities. Total available time, T, is used for working in the market L, for leisure F, or for political activities P:

$$T = L + F + P \tag{6}$$

The time used for political activities equals the various forms of expression multiplied by their time intensity t_i:

$$P = \sum_{i=1}^{n} t_i A_i. \tag{7}$$

Combining equations 4–7 yields the full income constraint:

$$wT = \sum_j p_j X_j + wF + \sum_i (p_i + t_i w) A_i, \tag{8}$$

where $t_i w$ is the time spent in political activities evaluated at its opportunity cost, w.

Maximizing equation 1 subject to equations 2, 3, and 8 yields the following first-order condition for the relative use of the different forms of expression A_q and A_r:

$$\frac{\sum_k \left(\frac{\partial U}{\partial G_k} \cdot \frac{\partial G_k}{\partial A_q} \right) + \frac{\partial U}{\partial E} \cdot \frac{\partial E}{\partial A_q}}{\sum_k \left(\frac{\partial U}{\partial G_k} \cdot \frac{\partial G_k}{\partial A_r} \right) + \frac{\partial U}{\partial E} \cdot \frac{\partial E}{\partial A_r}} = \frac{p_q + t_q w}{p_r + t_r w};$$

or

$$\frac{MU_q}{MU_r} = \frac{MC_q}{MC_r} \tag{9}$$

The left-hand side expresses the marginal utilities gained in the form of private goods and the public good (state of the economy) MU_q/MU_r; the right-hand side indicates the marginal monetary and time costs of engaging in the activities MC_q/MC_r. As shown in figure 1 (where the utility level U is kept constant), a relative increase in the cost of activity q (MC_q/MC_r rises) causes individuals to choose relatively less costly forms of expression (A_q/A_r falls). For a given utility level ($U = $ constant) equation 9 establishes a relationship between the various forms of expressing discontent for which

$$\frac{MU_q}{MU_r} = \frac{MC_q}{MC_r} = -\frac{dA_r}{dA_q} \tag{10}$$

holds. Equation 10 determines the marginal relationships between the forms of political activity in the optimal position.

A higher level of utility (say $\bar{\bar{U}} > \bar{U}$ in fig. 1) is associated with more private goods and/or a more favorable state of the economy (keeping the market goods and leisure constant):

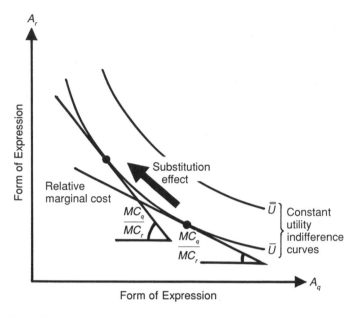

Fig. 1. When the relative cost of activity A_q rises, individuals substitute less costly activities.

$$U = U(G_1, G_2, \ldots, G_l, E) = f(A_1, A_2, \ldots, A_n). \tag{11}$$

Rearranging leads to:

$$A_1 = \Omega_1 (A_2, \ldots, A_n{:}G_1, G_2, \ldots, G_l, E). \tag{12}$$

The use of the form of expressing discontent A_1 depends on the intensity with which the other political activities are used, and on the level of private goods and on the public good state of the economy. Functions corresponding to equation 12 can be written for all A_i, $i = 1, 2, \ldots, n$. These expression functions form the basis for formulating theoretical hypotheses and econometric tests.

Comparative Analysis of the Forms of Expression

The exogenous changes in benefits and costs leading to systematic changes in the behavior of individuals with respect to how the forms of expressing discontent are chosen may reflect various factors: (1) the impact of differences between individuals, and (2) the impact of institutional differences.

Differences between Individuals

The formal model is useful for deriving testable propositions about which forms of expression are chosen by individuals living in varied circumstances. For the purpose of illustration, two types of individuals are distinguished, "young idealists" and "members of the middle class." The differences between these two groups of people are now applied to equation 9 describing the rational (utility maximizing) use of political activities.

Considering first the marginal utilities, it makes sense to assume that the young idealists are less interested than the middle class in the benefits from both private goods as well as the public good "general economic condition" ($\partial U / \partial G_k$ and $\partial U / \partial E$ are smaller). They are also likely to expect a smaller impact on the state of the economy from surveys and elections ($\partial E / \partial A_1$ and $\partial E / \partial A_2$ are smaller). Rather, they expect that policies can be changed only by unconventional and violent forms of expression ($\partial E / \partial A_3$ and $\partial E / \partial A_4$ are larger).

On the cost side, a major difference exists with respect to the cost of time: the young idealists have considerably lower opportunity costs than the middle class (w is lower) so that they are prone to use the more time-intensive political activities, i.e., demonstrations and internal war.

Considering both (marginal) costs and benefits the following testable propositions may be derived: (*a*) young idealists tend to engage in unconventional political participation (demonstrations, violence); and (*b*) the middle class shuns the time-intensive forms of participation and tends to engage in conventional forms, especially those with psychic rewards (voting in a social setting where this form of participation is considered a civic duty). These (and other) theoretical propositions may be empirically tested provided individual data are available.

Differences between Political Systems

This section develops theoretical propositions about the forms of expressing discontent with the government that tend to be used in democratic (*d*) and authoritarian (*a*) systems. The differences between the two political systems are reflected in the marginal cost and marginal benefits of equations 9 and 10, which specify an individual's optimal state. The differences in marginal benefits relate to the public good (i.e., the state of the economy) only. For the purpose of deriving comparative theoretical propositions, equation 12, describing the intensity with which a particular form of expression is used, may be simplified to

$$A_1 = \phi_1 (A_2, \ldots, A_n, E), \tag{13}$$

and analogously for the other types of political activity.

For the purpose of this analysis it is useful to group the forms of expression A_i into three basic forms.

1. Surveys as expressing satisfaction or dissatisfaction with the government concerning the state of the economy. In a democracy, this form of expression causes practically no (marginal) cost, not even in terms of time ($MC_s^d = 0$). In an authoritarian political system, on the other hand, this form of expressing dissatisfaction about the way the government deals with the economy may be quite costly, because the individual concerned may be easily identified and punished for opposing the government. Hence, $MC_s^a > 0$.

2. "Official" participation A_o in the form of elections and manifestations organized by, or on behalf of, the government. In a democracy, the cost of this form of expression consists in the time used ($MC_o^d > 0$). In an authoritarian system, the individuals run a (marginal) cost if they do not participate in this form of expression. The government monitors who is active in its support in these officially organized political activities, hence $MC_o^a < 0$.

3. Unconventional forms of expression A_u in the form of violent demonstrations and internal war. Such political activities are punished in both a democratic and an authoritarian system, and they require time, hence $MC_u^d, MC_u^a > 0$.

On the basis of these empirical observations about the differential marginal cost of the three forms of political expression between democratic and authoritarian systems, testable theoretical propositions about the relationships between the forms of expression can be derived. In particular, the (first) partial derivatives ($\partial A_q / \partial A_r \equiv \phi_{qr}:q, r = s, o, u, q \neq r$) in the expression functions

$$A_s = \phi_s(A_o, A_u, E);$$

$$A_o = \phi_o(A_s, A_u, E); \tag{14}$$

$$A_u = \phi_u(A_s, A_o, E)$$

are derived. As an example, consider an individual who minimizes the cost of achieving a given utility level U by using the optimal forms of expression A_q and A_r (see fig. 1). The slope of this cost or budget constraint is given by the relative marginal costs MC_r/MC_q, which are fixed within a political system, but differ across political systems. To remain in an optimal state, an individual reacts to marginal changes in the use of a form of expression and thereby to

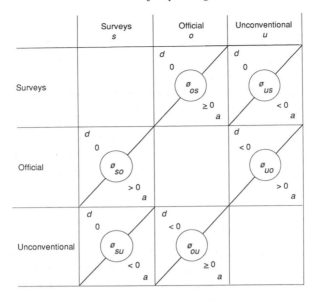

Fig. 2. The relationship between forms of political expression in democratic and authoritatian systems. The cells exhibit the marginal deriva-
tives ($\partial A_q/\partial A_r = \phi_{qr}$, q, $r = s$, o, u, $q \neq r$). The upper left-hand part of
each cell indicates the value of the partial derivative in a democratic
system (d), the lower right-hand part in an authoritarian system (a).

changes in total cost by appropriately adjusting the other forms of political
expression in order to reestablish the previous cost level.

Surveys. Consider the increased use of surveys to express dissatisfaction
with the state of the economy in a democracy due to an exogenous influence,
say greater opportunities to do so. The marginal cost of engaging in this form
of political activity being (practically) zero ($MC_s^d = 0$), the individual remains
in his or her optimal state and there is no incentive to adjust the other forms of
expression:

$$(\partial A_o/\partial A_s)^d = (\partial A_u/\partial A_s)^d = 0. \tag{15}$$

Conversely, if one of the other forms of expression (A_o or A_u) is changed, no
compensation of the disequilibrium is possible by surveys, hence:

$$(\partial A_s/\partial A_o)^d = (\partial A_s/\partial A_u)^d = 0. \tag{16}$$

These results are shown in figure 2.

In an authoritarian political system, on the other hand, it is costly for an
individual to express his or her opinion in a survey, because he or she risks

punishment ($MC_s^a > 0$). An increased use of surveys for expressing dissatisfaction drives up total cost, resulting in a suboptimal state. The individual concerned can only reach his or her preferred (optimal) position again by reducing cost. This can be achieved by either increasing A_o (as $MC_o^a < 0$) or by reducing A_u (as $MC_u^a > 0$). If risk of punishment by the government were the only relevant cost factor, this would mean that a greater exposure to risk by expressing one's dissatisfaction more freely in surveys must be compensated by supporting the government more strongly in official manifestations, or by reducing one's engagement in unconventional forms of expression, e.g., by participating less in (violent) antigovernment demonstrations. Thus, the partial derivates are:

$$(\partial A_o / \partial A_s)^a \geq 0; \; (\partial A_u / \partial A_s)^a < 0. \tag{17}$$

The equality sign for ϕ_{os}^a applies for the case in which the official form of participation is already at its maximum (e.g., the party in power is supported by 100 percent of the electorate). The derivatives (17) are again exhibited in figure 2.

Official Participation. Consider now an exogenous increase in official participation. In a democracy, there is some cost attached in the form of time and effort to be expended ($MC_o^d > 0$). An increase in this form of expression raises costs that can be compensated by a decrease in unconventional political participation:

$$(\partial A_u / \partial A_o)^d < 0. \tag{18}$$

In an authoritarian system, an individual who engages more strongly in officially sanctioned and prescribed forms of participation experiences a decrease in cost ($MC_o^a < 0$). He or she can therefore allow him- or herself to express dissatisfaction with the state of the economy by doing so more strongly in surveys or unconventional forms of participation:

$$(\partial A_s / \partial A_o)^a > 0; \; (\partial A_u / \partial A_o)^a > 0. \tag{19}$$

These results are again shown in figure 2.

Unconventional Participation. Engaging in unconventional political participation entails costs in the form of monetary resources, time, and risk of punishment in both democratic and authoritarian systems ($MC_u^d, MC_u^a > 0$). An increased engagement pushes up total costs that can be compensated by lowering official participation in a democracy (as $MC_o^d > 0$) and increasing it in an authoritarian system (as $MC_o^a < 0$):

$$(\partial A_o / \partial A_u)^d < 0; \tag{20}$$

$$(\partial A_o / \partial A_u)^a \geq 0. \tag{21}$$

The equality sign of ϕ_{ou}^a is relevant when official participation is already at its maximum.

In an authoritarian system, the rising costs of engaging in unconventional forms of political participation can also be compensated by reducing expression in the form of surveys (as $MC_s^a > 0$):

$$(\partial A_s / \partial A_u)^a < 0. \tag{22}$$

These results are again shown in figure 2.

Overall Pattern. The theoretically derived relationships between forms of expression yield the following overall pattern:

—There is neutrality between surveys and all other forms of expression in a democracy;
—There is a substitutive relationship between surveys and unconventional political participation in an authoritarian system, and between official and unconventional forms of participation in a democracy; and
—There is a complementarity between surveys and official participation, and official and unconventional participation in an authoritarian political system.

Effect of the State of the Economy. I now turn to the differential way in which the three forms of expression A_s, A_o, and A_u are used by individuals in order to express their discontent with the state of the economy. This determines the partial derivative $\partial A_q / \partial E$, $q = s, o, u$, in equation 14.

In an optimal state, the individual equates relative marginal utilities to relative marginal costs. Taking the effect of the forms of expression on private goods to be equal across political regimes, according to equation 9 the relative marginal utilities are:

$$MU_q / MU_r = (\partial E / \partial A_q) / (\partial E / \partial A_r). \tag{23}$$

Given relative marginal costs, the political activity A_q is used more intensively relative to A_r, the higher the (expected) effect of A_q on the improvement of the state of the economy ($\partial E / \partial A_q$), in comparison to the effect of the other activity ($\partial E / \partial A_r$).

In a democracy, the citizens can expect that survey results have an effect on the government's handling of the economy ($\partial E / \partial A_s^d > 0$), though the effect may be small. This effect has been established in the context of politico-economic models where the government takes popularity surveys as a current indicator of (expected) election outcomes. In the case of a popularity deficit, the government uses its policy instruments in order to improve economic conditions (see, e.g., Frey 1978). Accordingly, individuals in a democracy react to a worsening of economic conditions by expressing themselves in surveys: $(\partial A_s / \partial E)^d > 0$.

In a democratic setting, the citizens expect the greatest impact on the government's actions, and thereby on the economy, by using the "official" forms of expression, i.e., voting in elections and in referenda: $(\partial E / \partial A_o)^d > 0$. Hence, a worsening of the state of the economy leads to a reaction in official participation: $(\partial A_o / \partial E)^d > 0$. Finally, unconventional forms of participation may have some effect on the government's management of the economy, $(\partial E / \partial A_u)^d > 0$, but the effect may be expected to be rather small in the case of violent forms because of its illegitimacy. Consequently, the marginal utility of engaging in this form of political activity is rather small, but positive and hence $(\partial A_u / \partial E)^d > 0$.

Figure 3 presents the signs and approximate magnitudes of the reactions to changes in the state of the economy to be expected in a democracy.

In an authoritarian political system individuals cannot expect any significant impact from expressing their opinions in surveys: $(\partial E / \partial A_s)^a \approx 0$. Hence, their (expected) marginal utility of employing this form of expression is very small, and they are little inclined to engage in it when dissatisfied with the state of the economy: $(\partial A_s / \partial E)^a \approx 0$. The official forms of participation, elections and manifestations being employed by the government purely for its own purposes, cannot be expected to affect an authoritarian system: $(\partial E / \partial A_o)^a = 0$. Accordingly, no marginal benefit of using this form of expression exists, and individuals do not show any reaction to changes in economic conditions: $(\partial A_o / \partial E)^a = 0$. In a nondemocratic political setting, the only form of reaction that can be expected to influence the government's actions to any significant degree is that of unconventional political participation: $(\partial E / \partial A_u)^a > 0$. A worsening of economic conditions may therefore (ceteris paribus, i.e., under unchanged marginal cost) lead to increased unconventional political participation in the form of protest, violent demonstrations, or even guerrilla warfare: $(\partial A_u / \partial E)^a > 0$.

The theoretically expected forms of reacting to changing economic conditions are also exhibited in figure 3. It also shows that there are significant differences in expected reactions of individuals between democratic and authoritarian political systems.

Political Systems

	Democratic	Authoritarian
Surveys	> 0 (small to medium)	≈ 0 (small to zero)
Official	> 0 (large)	= 0
Unconventional	> 0 (small)	> 0 (medium)

Fig. 3. How individuals react to changes in the state of the economy in democratic and in authoritarian political systems ($\partial A_q/\partial E$, $q = s, o, u$)

Concluding Remarks

I have argued that there are good theoretical (and empirical) reasons to assume that the various forms of expressing discontent about the state of the economy are (at least partly) interdependent. There are both substitutive and complementary relationships between types of political activity, and there are significant differences according to whether individuals are acting in a democratic or authoritarian political system. These results suggest that existing econometric (politometric) estimates of expression functions, in particular popularity and election functions, may be seriously misspecified. In future works, the theoretically derived interdependence between the various forms of expressing satisfaction should explicitly be taken into account.

REFERENCES

Frey, Bruno S. 1978. "Politico-Economic Models and Cycles." *Journal of Public Economics* 9 (April): 203–20.

Frey, Bruno S., and Hannelore Weck. 1984. "The Hidden Economy as an 'Unobserved' Variable." *European Economic Review* 26:33–53.

Inglehart, Ronald. 1986. "Coercion and Consent: How Much Consensus Is Necessary for a Democratic Order? How Much Consensus Is Present?" Paper presented at the conference on Individual Liberty and Democratic Decision-Making, Herdecke, West Germany, October.

Monroe, Kristen R. 1979. "Econometric Analyses of Electoral Behavior: A Critical Review." *Political Behavior* 1:137–73.

Muller, Edward N., and Karl-Dieter Opp. 1986. "Rational Choice and Rebellious Collective Actions." *American Political Science Review* 80 (June): 471–87.

Paldam, Martin. 1981. "A Preliminary Survey of the Theories and Findings on Vote and Popularity Functions." *European Journal of Political Research* 9:181–99.

Rattinger, Hans. 1980. *Wirtschaftliche Konjunktur und politische Wahlen in der Bundesrepublik Deutschland*. Berlin: Duncker and Humblot.

Schneider, Friedrich, and Bruno S. Frey. 1988. "Politico-Economic Models of Macroeconomic Policy: A Review of the Empirical Evidence." In *Political Business Cycles,* ed. Thomas D. Willett. Durham and London: Duke University Press.

Schneider, Friedrich, Werner W. Pommerehne, and Bruno S. Frey. 1981. "Politico-Economic Interdependence in a Direct Democracy: The Case of Switzerland." In *Contemporary Political Economy,* ed. Douglas A. Hibbs and Heino Fassbender. Amsterdam: North-Holland.

Political Loyalties and the Economy

Gianluigi Galeotti and Antonio Forcina

1. Abstention from the Vote and Political Loyalties

Let P be the total of eligible voters, $v_h = V_h/P$ the share of votes going to party h's candidate (h = Democratic or Republican), and $a = A/P$ the share of people failing to register (or to vote), or voting for minor candidates. Hence, $v_D + v_R + a = 1$ are the results of a U.S. presidential election. With respect to previous elections, changes may occur either because voters shift to another party (party shifting) and/or because of variations in turnout (abstention shifting). These shifts can combine in different ways, and electoral data provide information only about net variations $\Delta v_D + \Delta v_R = \Delta a$. To get a better insight, we would need to know at least the internal variations of Δa, i.e., how many votes shifted from (to) abstention to (from) each party ($\Delta a = \Delta a_D + \Delta a_R$). Therefore we face a dilemma: either we ignore abstention and its variations, or we make some assumption about what occurs inside a. Whatever the solution, we should be careful of avoiding the fallacy of imputing all actual vote variations exclusively to party or to abstention shifting.

The prevailing convention is that of ignoring abstention ($\Delta a = 0$), though in the U.S. case it amounts to ignoring variations of up to 29 percent of eligible voters. Moreover, the symmetric vote shares implicit in the conventional transformation

$$d = v_D/(v_D + v_R)$$

and

$$r = 1 - d,$$

The order of the author's names was made by random selection. The authors wish to thank Vani Borooah, Paolo Guerrieri, and Allan A. Schmid for early discussions. Reprinted from *Review of Economics and Statistics* 71 (August 1989): 511–17. Copyright © 1989. Courtesy of Elsevier Science Publishers.

can be very misleading. Consider the last two presidential elections:[1]

	Basic Results			Conventional Transformation	
	Δv_D	Δv_R	Δa	Δd	Δr
1980	$-.0523$	$+.0099$	$+.0424$	$-.0636$	$+.0636$
1984	$+.0012$	$+.0401$	$-.0413$	$-.0329$	$+.0329$

In 1980, Reagan is awarded an increase of 6.36 percentage points, while the Republican vote increased slightly (less than 1 percent); in 1984, Mondale's small gain ($+.12$ percent) is transformed into a loss of 3.29 points. As the example shows, ignoring turnout can imply the fallacy of imputing all variations to party shifting.

Let us therefore follow the second path, and make some assumption about a_h. The economic theory of democracy can be helpful here. According to a well-known theorem, if we assume a unimodal distribution of voters' preferences along the policy space, candidates' platforms coincide at the median. It would follow that both a_h are univocally determined ($a_h = .5 - v_h$). If, however, candidates' platforms are different and voters perceive them as different (Hibbs 1977), we face the risk of the second fallacy: the convergence at the median precludes any party shifting and all vote changes would come to be interpreted in terms of abstention shifting. Let us then follow a different approach, capable of reducing the risk of either fallacy.

Still within a spatial interpretation, assume voters as sensitive to political distance (abstention by alienation). Then we can make use of the result that the relative distance between the platforms of vote-maximizing candidates is an inverse-u function of their supporters' average propensity to vote. It is only when those propensities are very high that we have the convergence at the median. But as they decrease, candidates' equilibrium positions first spread apart in an asymmetric way, depending on their relative values, before being pulled back (toward the mode, Comanor 1976) when those propensities approach 0 (Galeotti 1980). Thus, if we define $v_h + a_h = p_h$ as party h's area of political influence ($\Sigma p_h = 1$), these areas p_h are determined by, and move with, the middle point between the positions taken by vote-maximizing candidates. From p_h and v_h we can work out a_h, and in this way take into account both party shifting (following shifts of political platforms) and abstention shifting (following different propensities of the supporters of each area).

On the assumption that candidates assess their supporters' propensity to

---

1. For the source of data see table 1 (Δa includes votes for minor candidates: provided the few votes gathered by minor candidates in presidential elections, the simplification is not particularly troublesome).

TABLE 1. Loyalty Ratios and Aggregate Turnout

	1892	1896	1900[a]	1904	1908	1912[b]
Democratic loyalty ($100t_p$):	67.60	74.70	70.00	52.40	58.00	57.70
Republican loyalty ($100t_R$):	65.50	81.80	72.00	69.10	65.70	59.85
Aggregate turnout $100 (1 - a)$:	74.70	79.30	73.20	65.20	65.40	58.80

	1916	1920	1924	1928	1932	1936	1940	1944	1948
$100t_p$	60.60	31.50	43.10	47.20	62.00	67.20	63.60	60.00	51.50
$100t_R$	57.20	63.60	48.50	65.30	40.40	41.40	53.60	51.50	45.30
$100 (1-a)$	61.60	49.20	48.90	56.90	52.40	56.00	58.90	56.00	51.10

	1952	1956	1960	1964	1968	1972	1976	1980	1984
$100t_p$	56.40	51.30	62.40	70.10	51.90	41.70	53.80	41.60	42.50
$100t_R$	65.90	66.10	62.20	51.70	52.90	66.50	51.20	55.30	62.60
$100 (1-a)$	61.60	59.30	62.80	61.90	60.90	55.20	53.50	52.60	52.90

Sources: t_p, t_R: compiled by the authors; $(1-a)$: 1892–1928: *Guide to U.S. Elections,* 2d ed. Washington, D.C.: Congressional Quarterly Inc., 1985), 279–366.

[a]See appendix

[b]We followed Fair's aggregations (1978, 166).

vote (politicians' "animal spirits"?) reasonably well, electoral results represent the outcome of perfectly chosen vote-maximizing positions. Since the pair of values (v_D, v_R) is a function of the pair (a_D, a_R) and the relationship can be inverted (see the model presented in the appendix), we associate univocally a pair (a_D, a_R) to any given pair of electoral results (v_D, v_R) and find both parties' turnout (loyalty ratios):

$$t_h = \frac{v_h}{v_h + a_h} \tag{1}$$

We have carried out a numerical simulation of party equilibrium for the last twenty-four presidential elections and present the results in table 1.[2]

In what follows we intend to test the impact of economic variables on the strength of political links as expressed by t_D and t_R.

2. Political Loyalties and the Economy

In the standard analysis of the political-business cycle, voters are often seen (Kiewiet 1983; Schneider and Frey 1988) as engaged in redeciding their

---

2. Note that $(t_D + t_R)/2$ approximates $(1 - a)$ when the middle point between political platforms is at the median of the spatial distribution of preferences. The presence of votes collected by minor candidates (M) is included in the overall rate of turnout $(1 - a = t_D p_D + t_R p_R + M/P)$.

political alignment with each election. However, few people feel themselves born-again voters at regular intervals. Traditional links, previous searches, and past experiences are all elements that imply an "investment" in a political choice not cheaply disposed of by rational voters, and staying home might be the only rational option available. The incorporation of these elements in a model showing how political parties provide the trust basis required to support political exchanges is developed in Galeotti and Breton 1986. What is relevant here is that different loyalties fragment the market for votes and imply different political sensibilities.

The question then arises whether economic conditions come to strengthen or to weaken voters' attachment to their own party's candidate, as expressed in terms of their going to the polls. Here the incumbency-oriented voting rule (Fiorina 1981) acquires a specific meaning. In contrast with the referendum-like view of voters who are supposed to use the same measure of performance, in our approach an incumbent's economic performance may be appreciated differently by supporters and opponents. For example, do Democratic supporters react to unemployment as such or do they take into account whether it occurs under a Democratic or a Republican incumbent? The presence of partisan evaluations is therefore the important issue.

To summarize, two features of a voter's behavior are emphasized: the partisan choice between competing parties and the decision whether to go to the polls or to stay home. The first choice concerns only middle voters, while the core of party supporters is considered as having made a choice that cannot be cheaply changed in the short run: it is their attachment to their own party to be affected by short-run economic fluctuations. Economic conditions affect voters' decisions about whether to vote for the preferred candidate or to stay home (abstention shifting). Those decisions then influence candidates' equilibrium positions, and therefore the eventual shifts of middle voters.

Let us assume that the degree of allegiance of a voter belonging to party h's area of political influence is a random variable $L(h)$ defined as

$$L(h) = l(h) + \lambda = [\beta_o(h) + \Sigma x_j \beta_j(h) + \epsilon(h)] + \lambda, \tag{2}$$

where $l(h)$—which is the same for all voters in the area—is a linear regression function of economic variables (x_j), with an error term $\epsilon(h)$ depending on all other residual circumstances (such as the personal appeal of the candidate). Differences among voters are represented by λ, an individual bias depending only on the voter. The distribution of λ characterizes the aggregate model. Let us assume that this distribution is symmetric around 0, and that a voter goes to the polls only when her or his $L(h)$ exceeds a threshold level L^*. Therefore,

$$Pr[L(h) > L^* \mid l(h)] = Pr[\lambda > L^* - l(h) \mid l(h)]$$
$$= Pr[\lambda \le l(h) - L^* \mid l(h)] = \pi(h). \tag{3}$$

Under these assumptions, we have a binomial model with probability $\pi(h)$. Since the sample size $(v_h + a_h)$ is very large, t_h (above) provides a highly accurate estimate of $\pi(h)$. It is well known that for any given continuous distribution of λ, there exists a monotone transformation of $\pi(h)$ (or t_h) that is equal to $l(h) - L^*$. If we assume that λ has a logistic distribution, then

$$y_h = \log t_h/(1 - t_h) \simeq [\beta_o(h) - L^*] + \Sigma x_j \beta_j(h) + \epsilon(h). \qquad (4)$$

Let us note that $\beta_o(h)$ and L^* cannot be identified separately because an arbitrary constant could be added to $\beta_o(h)$ (and thus to $L[h]$) and to L^* without affecting the model.

3. Economic Influences

We are therefore able to consider two separate regression models with dependent variables

$$y_h = \text{logit}(t_h),$$

and the same set of explanatory variables. The basic assumption is that $\epsilon(h)$ has a normal distribution. Moreover, we assume that $\epsilon(h) = \epsilon(h,c) + \epsilon(h,r)$, where $\epsilon(h,c)$ is the random effect associated with personal characteristics of a candidate, while $\epsilon(h,r)$ is a random effect due to all residual circumstances acting on loyalty. In this way we can define two more parameters: $\sigma^2(h) = \text{var}[\epsilon(h)]$ and $\gamma(h) = \text{var}[\epsilon(h,c)]/\text{var}[\epsilon(h)]$; this relates to Fair's (1978) model where, however, it is assumed that $\gamma(D) = \gamma(R) = \gamma$ (Fair calls it λ). The joint maximum likelihood estimation of parameters $[\beta_j(h), \sigma^2(h), \gamma(h)]$ has been obtained by an algorithm based on the GLIM Program (see Forcina 1987 for details).

The explanatory variables that have been considered for potential inclusion in the model are the following:

G_t ($t = 0, 1, 2, 3$): real per capita GNP, t years before the election year;
u_t ($t = 0, 1, 2, 3$): percentage of unemployment in year t;
p_t ($t = 0, 1, 2, 3$): price index defined as the GNP deflator;
$GI = 100\log(G_o/G_1)$: percentage growth of real per capita GNP;
$GA = GI - 100\log(G_1/G_2)$: change in the percentage growth of real per capita GNP;
$UI = u_0 - u_1$: change in the percentage of unemployment;
$PI = \log(p_o/p_1)$: growth rate of prices;
$PA = PI - \log(p_1/p_2)$: change in the growth rate of prices;
$PAB = 100|PI|$: Absolute value of PI (in percent);
(h): a dummy variable denoting the incumbent party ($h = D, R$);

CR: a dummy variable specifying if a Democratic, Republican, or both
candidates are running for reelection; and

$T = 1, \ldots , 24$: a linear trend.

The annual data for the economic variables were taken from Fair (1978) for
the period 1889–1976; for the period 1977–1984, the data are:

Year	G	U	P
1977	6,146	7.1	141.69
1978	6,389	6.0	152.16
1979	6,498	5.8	165.34
1980	6,407	7.1	180.50
1981	6,505	7.6	197.83
1982	6,306	9.7	209.74
1983	6,491	9.6	217.86
1984	6,885	7.5	226.99

where G = real per capita GNP in 1972 dollars, U = civilian unemployment
rate, and P = GNP deflator (1972 = 100.00).

We fitted a large variety of suitable regression models, each one containing a different combination of explanatory variables. The selection among
different models was based on the asymptotic normal distribution of the
estimates and on their standard errors. No automatic selection procedure was
adopted and the interpretation of the resulting model was taken into account.
In the following, we first present the estimates for the model that we consider
most convincing for each loyalty ratio. The interpretation of the results will
then be discussed.

Results

In tables 2 and 3 we give the name of the variable, the estimate of the
corresponding parameter, its standard error, and the Durbin-Watson statistics.
If X is an economic variable, the term $X.(h)$ will denote the estimate of the
regression coefficient of X conditional on Democratic or Republican incumbency. Almost all coefficients are significant at or above the 5 percent level.[3]
Collinearity does not seem to be a problem, as the correlation coefficient
reaches a maximum value of .7 only between GI and GA (table 3). Stability of

---

3. It should be noted that the t-ratios have to be based on the asymptotic SE, adjusted for
the estimation of $\gamma(h)$; hence the significance tests should be based on the normal distribution and
not on Student t.

**TABLE 2. Parameter Estimates for the
Democratic Party, 1892–1984**

Parameter	Estimate	SE
Intercept	0.3550	0.0880
$GI.(R)$	−0.0589	0.0225
UI	−0.1830	0.0410
PI	−0.0524	0.0135
Candidate (γ_R)	0.6230	0.1860
Residual	0.0310	0.0100
DW = 1.69		

**TABLE 3. Parameter Estimates for the
Republican Party, 1892–1984**

Parameter	Estimate	SE
Intercept	0.6160	0.0850
$GI(D)$	−0.1666	0.0372
$GA.(D)$	−0.0368	0.0161
$UI.(D)$	−0.3180	0.0960
$PA.(R)$	−0.0549	0.0225
Candidate (γ_R)	0.0000	
Residual	0.0620	0.0180
DW = 1.66		

parameter estimates was tested against the presence of a linear trend, and the results were not significant.

As for explanatory variables not appearing in the tables, the time trend was clearly not significant; neither was a dummy for an incumbent running for reelection (see, however, the following discussion of candidates).

In tables 2 and 3, estimates are expressed in terms of transformed dependent variables. In order to make the interpretation easier, table 4 presents the same results in terms of loyalty ratios, by giving the values of intercepts and the variation of each ratio induced by a one percentage point increase in each explanatory variable, all others being set at 0. The discussion that follows will be based on table 4.

Discussion

As for the negative sign accompanying the growth of GNP, we call attention to how, for both loyalties, that sign is conditional on the incumbency of the other party. Take the case of a Republican incumbent: if, in an election year, the growth of per capita real GNP has increased one percentage point, the

TABLE 4. Estimated Percentage Effect on Loyalty Ratios of a 1 Percent Increase in the Explanatory Variables

Democratic Party[a]		Republican Party[b]	
GI.(R)	−1.44	GI.(D)	−3.88
		GA.(D)	−0.84
UI	−4.83	UI.(D)	−7.54
PI	−1.27	PA.(R)	−1.26

[a]Intercept = 58.78 percent.
[b]Intercept = 64.93 percent.

turnout of Democratic voters will be lower, ceteris paribus, by 1.44 percentage points (or the Republican one by 3.88 points, when that occurs under a Democratic incumbent). This result can emerge only when there is no forced symmetry between votes gained and lost by the two parties. But why do only the opponent's performances affect voters' loyalties in a significant way? An answer can be provided by reflecting on how, in terms of our model, loyalty implies a political commitment that bears a partisan reading of economic events. In other terms, voters are not uncommitted bystanders, and their previous political investments provide them with loyalty filters implying negative expectations for an opponent's performance, so that their partisan choice is weakened (confirmed) by the incumbent opponent's good (bad) economic performance.

That partisan reading seems to be, on the whole, weaker for Democratic voters because, for them, two out of three coefficients do not show any party label. More precisely, increases in prices and unemployment, as such, seem to discourage the political activism of Democrats. On the opposite side, the traditional Republican sensitivity to prices is fully confirmed. In fact, the variable PA.(R) is the only instance in our findings of voters reacting to their own incumbent's performance.

Throughout the elections under consideration, unemployment seems to be the one variable, among those that are significant, having the greatest impact on loyalties of both parties.[4] It could be inferred that, ceteris paribus, American voters tend to be politically less committed both with a growing GNP and with increasing unemployment. As for the latter, according to the above results, not fighting it would be a tempting choice both for a Democratic (the loss in terms of his own party loyalty is lower than the gain due to a lower Republican loyalty) and for a Republican president (because of

---

4. Surprisingly, Democrats' commitment does not increase with increasing unemployment, even when this occurs under a Republican president.

the fading loyalty of the opponents). However, if rising unemployment is accompanied by a decreasing real GNP, there is a compensation that makes the total impact closer to the one we would expect.

On the whole, the fact that the coefficients tend to be higher for Republican than for Democratic voters could be explained both in terms of different political commitments and in terms of different sensitivities to economic events. To obtain a more complete picture, however, we have to take into account that the degree of structural loyalty—as expressed by the value of intercepts in table 4—is lower for the Democratic than for the Republican party (58.78 percent vs. 64.93 percent). We can, therefore, see that Democratic loyalty tends to be both lower and less sensitive to the economic cycle if compared to Republicans' alertness (an alertness confirmed by their relatively longer memory shown by the parameter of $GA.(D)$, measuring the change in GNP growth rate).

A comment is in order on what Fair calls the Vote Getting Ability (VGA) (candidate, in our heading), i.e., on whether a candidate running in more than one election can explain part of the residual variation. In our findings, the relevance of this factor applies only to the Democrats (0.623), and is higher than that found by Fair (0.25). The difference is not surprising since that VGA should come out mainly at a partisan level, whereas Fair constrained it to be the same for candidates of both parties. In any case, his suggestion on the usefulness of this component is confirmed.

Concluding Remarks

In this chapter we have tested the impact of economic events on voters' loyalty in U.S. presidential elections. Instead of taking one party's share of the two-party vote as the dependent variable, we have presented a device to disaggregate the rate of voters' abstention in its party components. We have thus avoided the forced symmetry of reactions implied by the conventional transformation of electoral results in a zero-sum game. Consequently, each party turnout (i.e., the ratio between actual and potential votes) has become the new dependent variable, leading to the estimation of two separate equations.

Our findings support the view that voters react in different ways to the economic cycle, with Democratic loyalty appearing to be relatively more stable, and Republican loyalty more sensitive and selective. Our results appear to confirm, from the voters' point of view, the partisan theory of macroeconomic policy (Hibbs 1987). As for the incumbency-oriented versus policy-oriented voting rules (retrospective voting discussed in the literature), our analysis seems to clarify what comes to be inevitably mingled by the conventional handling of electoral data. Suppose that an incumbent's performance leaves unchanged supporters' loyalty and affects only opponents' loyalty: when electoral results are artificially constrained in terms of the two-party vote, it is only the latter effect that can appear, and with a reduced impact.

APPENDIX

Consider the following set of assumptions:

(i) The position of a voter is represented by a point along a one-dimensional axis. (ii) The overall distribution of voters follows a normal distribution that is assumed to have 0 mean and unit variance. (iii) Let x_D and x_R represent, at a given moment, the platforms of political parties D and R, respectively. The area of influence of D is the set of points x such that $x \leq (x_D + x_R)/2$; conversely, $x > (x_D + x_R)/2$ defines R's area of influence. (iv) The probability that a voter positioned at x will go to the polls depends on a parameter α_h ($h = D, R$) according to the following expression

$$\exp[-(x - x_h)^2/\alpha_h]$$

with $\alpha \in (0, \infty)$. (v) Each party tries to maximize its votes, given its α and the position of the opponent, under the constraint that $x_D \leq x_R$. Thus, party D chooses the platform x_D that maximizes

$$v_D = \int_{-\infty}^{(x_D + x_R)/2} (1/\sqrt{2\pi})\ \exp(-x^2/2)\exp[-(x - x_D)^2/\alpha D]dx.$$

v_R is defined in a similar way.

Remark 1. The equilibrium position may depend on the starting point. This difficulty can, however, be avoided by setting $x_D \leq 0 \leq x_R$.

Remark 2. When $\alpha_D = \alpha_R = \alpha$, the equilibrium point is such that $x_D = -x_R$; for $\alpha = 0$ and for $\alpha \leq 1$, $x_D = x_R = 0$.

A simple FORTRAN computer program that computes the equilibrium points x_h for any pair of α_h, is available from the authors. The same program also computes v_h and α_h, where, e.g,

$$\alpha_D = \int_{-\infty}^{(x_D + x_R)/2} (1/\sqrt{2\pi})\ \exp(-x^2/2)dx - v_p.$$

This algorithm can be viewed as defining (numerically) two functions $v_D = f_D(\alpha_D, \alpha_R)$ and $v_R = f_R(\alpha_D, \alpha_R)$. A pointwise inverse of f_D, f_R: can be defined for the set of (α_D, α_R) where the isovote curves f_D and f_R intersect only in one point. A numerical investigation of f_D and f_R showed that a unique inverse existed except for a very narrow strip around $\alpha_D \approx \alpha_R$ and $0.7 \leq \alpha_h \leq 0.8$): within this area, more than one solution to the inverse exists and the choice is somehow arbitrary.[5]

REFERENCES

Comanor, William S. 1976. "The Median Voter Rule and the Theory of Political Choice." *Journal of Public Economics* 5:169–77.

Fair, Ray C. 1978. "The Effect of Economic Events on Votes for President." *Review of Economics and Statistics* 60:159–73.

Fiorina, Morris. 1981. *Retrospective Voting in American National Elections.* New Haven, CT: Yale University Press.

Forcina, Antonio. 1987. "Correlated Observations with Normal Error." *GLIM Newsletter* 12:31–32.

Galeotti, Gianluigi. 1980. "Public Choice and Problems of Preference Aggregation: A Supply-Side View." In *Public Choice and Public Finance,* ed. Karl W. Roskamp. Paris: Cujas.

Galeotti, Gianluigi, and Albert Breton. 1986. "An Economic Theory of Political Parties." *Kikos* 39:47–65.

Hibbs, Douglas A. 1977. "Political Parties and Macroeconomic Policies." *American Political Science Review* 71:1467–87.

Hibbs, Douglas A. 1987. *The Political Economy of Industrial Democracies.* Cambridge, MA: Harvard University Press.

Kiewiet, D. Roderick. 1983. *Macroeconomics and Micropolitics.* Chicago: The University of Chicago Press.

Schneider, Friedrich, and Bruno S. Frey. 1988. "Politico-Economic Models of Macroeconomic Policy." In *Political Business Cycle,* ed. Thomas D. Willet. Durham, NC: Duke University Press.

---

5. It occurred in the 1900 election, and we chose the lower values.

Contributors

JAMES E. ALT, Department of Government, Harvard University

NATHANIEL BECK, Department of Political Science, University of California, San Diego

PAOLO BELLUCCI, University of Campo Basso, Italy

HENRY W. CHAPPELL, Jr., Department of Economics, University of South Carolina

PATRICIA CONLEY, Department of Political Science, University of Chicago

STANLEY FELDMAN, Department of Political Science, State University of New York, Stony Brook

ANTONIO FORCINA, Institute of Economics, University of Perugia, Italy

BRUNO S. FREY, Institute for Economic Research, University of Zurich

GIANLUIGI GALEOTTI, Institute of Economics, University of Perugia, Italy

GARY C. JACOBSON, Department of Political Science, University of California, San Diego

WILLIAM R. KEECH, Department of Political Science, University of North Carolina

GEBHARD KIRCHGÄSSNER, Department of Economics, University of Osnabrück, Germany

MANFRED KUECHLER, Department of Sociology, Hunter College of the City University of New York

JEAN-DOMINIQUE LAFAY, Faculty of Economics, University of Paris I, France

MICHAEL S. LEWIS-BECK, Department of Political Science, University of Iowa

DAVID MARSH, Department of Government, University of Essex, England

HELMUT NORPOTH, Department of Political Science, State University of New York, Stony Brook

MARTIN PALDAM, Institute of Economics, University of Aarhus, Denmark

HANS RATTINGER, Department of Political Science, University of Bamberg, Germany

DAVID SANDERS, Department of Government, University of Essex, England

HUGH WARD, Department of Government, University of Essex, England